Home Inspection

Paul Shaktman & Cory Bosy

ASHLEY CROWN
SYSTEMS, INC.

Publisher and Editor: Pollyanna Fields
Technical Advisor: Bill Parker
Research, Analysis, and Development: Judy Hobbs
Creative Editor and Production Coordinator: Judy Hobbs
Editor: Joan Manno
Senior Illustrator: Rey Dulay
Illustrator: Eric Sharkey
Senior Graphic Designer: Dria Kasunich
Graphic Designer: Susan Mackessy

Ashley Crown Systems, Inc.
22952 Alcalde Drive
Laguna Hills, California 92653

Printed in the United States of America
ISBN: 0-934772-37-1

PREFACE

The *Home Inspection* textbook provides you with a comprehensive perspective of all you need to know about inspecting a house. Although written for the beginning home inspector, anyone, consumers and investors alike, will find detailed answers to their questions about the value and condition of property.

This book is unique in that it presents the home inspection process from the "outside looking in" rather than just the nuts and bolts of building construction. It covers the inspection process from start to finish and concludes with the home inspection report. Each chapter is divided into illustrated topics to clarify important issues for your understanding and satisfaction.

Home inspection is becoming an integral part of the real estate transaction, and its value will increase in the future. Many states already have passed legislation to regulate the home inspection industry and more are continuing to develop regulations and procedures. Today's home inspector must be educated and have access to current home inspection information. Whether you are entering this profession part time or starting out in a new career, this book will provide you with all the information you need to compete in today's market place.

ABOUT THE AUTHORS

CORY BOSY

Cory Bosy is the co-author of *Home Inspection*, published by Ashley Crown Systems, Inc. He holds a Bachelor's Degree in Journalism after graduating from the University of Northern Colorado in 1997. Mr. Bosy has written extensively about the construction industry and served as the Senior Editor of a construction newspaper and online service that covered the eastern seaboard, Texas, and California from 2000-2003. He began writing about home building and commercial construction in Denver, Colorado in 1998.

In the process of authoring *Home Inspection*, Mr. Bosy did extensive research and interviewed numerous home inspection professionals on the nuances of the home inspection industry. He also interviewed home inspection students to determine what was necessary to become a home inspector. In March 2005, he passed the National Home Inspection Exam (NHIE) given by the Examination Board of Professional Home Inspectors (EBPHI). The exam is required by at least 14 states and numerous professional organizations such as the American Society of Home Inspectors (ASHI) as a means of assessing competence in the home inspection field.

PAUL SHAKTMAN

Paul Shaktman is the co-author of *Home Inspection*, published by Ashley Crown Systems, Inc. He became involved in home inspection after selling his business in North Carolina and moving to the Los Angeles area. Mr. Shaktman is currently living in Murrieta, California with his wife.

RESEARCH AND DEVELOPMENT

Judy Hobbs is the creative editor and production coordinator for Ashley Crown Systems, Inc. She also manages textbook research and development for new products, as well as improvement to existing products. This ensures that higher education materials are accurate and current.

Ms. Hobbs has over 10 years experience in textbook publishing from State University of New York at Buffalo and Buffalo State College. She has a Bachelor of Science Degree from Empire State College with graduate studies from Cornell University.

ACKNOWLEDGMENTS

Home Inspection is the result of teamwork from the publisher, educators, and other professionals who assisted in the development of this textbook and helped to make it the best in its field. Special thanks to Leigh Conway, Joan Manno, Rey Dulay, Dria Kasunich, Susan Mackessy, Eric Sharkey, Meagan Jones, Sue Carlson, David Waterman, Laura Dearman, Verity Fletcher, and Lisa Schoenle for their experience and skill in bringing together the material content, photographs, illustrations, and layout.

A special thanks to Bill Parker, the technical advisor, whose expertise in the field of home inspection was invaluable. Mr. Parker is curently the Area Manager of InspectTech of Orange County, California.

ACKNOWLEDGMENTS

Contents

1 Chapter

Home Inspection: Getting Started

Introduction

Mike is a construction foreman for a contracting firm. Through no fault of his own, he is injured while lifting lumber from one scaffolding to another. His doctors tell him that a new career would help him avoid future injury. He dropped out of college and has been working in construction for 15 years. His workers' compensation insurance runs out soon, and he needs to find a new job to provide for his family. What can he do?

Jenny works as an operations manager at a bank. She has been doing similar work since college. Her landlord is raising her rent and she needs more money or a new job to continue to put a roof over the heads of herself and her three kids. She knows there is something better out there, but cannot seem to find it or is too scared to look. What can she do?

They both can invest in their futures and learn something new. Home inspection is an up-and-coming industry due to the explosion of home sales, both new and existing. An estimated 77% of all homes sold in 2000, approximately 4.9 million homes, were inspected by professional home inspectors. That number is only increasing as the number of homes sold increases. This is creating a strong demand for qualified people to start careers in the home inspection field.

Why Are Home Inspections Important?

The purchase of a home is likely to represent the single-largest financial transaction for anyone in his or her life that has risk associated with it. A **home inspector** is the buyer's advocate and provides the potential homeowner with education about the condition of the potential home purchase. They are involved to protect the potential buyers' interests.

An accurate **home inspection** can save thousands of dollars and even years of regret. Even at the going average of $240 per home inspection nationally (range is usually $200 -$500), it is a bargain if problems like faulty roofing, wiring, or foundations are spotted. Each of those could cost a homeowner in the thousands of dollars to repair.

Every home has a list of some problems with it, whether it is a short, medium, or long list. A home buyer can save thousands of dollars on post-escrow discoveries and subsequent repairs by having a thorough home inspection performed by a qualified professional.

A home inspector is trained to spot problems and conditions which may compromise the safety of occupants like bad electrical wiring and fixtures, faulty ventilation in areas like fireplaces and chimneys, leaking gas appliances, substandard construction, fire rating non-compliance, improper glass glazing, and even railings that are dangerous. They are also trained to look for conditions that would affect the livability or resale value for the home.

Home inspectors do not point out every little problem with a home. Cosmetic or other minor problems should be apparent without the help of a professional home inspector.

Home inspection can also provide a potential home buyer protection by making the sale contingent upon a satisfactory inspection. This can allow for a buyer to get out of the contract if major problems with the home are found. Home buying contracts can also be written so that a monetary compromise is made for the problems found. An inspection, by comparison, is a deal if it helps to uncover some serious problems with the home and allows for an escape from a damaged home or compensates the buyer for problems.

Earning Potential of a Home Inspector

Home inspection offers Mike and Jenny, as well as many other like-minded people, the opportunity to improve their lives and provide for their families.

A huge need exists for qualified home inspectors in the industry. It is estimated that 15,000 homes are sold each year for every 1,000,000 people, or 1.5%. The percentage of these homes that are inspected can range in different areas of the country but was reported as 77% nationally in 2000. Exact figures for the number of inspections can be obtained from local real estate and home inspection agencies.

Approximately 290,000,000 people live in the U.S. If the same formula of 1.5% of the population selling a home is applied, then there will be 4,350,000 homes sold in any given year.

If the same 77% figure is used to represent homes inspected, then 3,349,500 homes will be inspected. Bear in mind this is but an average and actual home sales are much higher. In 2000, 6,027,000 homes were sold. In 2004, there were projected to be 6,490,000 existing homes and 1,150,000 new home sales. Together, this equals 7,640,000 homes that would be sold. Now if the 77% is used as the inspection rate, then there would be 5,882,800 home inspections performed nationally in 2004. That is a huge number and is up significantly in just four years when there were 4,900,000 inspections. That represents almost 1,000,000 more opportunities to earn money in the U.S. over the last four years for home inspectors.

Getting Started

Sounds good, right? Home inspection is an attractive career opportunity. However, before you can get started, you may need a home inspection course and a state license or certificate. Additionally, you will have to decide whether you want to work for an established firm or start your own home inspection business. Whether you work for yourself or a home inspection company, you will need some supplemental income to help you through the transition period, extra liability insurance, and the necessary tools to perform home inspections.

Education and Licensing

Even though many people enter the home inspection business from a related industry such as construction or real estate, it is important to take a home inspection course. You may wonder why someone familiar with construction would need to complete a home inspection course. It is because some states require education and training while others do not.

All states have varying education, examination, and licensing requirements for home inspectors. Some states require apprenticeship programs before becoming an actual home inspector. Knowing the requirements and following them is an important step in starting the home inspection business. Appendix A shows the state requirements for home inspectors.

Supplemental Income

You will need to have some type of supplemental income or savings to support yourself while getting started in the home inspection business. It will probably take around six months to become established and to have a steady flow of income.

Whether you are paid per inspection by a company or are in business for yourself, the good news is that inspection fees run between $200 and $400. Since an experienced inspector can usually complete two inspections per day, once you are established, the earning potential is there.

Insurance

You will need errors and omissions insurance, and if you own the business, you will need general liability insurance. **Errors and omission** (E&O) **insurance** will protect you from lawsuits arising from serious mistakes or even things you may leave off the inspection report. **General liability insurance** will cover the costs of any damage you might do to the property, like falling through the roof or attic while inspecting it. Purchasing E&O and general liability insurance will probably be your largest expense. It is difficult to estimate the premiums due to the specific information one needs to get a quote, but they can cost upwards of a few thousand dollars, so be prepared.

Tools

Your five senses are probably the most important tools you can bring to the job. Your sense of smell can tell you if there is mold or mildew present from a possible water leak. Your nose will alert you to possible gas leaks, or improperly vented sewage pipes. Your eyes will provide most of the data for your report. You can hear fan motors in need of new bearings, and your sense of touch will alert you to uneven surfaces or weak spots.

You should always be prepared to protect yourself with coveralls, boots, gloves, and a hard hat. Every home inspector should have the following **tools** to perform a professional home inspection. Although a company may furnish you some of these items, it is preferable to own your own equipment.

Necessary Tools to Perform a Home Inspection

- Two (2) powerful flashlights
- Extra batteries and bulbs
- Folding ladder (OSHA approved)
- Pair of pliers
- Pair of binoculars
- Electrical multi-tester
- Ground fault circuit interrupter (GFCI) circuit tester
- Outlet polarity tester
- Water pressure gauge
- Fireplace gas key
- Adjustable wrench - 12"
- Two (2) screwdrivers (Phillips and flathead)
- Dial thermometer (for checking HVAC)
- Mercury thermometer for checking ovens
- Camera (preferably digital)
- Telescoping mirror
- Lead paint test kit
- Hand-held tape recorder
- Painter's mask or other filtered mask

Figure 1.1
Water pressure gauge

Figure 1.2
Screwdrivers and flashlight

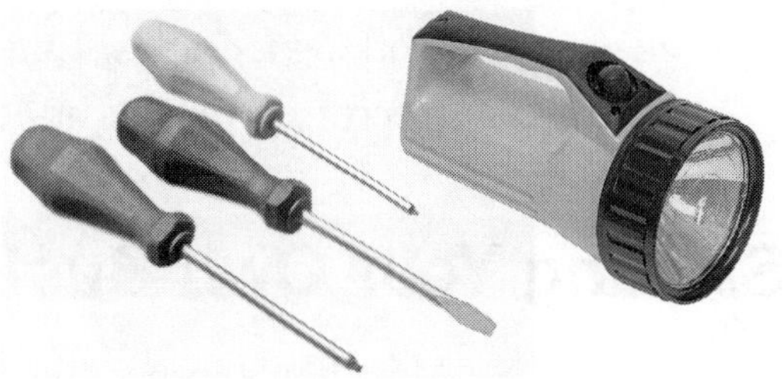

Working For an Established Firm

National and regional home inspection companies frequently will hire someone who has recently entered the field. Keep in mind most of these firms will require certification or special training to limit their liability should mistakes be made.

When working for an established firm, the home inspector will be paid a percentage of the inspection fee and the company will bear most of the costs associated with marketing, licensing, and insurance. The firm will also be responsible for scheduling appointments and/or acquiring the business. It will be the individual home inspector's responsibility to provide his or her own vehicle and the necessary tools to complete the inspection.

A good place to look for hiring notices is at the various home inspection associations, such as the American Society of Home Inspectors (ASHI), National Association of Home Inspectors (NAHI), National Association of Certified Home Inspectors (NACHI), and the Home Inspection Foundation (HIF).

Advantages of working for an established firm

- Avoiding initial start-up costs
- Gaining experience
- Gaining a network of potential clients and REALTORS® to work for
- Earning a steady income
- Steady customer flow/work schedule
- Company provided benefits received
- Company provided insurance to work under

Working for an existing firm is not nearly as common as the new home inspector starting his or her own new business.

Starting Your Own Business

Most home inspection companies are run by an individual because people who become home inspectors usually like the idea of being in business for themselves. The kind of person who is self-motivated and enjoys making decisions may want to consider owning their own company.

So, before starting your own home inspection business, you should ask yourself the following questions:

- What are the advantages and disadvantages of starting my own home inspection business?
- What are the most important facts I need to know to become a home inspector?
- What kind of training or certification is needed?
- How can I determine that my interest in the field will bring me success?
- Can I make a living in the home inspection business?

It is important to realize that although there are a lot of significant advantages to owning your own business, there are also some substantial risks. As a home inspector you will be making judgments that affect the value of properties selling for hundreds of thousands of dollars. You may perform an absolutely flawless inspection and still find yourself in the crosshairs of a legal battle. You may find yourself liable for thousands of dollars in damages all because one of the parties did not like the results of your findings.

Review - Advantages and Disadvantages of Starting Your Own Business

Advantages

- Increased earning potential
- Being your own boss
- Freedom to fully express ideas and thoughts
- Having a flexible schedule
- Personal satisfaction of owning own business

Disadvantages

- Financial risk of initial investment
- Possible shaky income
- No medical insurance provided
- All taxes have to be paid by sole owner
- There can be long and hard hours at first in order to get established

Capital Requirements

Prepare a business plan and budget so that you can determine the initial capital outlay to start the business and the ongoing operating expenses. Initially, **expenses** will always be more than you expect and revenue will generally be less.

The following is a list of items and costs that you should include in your budget. The only item not included in this budget is a vehicle expense because you can put a folding ladder into almost any car.

Item	**Low**	**High**
Training	$1,000	$3,000
Legal/Accounting	$500	$1,000
Licenses/Permits	$100	$300
Error and Omissions Insurance	$3,000	$5,000
Cards/Brochures	$400	$600
Inspection Reports/Software	$300	$800
Computer/Printer/Fax	$1,200	$2,500
Digital Camera/Binoculars	$400	$1,000
Tools/Ladder	$500	$1,000
Organization Memberships	$250	$1,000
Total	**$7,650**	**$16,200**

Types of Business Ownership

Once you make the decision to start your own business you need to decide which type of **business ownership** is appropriate for you. It is highly recommended that you secure the services of both an attorney and an accountant to assist you in making your final decision.

Sole Proprietorship

A **sole proprietorship** is the simplest and cheapest business format. It is designed for a one-person operation. Normally all you would need to do is choose a name and secure a business license in the municipality where your home office is located. If you choose to use your name as part of your business name, such as "Your Name Inspection Services." there is little likelihood that someone else will be using the same name in your market area. To ensure that you have chosen a unique business name, you should search the web or the county and state recorders office to see if the name is already registered.

In a sole proprietorship, all income received is treated as personal income and taxed accordingly. All expenses related to starting and operating the business are deductible. There is no liability protection in this form of business ownership. In the event that a substantial judgment is awarded against you, all of your personal assets could be seized.

Partnership

A **partnership** is formed when two or more individuals share in the operation of a business. Revenue flows into the partnership and out to the partners based on their percentage of ownership of the company. Percentage of ownership can be based on any mutually agreed-upon formula, such as capital contribution, time devoted to the partnership, or a combination of these.

The partnership itself does not have any tax liability but does exist as a reporting entity for various government agencies. Your share of the partnership revenue will be treated as personal income and taxed similarly to a sole proprietorship. You will also have the same liability issues of a sole proprietorship.

Corporation

A **corporation** is the most complex and expensive business format to create. A corporation is a business entity, created under state law that has an existence independent of the people who run it. The chief advantages of the corporation are that it effectively shields personal assets from claims by creditors or judgments, and the issuance of stock makes it easy to allocate ownership in any ratio.

The major disadvantages are that it is the most expensive form of business to start and maintain, it has very strict reporting and filing requirements, and it is subject to double taxation. **Double taxation** means the corporation's income is taxed and then the salaries of the employees, including the owners, are taxed as well.

Limited Liability Company (LLC)

This is a relatively new form of organization. The **limited liability company** (LLC) combines the simplicity of a sole proprietorship with the liability protection of a corporation. Like a corporation, the LLC has a separate and distinct identity that serves to protect the assets of the individual or individuals who operate it from being sued. An LLC is relatively easy to form and has modest reporting requirements. It is not subject to double taxation, as corporations are. Revenue flows into the LLC and out to the principals as ordinary income. The partners pay taxes on their income, but the partnership itself does not pay taxes. This form of business is a good choice for aspiring home inspectors.

Franchise

This is not exactly a business format in the same sense as a corporation or partnership. When you purchase a **franchise**, you will be buying the rights to use an established trade name and usually a protected trade area. Franchises are not cheap, but for someone with limited business experience they can often provide an effective way to get into business without the usual start-up risks. Most franchises will offer training and marketing aids to get customers.

Business Name and Registration

After consulting with an attorney and accountant, and selecting a business format, you will need to choose a name for your enterprise, register it, and secure the necessary licenses and permits to operate it. If your state requires that individual inspectors be licensed and/or insured, then you will need to satisfy those requirements. A list of states' requirements for licensing and insurance will be discussed later in this chapter.

When selecting a name for your business, keep the following guidelines in mind:

- The name should reflect what you do, it should be easy to say and easy to remember.
- As stated earlier, including your own name in your business name will almost always assure availability. For instance, "Jones Accurate Inspections" fulfills the requirements.
- If you choose to set up a sole proprietorship or partnership, you will need to file a fictitious business name statement with a local government agency. This name is often referred to as a DBA, which stands for "doing business as." If you set up a corporation, the business name will be registered when you file the documents of incorporation.

Communication

Communication with all parties is crucial. You will earn the respect of both buyer and seller if all the interested parties are present during the inspection and if you are diligent and forthcoming about your findings.

To avoid any legal issues, perform a thorough and competent inspection and make sure your client knows exactly what you are going to inspect and what the report will include. You should also explain what will not be included in the written home inspection report. Make sure you have the appropriate disclaimers in your contract and carry insurance.

Marketing and Selling Your Business

The most important factor in determining your success in this business is your ability to persuade people to try your services for the first time. Becoming a home inspector is not like opening a newsstand in a busy airport. You will have to go to the market because it is not going to come to you.

Marketing

A good way to begin **marketing** your business is to determine the geographic boundaries of the market you want to serve and then create a list of all the REALTORS® in the area. You can do this with the phone directory, the Internet, or the Chamber of Commerce. Once your area of marketing is determined, you can then start writing to prospective clients.

Write an introductory letter including a brief biographical sketch, a description of your services, and your intention to call the recipient soon to introduce yourself personally. Remember to keep updating the list of prospective clients to whom you want to market.

Stay current of any developments in the business so you have something informative to discuss on your visits. Soon you will be regarded as a familiar part of the scene. Familiarity produces trust, trust is the basis of relationships, and relationships are the foundation of business.

Make sure everyone you know is aware that you are now in the business of home inspecting and never leave the house without a stack of business cards and brochures.

There is a trend nowadays to produce and distribute the inspection report at the completion of the job but you may want to consider setting an appointment to present the report a day or so later. This gives you an opportunity to make sure that the report is complete and accurate in the calm surroundings of your own office. It also gives you another opportunity to get face to face with your client and possibly the REALTOR®. Always include a few extra cards with the report and ask for referrals. Also, during an inspection where the buyer, the seller, and each of their respective agents are present, use the opportunity to create new business.

You do not need to spend a lot of money on advertising, but you certainly should be in the local yellow pages. It is recommended that you have a web site and invest in magnetic signs for your vehicle.

Sales

Good marketing will lead you to selling your services. This is especially important if you own a one-person company. You have to sell, even if you do not like the idea of it. Most people have a negative impression of sales because they think it requires nagging people into doing something that they don't want to do. Successful selling is giving people the opportunity to do or buy something that they need or want from you. In most cases the prospective purchaser will select the inspector that their real estate broker recommends, so it is imperative that you concentrate your selling efforts in this area.

Selling is a numbers game. You need to speak to enough prospects, and sooner or later you'll meet up with someone who needs what you're offering. When you get that first job from a new client, go out of your way to be thorough and professional. If you were referred to by a REALTOR® then make sure to follow up with the REALTOR®, and thank them for the opportunity.

Your competition may have grown complacent and may be taking these relationships for granted. It is rare in this day and age to find someone who actually does what they say they are going to do, when they say they are going to do it, and for the amount they quoted. If you can deliver on these commitments, you will soon find yourself with more business than you can handle.

It may be your first inspection, but chances are you know more about the home and the systems than either the buyer or the seller. Take the time to go over your findings in clear language with your client in an objective manner, without making specific recommendations regarding repair cost. You do not need to dwell on cosmetic items, but make sure that safety or structural issues are pointed out to all interested parties. A great way to get experience and practice of the dialogue is to offer to inspect your friends' and family's houses free of charge.

The Inspection Process

A thorough inspection should include an assessment of the exterior and interior of the house, from roof to foundation, as well as a performance analysis of the electrical, plumbing, heating, and air-conditioning systems. In home inspection, you should use your five senses to listen, smell, hear, feel, and see possible problems in the home. There really is no substitute for the five senses in home inspection. The tools suggested previously will help boost the efficiency of these senses and improve the accuracy of the home inspection. Although home inspection is to be non-invasive, you may have to probe and even disassemble some systems in order to get an accurate look at their condition.

Since most homes are made from wood, there is a chance that over time, the wood has incurred some damage. Remember the roof structure, wall studs, mudsills, floor joists, and even sub-floors are made from wood. Due to their structural importance, they must be checked for rot, decay, or insect infestation that could weaken them and cause failure.

As previously mentioned, your five senses will be the first tools you use in home inspection. If you smell mildew or musty wood, you need to probe the wood to see if it has rotted. Wood can be probed by poking or stabbing the wood using your ordinary screwdriver. If the screwdriver goes into the wood more than a 1/4 inch to 1/2 inch, then there is rot or decay of some kind.

What about areas where wood is covered by paint, or wood sub-flooring is covered by carpet? You can easily press on the wood with your fingers. Damaged wood will be spongy and give way. Floors that are spongy and give way when walked over slowly may also have damaged wood underneath them.

If you smell burnt electrical wiring, you may need to open an electrical outlet using a screwdriver and visually inspect the wiring. For safety, you will want to touch the electrical outlet cover to make sure it is not electrically charged or hot before opening it up. After the visual check, you may need to pull the wiring out from the outlet so you may further inspect the condition, type, and size of wiring being used. This may tell you something about other problems like flickering lights or even blown fuses in the home.

Home inspectors look for potential problems and safety issues in homes for their clients. However, inspectors must also look to their own safety while inspecting a property. There are potential safety hazards when inspecting a home, particularly the remote areas of a property such as the roof, attic, or crawlspace. It is important for an inspector to be alert when performing home inspections and to know the proper use of tools. Following safety procedures protects both the inspector and the client.

Chapter 2
Soils, Foundations, and Floors

Introduction

In order to do a thorough job, a home inspector needs to know about more than just the building and its construction. Having knowledge of local soils and their associated conditions can go a long way in aiding the home inspector when trying to determine other problems in the home.

Factors Affecting the Foundation

Many factors affect the foundation of a home. The type of **soil** and its movement can affect the overall function of the foundation. Location can restrict the type of foundation that can be used. For example, the foundations of homes in colder climates will have to deal with frost in the soil and will need a foundation type that extends below the **frost line**. **Grading** and **drainage** also affect the stability of a foundation.

Types of Soil

Soil formation is a product of time, climate, and the characteristics of the native plants and animals. All soil is composed of one or more of the following ingredients: sand, clay, silt, and gravel. Soil is usually classified as sandy, clay, or loam. **Sandy soil** contains mostly sand and does not hold water very well. Most sand is small pieces of quartz. **Clay soil** is mostly clay and is made mostly of small pieces of mineral other than quartz. Clay soil holds water very well. The third type of soil is loam. **Loam** is made of gravel, sand, clay, and a lot of humus. Examples of loam would be sandy loam (sand and silt) or clay loam (clay and other soil types). There is a great deal of variation in soil composition in different parts of the country, and the home inspector needs to be familiar with the local conditions.

Weight-bearing Ability of Soil

The ability of the soil to carry the weight of the structure is largely determined by its composition. Physical properties of soil include plasticity, grain size, and other relevant factors. **Plasticity** is the range of moisture content within which the soil will remain plastic. **Grain size** refers to the dimensions of the individual soil grains.

One soil grain type is **coarse-grained soil**. Sand and gravel are considered coarse-grained soils because individual grains can be seen with the naked eye. Course grained soil has few voids (spaces) when compacted. This makes it stable and resistant to shifting when bearing the weight of a building or other structure.

Another type of soil grain is **fine-grained soil**. Silt and clay are examples of this type. These types are almost fluid in nature and must be checked to ensure the amount of moisture is stabilized. **Expansive clay** has the ability to swell and to shrink dramatically depending on the existing moisture conditions. Therefore, expansive clay requires careful planning regarding drainage, landscaping, and irrigation. When a building is located in an area that has fine-grained soil and seismic activity, then seismic bracing or anchoring may be necessary to keep the foundation stable and structure safe from failure.

Causes of Soil Movement

Soil movement occurs when soil expands or contracts and exerts pressure on the foundation. When the soil moves uniformly exerting force on the entire foundation, it is usually not harmful. When the forces of soil movement are uneven on a foundation, the inside of the attached structure can be bent or twisted. This is usually caused by a change in the moisture content of the surrounding soil. Over watering, poor drainage, and even leaking plumbing can be a result of this. Common examples of this condition are interior or exterior wall cracks, ceiling cracks, sticking doors or windows, pulled roof trusses, or broken windows.

Figure 2.1
Improper grading can cause erosion

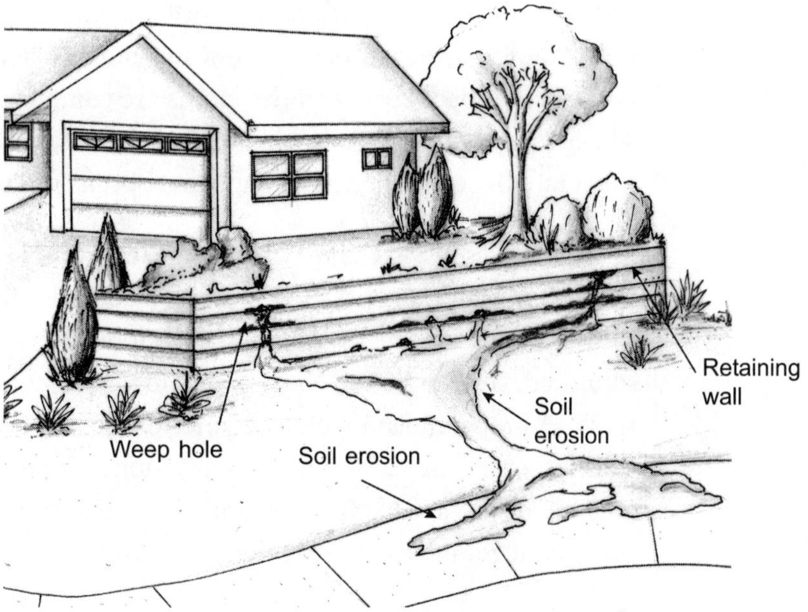

Moisture Content

To keep a building's foundation safe, the moisture content of the soil must be kept stable—it can be neither too dry nor too wet. **Moisture** is a small amount of water that causes something to become damp.

Dry Soil

If the soil surrounding the foundation is allowed to get too dry, it will form cracks and begin to shrink away from the building. The cracks will allow greater evaporation of the moisture in the soil around the building perimeter. When it rains, the cracks provide a path for water to erode the soil under the edge of the building. This could lead to possible cracking of the foundation or slab.

Tree roots can cause movement in foundations and can harm plumbing systems. In addition, trees and vegetation can dry out the soil beneath a foundation by **wicking** the water out of the soil. A general guide is to have a tree no closer than one and one-half times its mature height. This becomes more difficult as lot sizes decrease.

Saturated Soil

When water contacts dry soil, the grains become coated with **moisture**. Once the spaces between the grains are filled with water, any additional water that is added to the soil will drip down until it contacts the ground water at the **water table**. The area below the water table is called the **saturation zone** because the spaces between the grains are completely saturated with water. The area above the water table is called the **aeration zone**. The level of the water table is determined by how much moisture is in the soil at any given time.

Fine-grained soils, like clay, will become fluid when saturated with water and may be unable to support a load such as a building. Expansive clay soils, such as those found in the Southwest, may double in volume when thoroughly saturated. This dramatic change in volume can put severe stress on foundations. A proper moisture maintenance program is critical with these kinds of soils to control expansion and contraction. Coarse-grained soils, like sand and gravel, are less likely to expand and contract with the addition of water due to the granular nature of their composition.

Soil Moisture Control

Moisture is removed from soil by evaporation. Additionally, trees and large shrubs can remove hundreds of gallons a day by themselves. To keep a building's foundation safe, the moisture content of the soil must be kept stable. The most effective method for controlling foundation movement in expansive soils is a controlled watering program. The purpose of this program is to maintain a constant level of moisture in the soil around and under the foundation.

An automatic lawn sprinkling system is a very effective way to introduce a controlled amount of moisture to the foundation. The sprinkler heads should be located at least 18 inches from the foundation and aimed so that they do not spray on the building itself. The reason for locating the sprinkler heads at least 18 inches from the foundation is to set up the capillary action that will draw the water to the foundation. The irrigation system should not spray water on the foundation directly as this could create erosion. Erosion weakens the foundation causing settling and cracks.

The home inspector should operate the system manually and check the following: missing or damaged sprinkler heads, misplaced or misdirected sprinkler heads, missing or damaged connection parts, watering of the structure or foundation, and standing water. Any missing heads or leaking connectors should be noted and reported.

Reportable Deficiencies - Soil Moisture and Control

- Missing or damaged sprinkler heads
- Misplaced or misdirected sprinkler heads
- Missing or damaged connection parts
- Watering the structure or foundation
- Standing water

Drainage

The **drainage systems** direct surface and **subsurface water** away from the property. Another purpose of the drainage system is to maintain a constant level of moisture at the foundation. A system of **inlets**, **catch basins**, **French drains**, and **perforated pipes** should be used to move surface and subsurface water away from the perimeter of the building. In addition to these mechanical features, swales should be cut to direct the water to these collection points. A **swale** is a shallow depression cut into the soil to direct the flow of water.

Inadequate drainage can allow water to penetrate the structure. An improperly designed drainage system can contribute to premature foundation failure, and in extreme cases can cause the structure to collapse.

Figure 2.2
Arrows demonstrate grading methods to divert water away from a home's foundation.

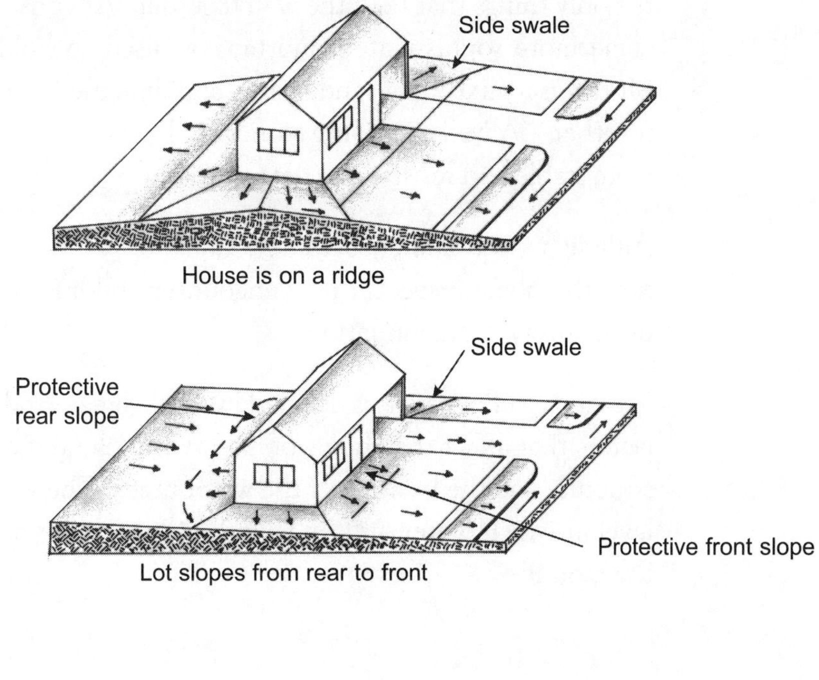

Suitable drainage starts with the proper grading of the site. The lot should be graded to produce a **slope** or decline away from the building. This slope should be from 2 percent to 5 percent (a 4 percent slope will lose 5 inches in 10 feet). If the slope is too steep, the surface water will drain too quickly and will soon erode the site. Proper drainage is as important as proper footing design to the integrity of the foundation.

In certain cases, the runoff will have to be collected in a **sump** and pumped to the storm sewer. **Gutters** and **down spouts** should be adequately sized and positioned to handle the anticipated flow. The down spouts should direct the water to an area away from the foundation walls.

Foundations

Since the foundation supports the entire structure and its weight, it is obvious that this area of the building requires the most rigorous of safety inspections and strict adherence to all applicable building codes.

The **foundation** of a structure has two purposes: (1) it supports the entire building, and (2) it transfers the weight of the building to the ground. It is imperative that the home inspector pay particular attention to this feature. Foundation problems can be the cause of plumbing leaks, squeaky and uneven floors, sticking doors, and cracked walls.

Typically, foundations are made of poured concrete, cinder or concrete blocks, or wood. The earliest foundations were dry laid stones, which were simply piled one on top of another without any mortar. Gravity and friction were the only things that held the wall together. As construction techniques became more sophisticated, mortar was used to hold the stones together. **Mortar** is a mixture of sand, water, and lime used to bind stones or masonry together. A wall where the stones are bound together with mortar is much more stable and resistant to deformation.

Although stone is rarely used for foundations in modern residential construction, the home inspector may encounter buildings in older neighborhoods using this type of foundation.

The choice of materials is dictated by local climate and soil conditions. Other factors that affect the choice of materials include the size and weight of the structure and the location of the water table. The **water table** is the natural level at which water will be found, either above or below the surface of the ground.

Slab-on-Grade Foundations

Depending on the climate, soil conditions, and architectural requirements the builder may use a slab-on-grade foundation. A **slab-on-grade foundation** is a foundation built directly on the ground with the foundation and footing as an integral unit. A **footing** is the spreading part at the base of a foundation wall or pier. A properly designed slab supports the weight of the entire structure, and is unaffected by soil movement.

A **monolithic slab** is poured in one piece. It requires a wide base and steel reinforcement. The slab floor alone will not support interior loadbearing walls so an interior footing is trenched in before the slab is poured. A **floating slab** is composed of one section for the floor and another for the foundation wall, each poured separately. The two parts are separated by an expansion joint. A **screeded slab** is a wooden floor built on a **concrete slab** with no crawlspace underneath. The space under the wood flooring is usually used as a return for the heating and cooling system.

Figure 2.3
Monolithic slab

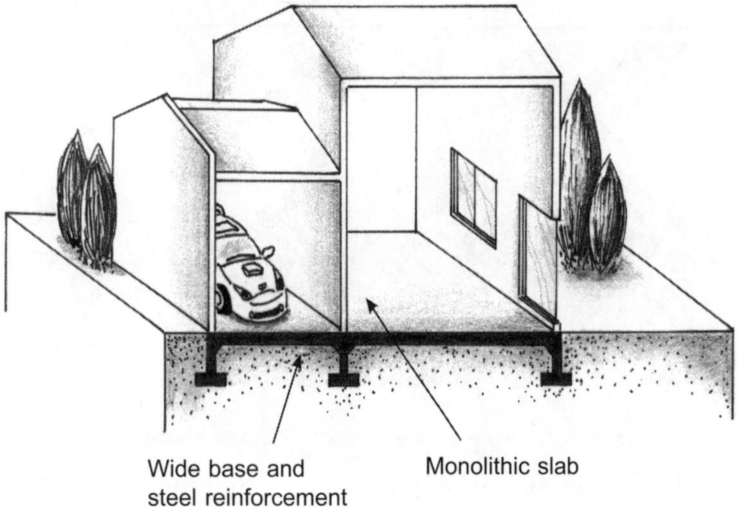

Poured concrete slabs are generally reinforced with steel bar or mesh, and in some cases, a technique called post tensioning is used. In a **post-tensioned slab**, cables are laid in the wet concrete and put under tension after the concrete has cured. This technique increases the strength of the finished foundation. Inspectors need to make sure someone has not cut or drilled into a post-tensioned slab.

The slab should be poured on top of clean soil, sand, or gravel. If sand or gravel is used it will stop the capillary action and prevent ground water from contacting the slab. Polyethylene will accomplish the same thing, but care must be taken where the sheets overlap and penetrations are made. In some cases, heating ducts may be incorporated as part of the slab. A slab should be at least 4 inches thick but may be thicker in areas where a greater load is carried, such as chimneys and interior bearing walls.

Cinder or Concrete Block Foundations

Concrete masonry units (CMUs) are a very common material for foundation wall construction. Commonly called concrete or cinder block, this material is strong and durable if proper techniques are employed during its construction. Both poured concrete and CMUs are absorbent and need to be coated with waterproofing material when used as foundation construction material.

Figure 2.4
An example of rebar

To increase the strength and resistance to cracking, reinforcing steel should always be used in conjunction with masonry or poured concrete. Reinforcing steel, commonly called **rebar**, is sold in various diameters starting at $^1/_8$ inch. It is identified by using the numeral 1 for $^1/_8$ inch, 2 for $^2/_8$ inch, 3 for $^3/_8$ inch, and so on.

The foundation itself rests on a footing that should be at least 1 foot below the finished grade or the frost line, whichever is deeper. The pressure exerted by the soil increases with depth, so the deeper the foundation wall is placed, the thicker the construction needs to be. For example, a concrete foundation wall only needs to be 8 inches thick for depths up to 5 feet, but must be 12 inches thick at 7 feet. Similar increases hold true for poured concrete. **Efflorescence** is a white powdery substance that forms on the surface of masonry by water leaching out certain chemicals. If efflorescence is found on the interior of a basement wall, it is a sure sign of water intrusion.

Wood Foundations

In areas that are free from wood-destroying pests such as termites, wood can be an excellent foundation material. Wood is very simple to use, is a great insulator, and allows for flexibility of design. The depth of the foundation wall will determine the size of the studs to be used and their spacing.

As with other foundation systems, adequate drainage is essential to maintain the integrity of the structure. A 4 inch layer of gravel should be placed under the foundation floor and covered with a polyethylene vapor barrier. Wood foundation materials need to be pressure treated and can last up to thirty years if kept free of standing water. The home inspector will learn to recognize the distinctive odor of damp or decaying wood.

Pier and Beam Foundations

Pier and beam construction uses a system of piers and girders together with the foundation walls to support the structure. **Girders** are needed when the span is too great for the use of floor joists alone. Girders are secured to foundation walls either by using pockets or by placing the girders on top of the walls. The girders themselves may be formed from a solid piece of wood or built up from laminated planks.

Piers

Vertical columns that support a foundation are called **piers**. In areas with stable soil conditions, piers can be used economically to support the foundation system. In some cases, piers will be used similarly to pilings to bypass weak soil and reach a firmer bearing area. Typically, the pier will rest on a footing and may have the lower end "belled" out to increase the bearing area.

Piles

In cases where the underlying soil is not capable of supporting the structure, piles may be employed. **Piles** are vertical foundation members that transfer the load to the ground and may be made of wood, steel, concrete, or a combination of these materials. Piles are driven into the ground until either bedrock or friction will allow no further driving. The ends are then cut level, and the foundation system is attached to the piles. The inspector should examine any exposed piles for signs of deterioration or structural problems.

Crawlspaces and Basements

Buildings with raised foundations will have either a crawlspace or a basement. A **crawlspace** is a low space beneath a floor of a building to give workers access to wiring and plumbing. A **basement** is the lowest story of a building partially or entirely below ground.

Figure 2.5
Crawlspace with concrete footing and air vents.

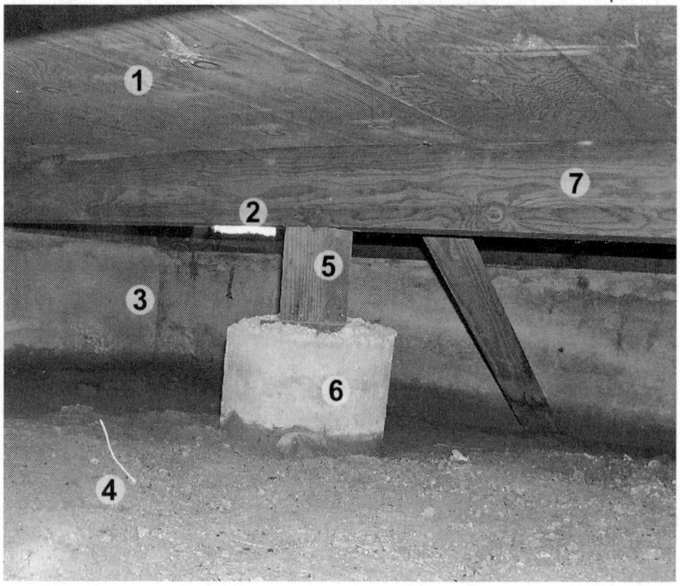

1) Floor sheathing
2) Crawlspace vent
3) Concrete crawlspace foundation
4) Grade
5) Wood column
6) Concrete footing
7) Floor beam

Crawlspace

In areas where more moderate climate prevails, homes built with pier and beam foundations will have a crawlspace that may be 18 inches to 4 feet tall. The crawlspace is not large enough to be a finished or livable space. It serves the same purpose as the basement in that it connects the foundation of the home to footings and piles that are pounded into the earth below the frost line. There should be access into the crawlspace. The size of the opening may be dictated by local code. It is usually between 18 by 24 inches or 20 by 28 inches. In any case, it should be big enough to allow access to check the crawlspace.

Under-floor Ventilation

Homes need air to circulate in subfloor areas to keep wood and other structural components free from mold and fungi growth, insect infestation, and even wood rot. Under-floor ventilation is especially important in homes where crawlspaces are present.

Sub-floor ventilation is divided into two types: (1) natural cross flow ventilation where the air flows in from the outside via natural air currents and (2) mechanical ventilation, where fans are installed to manipulate air in or out to help ventilation. Both types may be needed in order to get proper under floor ventilation for a home. This is a critical area for the home inspector. The inspector should check for adequate ventilation, moisture penetration, plumbing leaks, evidence of pest infestation, and efflorescence. Home inspectors should look for proper screening on vents and fans to ensure animal and insect infestation can be controlled or limited in the crawlspace or basement.

If possible, the home inspector should enter the crawlspace to perform a thorough examination, but if there is evidence of standing water or other potential hazards such as wiring on the ground, an examination from the entrance will have to suffice. The home inspector should also note access to crawlspaces that are not large enough or too big to meet code standards.

Reportable Deficiencies - Crawlspaces

- Inadequate ventilation
- Moisture penetration or standing water
- Plumbing leaks
- Pest infestation
- Efflorescence
- Lack of screens on vents
- Crawlspace size that does not meet code standards

Basements

In the colder parts of the country where the frost line may be 5 or 6 feet deep, many homes are built with basements. **Basements** are the stories of a building that are below grade or below ground level that can be finished spaces or unfinished spaces. Good building practice and codes require the footing for the foundation to be below the area where the ground freezes. The reason for requiring footings to be placed below the frost line is to minimize the movement associated with the cyclical freezing and thawing of the soil during the winter.

Figure 2.6
A basement is built below ground level and can be used as living and/or storage space. Basements can be solid concrete or a combination of concrete and stone.

Water and Dampness Problems

Water or moisture in the basement or the crawlspace should always be reported. Water may collect in the basement or crawlspace due to gravity, ground water intrusion, or wicking. **Wicking** is a capillary action phenomenon caused by surface tension. It is not affected by gravity or pressure. This process can be interrupted by using a vapor barrier such as polyethylene or a layer of course-grained sand or gravel.

Water in the basement may be constant or intermittent depending on the cause. There will be traces left behind to alert the home inspector such as efflorescence, fine sand, or dirt on the floor.

If the basement floods every time it rains, then the time delay between the onset of the rain and the onset of the flooding can be a clue as to the cause of the wet basement. If there is a considerable delay, then the cause is likely to be associated with the water table. This is because it takes some time for rainwater to get to the water table and raise it to the level of the basement. If the onset is almost immediate, then the roof drainage system is the likely culprit. Look for clogged drains, downspouts, and reverse slope grading next to the house as signs of drainage problems.

While not as obvious or serious as water in the basement or crawlspace, dampness also should be noted on the inspection report. **Dampness** is caused by the condensation of moisture out of the air. **Condensation** occurs when the temperature of the air is cooled by contact with a cold water pipe or cool basement wall and the moisture that was held in the air is deposited on the pipe or wall.

One way to control basement dampness is to use a good quality vapor barrier such as tar or polyethylene on the outside surface of the foundation wall during construction. This serves to keep the moisture found naturally in the soil from entering the basement via capillary action. The problem is that tar or bitumen coatings will deteriorate in time and lose their effectiveness.

Drainage Systems or Sump Pumps

Foundation drainage systems are located below basements or crawlspaces. The main components of the drainage system are a drain and a sump.

A **sump** is a container that collects water. When a certain water level is reached, the water is pumped out by a **sump pump** to a storm sewer or a drain leading away from the structure. Sump pumps are essential in keeping a basement or crawlspace dry, thereby preventing moisture and mildew problems. They also help to keep these areas from flooding altogether.

Home inspectors should run the sump pump to make sure it works. In order to do this, they may need to put water in the sump and check the float switch. They should also look for signs of debris that could clog the system or damage it so that it would not function properly.

Footing Drains

Footing drains are used to remove unwanted subsurface water that might otherwise flow against a building's foundation. A footing drain consists of a waterproof membrane placed against the masonry. Porous material, such as gravel, is placed next to the membrane to allow water to flow through the gravel and away from the foundation. Any indication of a clogged outflow drain should be reported. Damaged or missing drain covers should also be noted.

In a process known as **cold flow**, a wall may become severely distorted and not crack. These walls can have serious bulges, bows, and sags. A wall whose center of gravity has been displaced from over its base is subject to collapse.

Inspection Items for Foundations

When examining foundations the inspector should check for cracking, settling, tilting, or shrinking. **Cracking** occurs when stresses on the foundation make it separate or fracture in spots. Cracks can be caused by many forces like settling. **Tilting** of the foundation, or not being level in all areas, can happen when it settles at different rates in some parts due to varying amounts of groundwater and other forces. **Settling cracks** occur when a foundation comes to rest or falls down into the soil. The stresses and weight of a building can cause cracks. Yet another area to look for in foundations is **shrinking cracks**. These occur when the concrete of the foundation naturally cures over time and decreases in size. The inspector should look for cracked or missing stones, bulging walls, and weak or crumbling mortar in older foundations. Newer foundations are primarily made of concrete. Therefore, the inspector should report cracking, rising up, tilting, sinking, or wetness if found.

Figure 2.7
Tilting of a foundation

Wood foundations will have problems like bowing, cracking, and signs of dry rot or insect infestation. Additionally, a wood foundation should not be placed directly on the soil. An important construction feature is to make sure that the walls and floors are properly connected to the foundation to resist the lateral forces generated by the backfill.

Cracking

Depending on how the stress load is distributed on the wall, it is possible for the concentration of force to overcome the strength of the wall. This will cause a failure or crack. Cracks will tend to appear where there is a change of materials or direction in a wall especially at windows, doorways, and corners.

Cracks in foundation walls are caused by overloading, settling, or heaving. Cracks on an angle or straight up and down are usually caused by settlement or heaving. Horizontal cracks are caused by load pressure or backfill pressure. The inspector will learn to recognize the pattern made by cracks with similar causes. Cracks that do not penetrate the wall, and are not accompanied by directional displacement, are considered cosmetic and not serious. They should however be noted on the inspection report.

Cracks are not usually singular in nature and if one is observed the home inspector should be on the lookout for more. If a crack is detected, there will be clues as to how long ago it was formed.

An old crack, which does not exhibit any signs of recent movement, is less of an issue than a new one. Evidence of dust and dirt accumulation in the crack will indicate that it was formed some time ago, while fresh clean edges suggest a more recent occurrence.

Settling

A wall that is subject to opposite adjacent forces will crack vertically. These cracks are commonly caused by settling, expansive soil, frost, or seismic activity. **Angle cracks** are created when the loads on the wall are offset from each other. These cracks are usually formed when there is dissimilar soil or piling failure. The angle of the crack points toward the load.

While most buildings experience some settling during the first few years, this should not produce dangerous cracks. If there is any doubt as to the structural integrity of the foundation, the services of a structural engineer should be recommended.

Shrinkage

V-cracks are formed by bending forces and require the presence of stress at three locations. If the crack is wider at the top but does not continue all the way to the bottom, then it probably was caused by shrinkage during the curing process.

Horizontal cracks may form when the pressure on the wall is exerted from the outside toward the inside. These cracks can be the result of expansive clay, improper backfilling, or frost expansion. Horizontal cracks often follow the mortar joints in block walls. The cracks will be in the center of the wall and will appear to be wider at the inner face.

Figure 2.8
Vertical V-cracks simple, equal loading

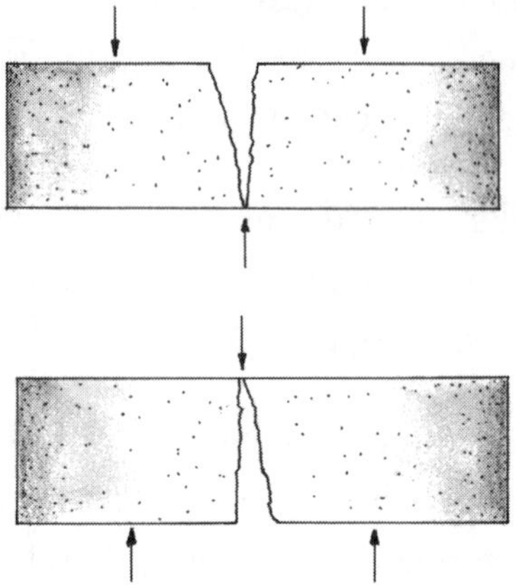

Cracks are commonly observed at openings for doors and windows where the load is being supported by a sill or header. These cracks are usually not serious but are cosmetic in nature.

Tilting

Cracks may also occur if the fill washes out from under the foundation or slab. Pay close attention to the area where downspouts drain or where there is any other source of running water. The home inspector cannot always determine the origin or severity of a crack, but it should be noted on the report. Cracks in concrete floors that are covered with carpet can often be discovered by walking on the floor without shoes. In certain areas, such as an ocean front property, where there is a high salt content in the moisture, a condition known as concrete spalling may be found. **Spalling** is the chipping, scarring, crumbling, or splitting of concrete, and is often the result of the reinforcing steel in the concrete rusting out.

Figure 2.9
Tilting foundation

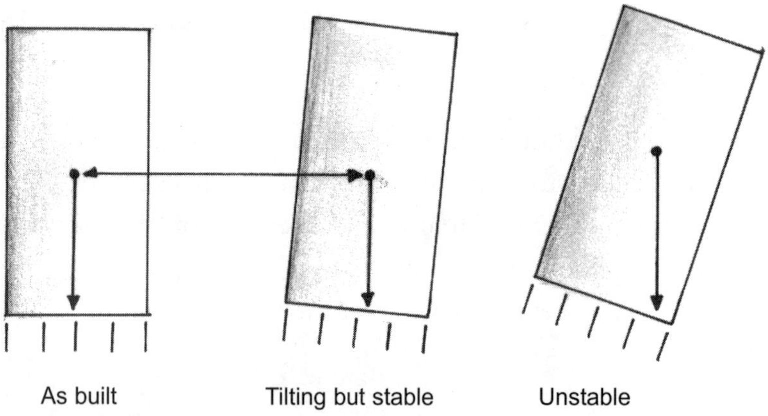

Reportable Deficiencies - Foundations

- Cracked or missing stones
- Bulging walls
- Weak or crumbling mortar
- Cracking, tilting, and sinking in concrete foundations
- Bowing, cracking, signs of dry rot, or insect infestation of wood foundations

Seismic Bracing or Retrofitting

Almost all of North America has a history of being seismically active. Most states outside of those on the West Coast do not have seismic requirements for bracing even though they are on faults. One area due for a quake is the New Madrid fault in the Midwest. When a quake hits, this will be a catastrophic event due to the large numbers of old masonry and brick buildings and the lack of seismic codes.

Figure 2.10
An earthquake can be a catastrophic event for old masonry and brick buildings.

For those people on the West Coast, seismic bracing and anchoring is factored into most new homes. Seismic bracing transfers the lateral and vertical forces of earthquakes to the foundation and makes walls and footings into one structural unit. The Uniform Building Code specifically states the need for a $^{1}/_{2}$ inch **anchor bolt** every 6 feet. In seismically active areas, the bolts are increased to $^{5}/_{8}$ inch diameter anchor bolts every 32 inches instead of every 6 feet. While these anchor bolts do a good job of holding the sill onto the foundation, they will not prevent walls from literally jumping off sub-flooring during seismic events. For this, seismic anchors or braces are needed. Most new residential structures in areas of seismic activity will have between 10 and 50 tie-downs.

For older homes, they can be retrofit to stabilize their structure during seismic events. The retrofitting adds structural stability to existing components without having to start over or rebuild entire parts. Some seismic braces can be added to already damaged parts of a home and make them immediately stable.

Home inspectors should be aware of the presence of seismic bracing and be checking for retrofitted components to ensure their proper installation and if needed, maintenance.

Foundation Repair

Although repair procedures are beyond the scope of a home inspection, the inspector should at least be able to discuss the possibilities with the client if the need arises. The most challenging situation is where the slab has shifted upward due to soil movement. This condition can sometimes be remedied with a process called **mud jacking**. In this process, cement is pumped through holes drilled in the slab and the slab floats to a level condition. In extreme cases, the old slab may have to be broken out and replaced.

Movement in a pier and beam foundation is caused by settlement or upheaval. The preferred repair procedure for both conditions is to shim. **Shimming** is the process of raising the level of the lower piers by inserting wedge-shaped pieces of material under the pier. This brings low piers to the level of the high ones. Only in extreme cases are the high piers cut down to the level of the low ones. It should be noted that shimming is only a temporary fix unless the cause of the soil movement is addressed. Most settling and foundation movement occurs early in the life of the home. If most of the movement has already occurred, the fix will be effective.

Floors

Floors transfer the loads in the house to the walls, foundations and on to the soil. They provide support for foundation walls. In order for floors to perform their function in construction, they must have strength and stiffness.

Strength in this instance refers to the ability of the floor to withstand the load placed on it. This refers to how much weight of the building the floor will hold before breaking or collapsing. The **stiffness** of floors refers to how much bending (deflection) happens when a weight load is applied to the floor. **Deflection** is the amount of bend in a board when under the stress of a load. Often building codes state how much deflection is allowed and how much drywall and plaster the floor will tolerate before breaking or cracking.

The two most common types of floor structures are the suspended wood flooring system and the concrete slab.

Suspended Wood Flooring Systems

Suspended wood flooring systems have five parts: sills, columns, beams, joists, and the sub-floor.

Sills

A **sill** is a board placed level on the foundation that is used to connect the exterior wall studs and floor joists. Sills are often separated from the foundation by a barrier or sill gasket. The **sill gasket** is a barrier used to separate the wood from the concrete and to stop air leakage between the sill and the foundation.

When sills are below the grade or ground level, serious consequences can arise. Insect infestation and damage, wood rot and building settlement all could result from the sill being below grade. Insect damage or wood rot weaken the strength of the wood and cause failures.

Crushed sills result from the weakening of the wood. This can occur if the proper type of wood is not used, water has harmed it, or insects have weakened it.

Some types of construction do not require the use of sills. One such example would be solid masonry construction. Here the joists may be connected directly to the masonry in pockets in the foundation or other walls. Rot is common in this scenario, so be sure to check these connections where possible.

Sometimes sills are not properly installed or anchored with the proper bolts. Bolts are sometimes hammered through sills instead of being inserted through drilled holes. This can cause failures in the sills. If the sills are not connected by evenly spaced holes or the bolts miss the sills when being installed, this could also be a problem for the structure.

Gaps in between the sills and the foundation can cause excessive heat loss and the structure to settle unevenly. This can cause the deflection of the floors to be less than needed.

Reportable Deficiencies - Sills
- Sills below the ground level or grade
- Crushed sills
- Insect damage to the sills
- Rotted wood sills
- Missing sills
- Improperly installed or anchored sills
- Gaps between sill and foundation

Columns

A column is a vertical structural member that provides support for the framing. Columns are made of wood or steel, but may also be concrete, concrete block, brick, or any combination of these materials. Columns are found inside the interior supporting walls. Columns that are integrated into exterior walls are known as pilasters.

Figure 2.11
Wood columns deficiency

1) Cracked wood foundation column
2) Underfloor insulation
3) Floor beam
4) Crawlspace ducting

Reportable Deficiencies - Columns

- Leaning columns
- Spalling concrete or brick on columns
- Missing columns
- Crushed columns
- Rusting columns
- Rotting columns
- Insect-infested columns
- Heaving, settled, or buckled columns
- Poorly secured columns
- Deteriorated mortar on columns
- Columns that have been previously repaired

Beams

Beams are horizontal structural components and bear the load of the floors, walls, and/or roof of a building, transferring it to the columns and/or foundation walls. They are normally made of wood, steel, or engineered wood products. Beams require $3^1/2$ inches of end bearing due to the loads they carry.

Reportable Deficiencies - Beams

- Sagging
- Rust
- Rot or insect damage
- Rotation or twisting
- Splitting
- Holes
- Poor connections
- Previous repairs
- Weak connections to columns or joists
- Lack of lateral support
- Missing sections

Joists

Joists are structural parts of the floor laid on beams to transfer the load of the floor, people, and items inside of the structure to beams, walls, or foundation walls. The joists that go around the outer edges of the structure are called **rim joists**, header joists, or band joists. Joists carry a lighter load than beams and require only $1^1/2$ inches of end bearing.

Reportable Deficiencies - Joists

- Sagging
- Rotting or insect infestation
- Poor or insufficient end bearing
- Rotating or twisting joints
- Splitting
- No strapping or poor connections
- Holes
- Missing components
- Previous repairs
- Weakness around opening in the joist system due to stairwells or chimneys

Subflooring

Another component of the wood floor system is the subfloor. **Subflooring** is the name given to boards or plywood sheets placed on joists over which a finish floor is to be laid. They commonly span 12 to 24 inches and are laid over and attached to joists with glue and nails. Boards can be installed either at right angles or diagonally across the joists, while plywood will be placed only at right angles.

Finished flooring is then attached to the subflooring boards or sheets at right angles to the subfloor to add strength. Small gaps are left to permit swelling due to moisture variations without causing buckling.

Reportable Deficiencies - Sub-Flooring

- Squeaks
- Rotting and insect infestation
- Cracking applied tiles
- Sagging or sponginess due to boards being undersized or over stretched
- Previous repairs
- Unsupported end of boards

Concrete Slab Flooring

The other type of floor system is the concrete slab. **Concrete slab flooring** is created when concrete is poured directly onto either supporting native soil or fill dirt. Slab floors can be suspended with living spaces or garages below, but this application is rare in homes. Concrete slab floors vary in thickness depending on their applications. The most common thickness for this type of floor is between 3 and 4 inches. Like sidewalks and even foundations, these concrete floor applications experience similar types of troubles.

Reportable Deficiencies - Concrete Slab Flooring

- Cracking
- Settling
- Concrete erosion
- Loss of soil support below the floor slab
- Rusting of support rebar
- Spalling

Figure 2.12
Concrete slab flooring and columns found typically in underground garages.

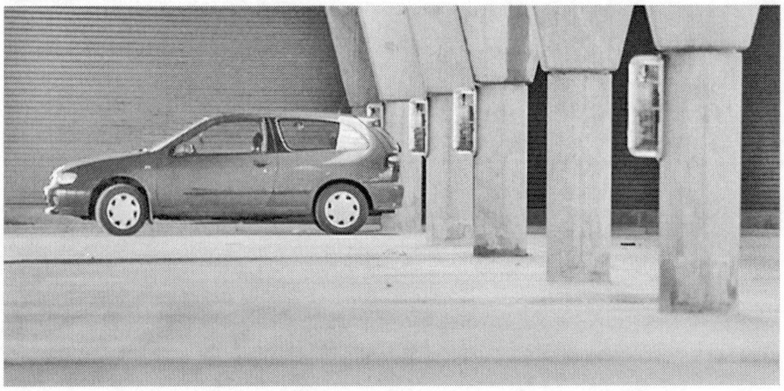

3

Chapter

The Exterior

Introduction

In order to examine the exterior of a home properly, the inspector must observe the grading, landscaping, walkways, driveways, attached structures, and retaining walls within 6 feet of the primary building. While not all of these items are necessarily within the scope of the home inspection, their appearance can often give a clue to items that are.

Once the exterior of the home and its associated structures have been described, the framing or backbone of the home will also be examined.

Grading

The grade of a property is important because proper grade causes water to run away from the foundation and the structure. **Grade** is the level or surface of the ground expressed as a percentage. For example, a 2-percent grade slopes 2 feet for every 100 feet of horizontal distance.

If the slope of the ground is toward the house, this may cause standing water, flooding of basements or crawlspaces during storms, and foundation damage over time.

Sometimes the level or elevation of the ground has to be changed or altered using bladed machines that literally scrape the earth in a process known as **grading**. A common recommendation for the grading on a home lot is 1 inch per foot for a minimum of 6 feet.

Improper grading and drainage may cause erosion and standing water. These are the most commonly reported problems by home inspectors. Home inspectors are not required to measure the slope or grade, but simply eyeball the land and observe. It should be apparent if improper grading is present.

Erosion

One consequence of improper grading is **erosion**—the wearing away of soil due to natural forces like rainwater and wind. Erosion can cause soil movement as well as soil loss, thus affecting the foundation and even the structural integrity of a house.

Indicators of erosion and soil movement

- Freshly exposed areas of topsoil in the middle of vegetation
- Leaning tree trunks
- Deep cracks in the soil
- Cracking in the walls of the house
- Cracks or gaps where porches and decks attach to the house

Standing Water

Standing water can occur when the slope away from a house does not allow for proper drainage. This water can cause damage to many areas around a home including the basement or crawlspace, foundation, and even the siding. Visual confirmation or evidence of standing water should be noted in the home inspection report.

Landscaping

Landscaping is the art of arranging rocks, lumber, and plants around the outside of a property for an aesthetic purpose, such as an appealing look, or for practical purposes, such as to prevent erosion or provide parking areas. Landscaping often involves work with both hardscape and softscape components. Since these components must also be maintained, landscaping includes yard maintenance.

Softscape

Softscape is landscaping that uses plantings around a house to prevent erosion and improve aesthetic appearance. Different types of plants are appropriate for different climates. Desert climates use a form known as zeroscaping, where little or no water is needed. Another type is **xeriscaping™**, where water efficiency is achieved by using plants appropriate for a naturally dry environment.

In any case, there are some areas where landscaping can affect a home inspection. Large trees should not be planted too close to the home because their root systems can crack foundations, retaining walls, and water pipes. Shrubbery should be far enough away from foundations so that the plants do not trap water against the building. If the branches of a shrub or tree touch a home's exterior wall, they can wear away siding.

Ivy growing on a wood-siding home can literally force the clapboards off the wall, and the tendrils can punch holes in wood shingles. Plants like ivy, trees, and even shrubs that are planted too close to a home can prevent the wind and sunlight from drying wet siding.

Fresh sod may be an indication of recent septic tank work or sewer line problems. Asking the homeowner to learn why the sod has been replaced is important to complete a thorough inspection.

Sprinkler Systems

Sprinkler systems are the easiest way to irrigate landscaping. However, they are not free of problems. It is recommended that sprinkler heads be at least 18 inches away from a home. If the home is equipped with an automatic sprinkler system, try to turn it on and make note if any of the sprinkler heads are watering the building instead of the lawn. Sprinklers that are broken, leaking, or watering the home or its foundation should be noted.

Hardscape

Hardscape, in landscaping, refers to structures and features such as retaining walls, pathways, pools, sidewalks, curbs, and gutters. The hardscape of a landscaping project compliments the softscape design elements and consists of materials such as stone, brick, slate, pavers, rock, wood, river wash, and gravel. For example, tile paths, concrete or brick patios, wooden decks, stone walls, and wooden arbors would all be considered part of the hardscape.

Walkways and Driveways

Walkways can be paths leading up to a house or even the sidewalks near the street. **Driveways** are pathways for cars typically found leading up to a garage. Both can be solid materials like concrete or asphalt or even parted materials like stones, pavers, bricks, or gravel.

Figure 3.1
Pathways leading up to a house can be walkways, driveways, or sidewalks.

Walkways should be free of trip hazards where concrete is uneven due to cracks, heaving or uplifting, and possibly even spalling. Driveways should not have any major cracks and should be sloped to drain water away from the home and garage. Suitable grading, drainage, and supports are needed to ensure the function and longevity of these components.

Patios

Patios are usually surfaced exterior areas used for outdoor enjoyment of the home. Barbecues and even patio furniture are often located out on these areas. Their construction type varies, as some are concrete, brick, stone, asphalt, wood, or even simple paving stones placed in a sand base. No matter the type, they are usually at ground level. If the patio is more than 2 feet off the ground, it should have a guardrail that is at least 36 inches high.

Problems reported in patio areas are typical to those in pathways and driveways. These include trip hazards, improper slopes and rises, cracking, and even spalling. Patios that have missing guardrails should also be reported. The inspector should look for cracking, heaving, spalling, and settling of these components. These are not only safety hazards, but could be indicators of more serious problems.

Porches

When inspecting a home with a **porch**, the critical areas are where wood meets the earth and the porch meets the house. The inspector should be aware of poor drainage or incorrectly pitched floors because these conditions support dry rot. If the porch construction includes concrete work, the inspector should look for cracks, shifting, or deteriorating mortar joints. Railings should be securely attached and strong enough to bear the weight of an adult falling against them.

Balconies

Balconies are second-story porches. They are often constructed using a cantilever system for support. **Cantilever** refers to any structural part of a building that projects beyond its support and overhang. Occasionally the balcony is supported from above, but if it is supported at all, it will be done with posts extending to the ground. When supported by posts it becomes, in effect, a second-story deck.

The important areas for the home inspector to observe are where the cantilevered posts pass through the building. Look for any decay or rot in the posts themselves and distortion or crushing of the supporting area. Since a balcony is usually at least one story up, the integrity of the flooring and guardrails is very important. The drainage of a balcony is critical. You will want to be sure that the drainage is adequate to prevent water damage.

Decks

In its most basic form, a **deck** is nothing more than a floor attached to the exterior of the home, used primarily for outdoor leisure activities. The deck is supported by piers or posts and is fastened to the house. The inspector should check that the supporting joists are sized properly for the load, and any wood-to-earth contact is adequately protected from water and insect damage. The deck should be equipped with sturdy handrails. Wooden decks or balconies are susceptible to rotting and can pose a serious safety hazard if not properly maintained.

Figure 3.2
Deck components

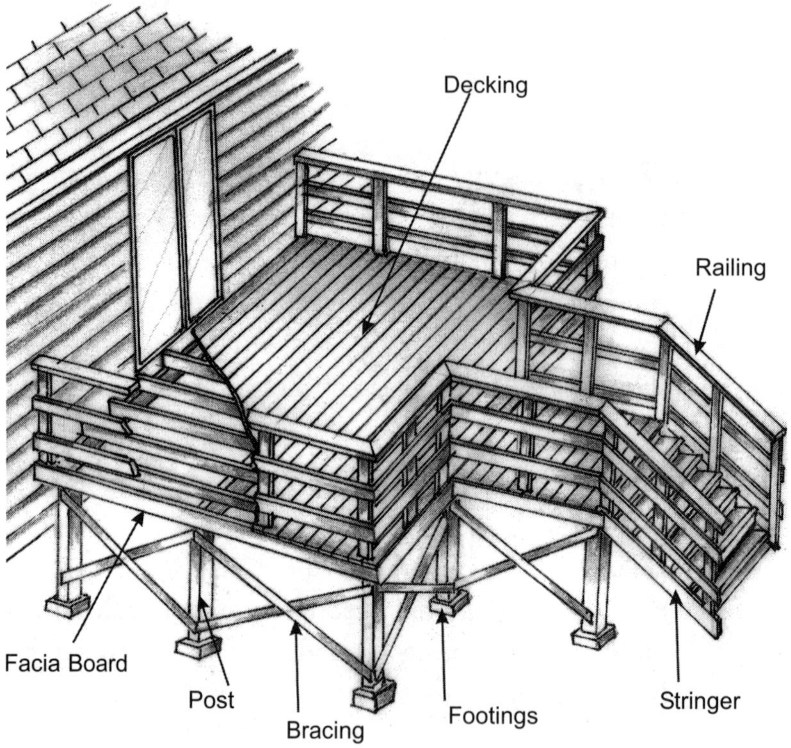

Since many decks are "do-it-yourself" projects, the inspector should pay strict attention to the construction techniques employed and be prepared to report any deficiencies.

The distinction between a porch and a deck is largely semantic. **Decks** are built as a subsequent addition and porches are included in the original design of the home.

Retaining Walls

Retaining walls are constructed to hold back soil and prevent erosion. Usually, they are found where elevation differences on a property and soil must be held back. Retaining walls are built from many types of material. There are numerous guidelines for their construction. Most retaining walls should have some type of reinforcement and drainage via spaces or weep holes in the face of the wall. **Weep holes** are openings that allow trapped water to escape and for ventilation of brick. It will be impossible to see the interior of these walls to check for possible problems, so the easiest way to check a retaining wall is to see if it is performing its function.

Retaining walls should lean towards the hill or surface they are holding back. If they are straight or leaning away from the surface retained, some sort of soil movement has occurred and the retaining wall could fail. Cracking also can cause failure by weakening the wall. When reinforcement components like steel begin to rust out in spalling, failure of the wall can also occur. A lack of drainage in a retaining wall can make it lean outward or even bow. This is a sign that a build-up of water has occurred and wall failure is possible. In any case, the eventual failure of a retaining wall can lead to failures in other support structures of a home, so it is important for a home inspector to note any signs of trouble in the retaining walls.

Other exterior components, such as downspouts and gutters, are covered in the following chapter on roofs.

Reportable Deficiencies - Retaining Walls

- Leaning away from the slope
- Cracking
- Bowing
- Spalling
- Lack of drainage

Cladding

Cladding in general can refer to any external protective skin or device for the exterior surfaces of the home. One of the most important functions of the cladding system is to prevent racking or twisting of the house frame. Underneath the cladding are vapor barriers. Cladding includes the **surface coatings**, siding, doors, windows, trim, shutters, entryways, flashings, and caulking.

Figure 3.3
Cladding includes the external protective skin of the exterior surfaces of a home (surface coatings, siding, doors, windows, trim, shutters, entryways, and flashings).

Surface Coatings

The outer most layer of the skin of the house is a layer of paint or similar coating and is only a few thousandths of an inch thick. Some major types of protective finishes are enamel, latex, epoxy, lacquer, shellac, and stain. If properly applied and replenished, this "skin" will protect tens of thousands of dollars worth of siding. Although there are several different chemical systems used in common home coatings, they are all applied as a liquid and when dry form tough plastic-like layers of protection on the surfaces to which they are applied.

Problems with coatings are caused by either the coating itself or the application. Of the two, problems with the application are most common. In application-related problems, the most common cause of inferior performance is poor preparation. If the surface being coated is not properly prepared and cleaned, the coating may crack and peel prematurely. As far as the home inspector is concerned, the symptoms are more important than the cause. The inspector is only required to report deficiencies in the surface coating and not to diagnose causes.

Reportable Deficiencies - Surface Coatings

- Blisters and surface bubbles
- Peeling
- Paint becomes chalky to the touch
- Staining

Siding

Siding is used to protect the interior and framing from temperature and weather. Another critical function of the siding system is the management of condensation, which forms between the inner and outer walls. In older homes with looser construction, air can pass relatively freely between the inner and outer walls, thus balancing the temperature between those surfaces and eliminating the cause of condensation. During the energy crisis of the 1970s, building practices changed drastically to create more energy-efficient homes. While this resulted in tighter, draft free, more economical environments for homeowners, it produced a potential moisture management problem.

There are common problems with homes that have been re-sided. Sometimes the old siding is covered up instead of being removed. Check to see if the attic and basement ventilation areas are blocked. Other problems like improper caulking and inadequate drain holes also can be found in re-sided homes and should be reported. There are several types of siding including wood, steel, aluminum, vinyl, masonry, stucco, and Exterior-Insulation and Finishing Systems (EIFS).

Wood Siding

Wood is one material used in siding and if properly maintained, can last a long time. **Wood siding** must be tight enough to prevent water and vermin infiltration. Conversely, it must also be loose enough to allow for drying in both front and back. Cedar and redwood are good woods to use for siding due to their natural resins that resist decay.

When inspecting siding it is a good idea to examine closely the fastenings, paint, and general condition of the wall. An inspector should look for signs of rot, split, or warped wood siding. Rotting wood loses its structural integrity. Probing the wood siding or pressing on it will usually indicate whether rot is present or not. Split wood siding will allow water a path into the home so it is important to note this if this is occurring. Warped wood will also lack water tightness and possibly allow for vermin infestation. Your inspection should include the area where two dissimilar surfaces meet, construction materials change, and any occurrence of penetration is visible.

Reportable Deficiencies - Wood Siding

- Signs of rot
- Split wood
- Warped wood siding
- Peeling or missing paint

Aluminum Siding

At one time, steel was used as a siding material, but because it corrodes easily, it has been largely replaced by aluminum. **Aluminum siding** is almost maintenance free and relatively inexpensive but not completely without drawbacks. Aluminum siding is noisy, prone to denting, and will lose its luster after time. Generally, aluminum is used as an aftermarket re-siding material, and the home inspector should look for installation defects.

The inspector should check for the proper use of moldings and caulking. There should be adequate drain holes at the bottom of the wall to allow the condensation to drain. These conditions should be reported if found in the home.

Reportable Deficiencies - Steel and Aluminum Siding
- Improper installation
- Lack of drain holes at the bottom of the wall

Vinyl Siding

Vinyl siding is similar to aluminum but is not as noisy. Vinyl siding maintains the same color throughout the material unlike aluminum siding, which needs to be repainted. Ideally, vinyl siding will be applied with a backing layer of bead board for better insulation from temperature and noise.

The inspector can tell if the siding has this extra layer of insulation by pressing against the surface. If the bead board has been installed, the inspector will be able to feel it underneath the siding. Plastic materials become brittle as the temperature drops, and unless securely fastened, they can break during a cold winter storm. Broken vinyl pieces or missing bead board should be noted.

Reportable Deficiencies - Vinyl Siding
- Broken vinyl pieces
- Missing bead board

Masonry Siding

When the exterior of the residence is stone, brick, or block, it is a type of **masonry siding**. The inspector must determine whether the material covering is simply a **veneer** (layer applied as decoration or for protection) or the load-bearing masonry that supports the wall. In either case, the symptoms of damage may be the same, but the impact on the integrity of the building will be different.

Masonry Veneers

When using masonry as a decorative accent or veneer, the method of attachment to the framing is critical. Corrosion resistant wire or straps are used to bind the veneer to the wall. Due to the relatively heavy nature of brick and stone, it is necessary that this material be supported by the foundation.

The inspector should be aware of any sign that the veneer is separating from the wall. Because the wood and brick have different thermal characteristics, there must be a way for the condensation moisture to drain out of the cavity between the two surfaces. Typical flaws to look for include cracking, mortar deterioration, efflorescence, spalling, missing weep holes or flashings, and bowing or leaning walls.

Cracking is the most prevalent type of defect in masonry construction. Cracking occurs for a variety of reasons. Cracking is caused by settling, poor quality of materials, improperly mixed mortar, and corrosion of steel reinforcing materials. Cracks can be nothing more than cosmetic or structural in nature.

Mortar deterioration occurs when the mortar that connects masonry wears down. It can cause leaks and allow moisture into the walls. This weakening of the mortar can also lead to failure of the masonry in extreme cases. A home inspector should check the masonry joints for signs of crumbling, failing connections between the mortar and masonry units, or for softening mortar. To do so, a screwdriver can be dragged across the mortar joint to see just how soft it is.

Efflorescence is a powdery, salty deposit, often white, on the surface of masonry walls. Its presence indicates that water has passed through the surface or may be in the masonry itself. The inspector should try to identify the water source causing the efflorescence and recommend that it be fixed. Efflorescence can be a sign of spalling or future spalling.

Spalling occurs when masonry cracks or flakes usually due to water penetration and efflorescence. Spalling in masonry veneer is not as troublesome as spalling in load-bearing masonry units where structural weakness can result. A home inspector should be able to identify any spalling via the visual inspection. Particular attention should be paid to those areas where masonry extends down to the soil, and where masonry is covered by vines or shrubs.

Weep holes let water drain out, air to flow in, and equalize pressure in masonry walls. Behind these holes are metal flashings which guide the water to the holes for draining. A problem arises if these weep holes are missing. Water could still get into the walls and not drain out if the flashings are not functioning properly. Water then gets out by efflorescence and causes damage. The inspector should be able to see these in the visual inspection.

Bowing and **leaning** can result when masonry walls are out of plumb (not exactly perpendicular or vertical). When this happens, the repercussion can be the failure of the wall. Bulges in masonry and any evidence of repairs to the masonry walls should be noted on the inspection report.

Reportable Deficiencies - Masonry Siding or Walls

- Cracking
- Mortar deterioration
- Efflorescence
- Spalling
- Missing weep holes or flashings
- Bowing or leaning walls

Stucco

Stucco is a popular wall cladding in the southwest. It is durable, weather-proof, and relatively inexpensive to apply. **Stucco** is a cement-like substance that is sprayed on the sheathing after a wire mesh lath is applied to **building paper** (felt or sheathing paper) that is permeable to water vapor. At the bottom of a stucco wall there should be a metal **drip screed**, which is a metal stop exposed below the stucco. The drip screed allows drainage and prevents water from being drawn up the wall.

Typical defects with stucco are cracks and separation of the stucco facing from the supporting wall. The inspector can check for separation by tapping the wall with a screwdriver handle and listening to the sound. Stucco that is firmly attached to the substrate will have a live crisp sound, while loose stucco will sound dead and flat.

In addition, flashings may be in direct contact with stucco and rusting out. A visual inspection of these will locate problems. The inspector should also check to see that drip screeds are present and functioning properly.

Reportable Deficiencies - Stucco

- Cracks in the stucco
- Separation of the stucco facing from the supporting wall
- Rusting flashings that are direct contact with stucco
- Missing drip screeds

Exterior Insulation and Finishing Systems (EIFS)

Exterior insulation and finishing systems (EIFS) is synthetic stucco and is commonly referred to as softcoat or thincoat. The main difference is the flexibility of EIFS versus the rigidity of traditional stucco.

EIFS is a multi-layered cladding system. It begins with a polystyrene layer that acts as insulation. Next is a base coat with fiberglass mesh set in it that adds strength. The outer layer is an acrylic finish coat that performs as a water barrier and protects the inner layers.

The home inspector should be able to identify EIFS and its types. EIFS must be 2 inches from the roof and 8 inches from the ground. Proper flashings should also be in place. This will aid in identifying potential areas of water and moisture damage where EIFS applications are being used.

Reportable Deficiencies - EIFS

- EIFS more than 2 inches from the roof
- EIFS less than 8 inches from the ground
- Missing flashings

Windows, Doors, and Entryways

Openings are created in the wall structure to allow for the passage of people (doors) and light (windows). These openings must be sealed, caulked, and flashed to perform their intended function without leaking. It is also important to note that the opening for a door or window interrupts the structural integrity of the wall system. In order to restore the strength of the wall system, **headers** of the proper dimensions must be installed.

Windows

Windows allow light and air into a home. They also help to improve airflow and circulation. Most windowpanes are conventional glass but some may be laminated glass, tempered glass, or even wired-glass. Acrylic coatings are used in many skylights and polycarbonates are used to strengthen windows in security applications. Window panes come in single, **dual,** or triple-pane styles, all of which can be glazed.

Windows are usually described by the materials that make up frames and **sashes**. For example, most window frames and sashes are wood, metal, vinyl, or fiberglass. Windows are available in many styles. The main difference is how they open. Windows will be discussed more thoroughly in Chapter 5.

Common Types of Windows

- **Single-hung** bottom portion moves up and down to open and close
- **Double-hung** both top-and-bottom parts are able to open and close by moving up and down
- **Casement** windows are hinged at the side and swing in and out to open and close
- **Hopper** windows are hinged at the bottom and the top opens in or out
- **Awning** windows are hinged at the top and the bottom opens out
- **Jalousie** glass slats are used and each slat rotates to open or close the window
- **Fixed** windows do not open or move at all, as in many modern office buildings

Windows should open and close easily and securely, and the locking hardware should be in good operating order. All of the edges of the window installation should be caulked with no drafts or air leaks.

Figure 3.4
Window styles

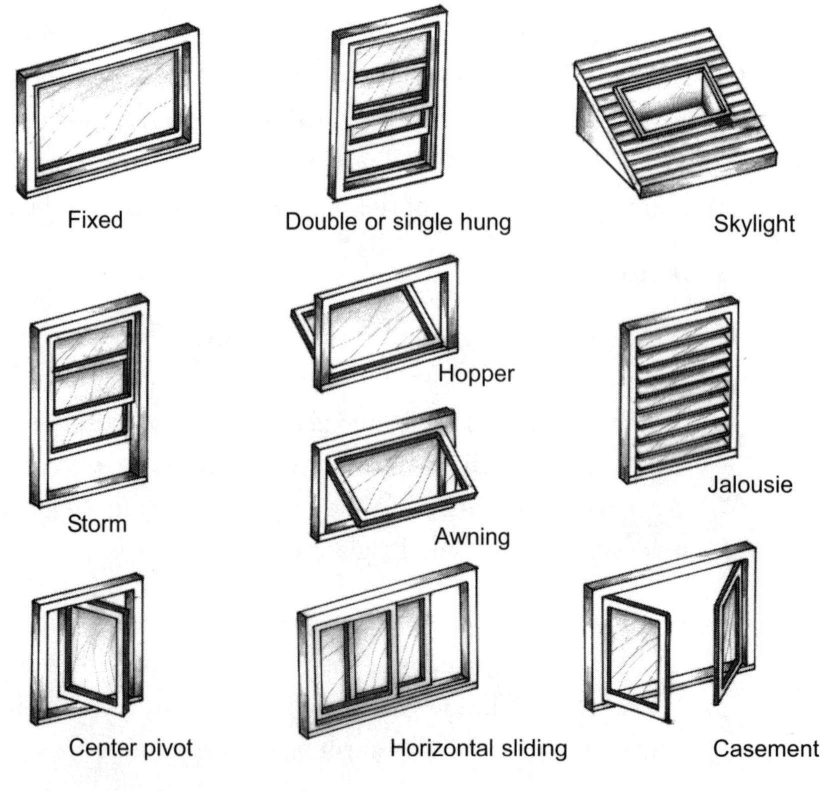

Window Screens

Window screens are on windows to keep insects and animals out of the home while allowing windows to be open for added air ventilation. The inspector needs to make sure they are intact and not bent, torn, ripped, rusted, or loose. The window screen must completely cover the window in order to perform its intended function. The inspector should report any deficiencies in the window screen.

Reportable Deficiencies - Windows

- Rotting wood
- Broken or cracked glass
- Leaking air or water
- Missing or damaged weather stripping, caulking, or flashing
- Loose or poor fit for opening
- Inoperable
- Missing or damaged trim
- Missing or damaged glazing
- Damaged or sloping window sills
- Damaged tracks
- Torn or missing screens
- Storm windows cracked or missing
- Ice damming of skylights

Figure 3.5
Broken or cracked glass is a window deficiency.

In many areas of the country, it is common for homes to be equipped with storm windows and doors. The home inspector should evaluate these using the same criteria as for the permanent windows and doors.

Dual pane windows are required by building codes in many areas of the country. The inspector should note any moisture between the panes as evidence of seal failure and air/moisture leakage.

In regions where homes have basements, the home inspector should pay careful attention to the basement windows. These windows are particularly subject to neglect. Check for leaks, standing water in the wells, and wood rot in the frames.

Doors

Modern doors and windows are sold as pre-packaged units and come with all the necessary framing and hardware. The door and window units are fit into the rough-cut openings and fastened into place. This method assures that doors and windows will function smoothly and lock properly.

Doors are usually packaged units that need to fit squarely in their frames, and open and close smoothly without binding. They can be solid or hollow and can be made from wood, metal, glass, vinyl, or hardboard. Doors have different surfaces as well. Some may be flush or level, glazed, paneled, or even louvered.

Doors can also be hung in different ways. Some doors are hung traditionally with hinges. **French doors** are double doors hinged at either side. Sliding doors run in tracks. A **pocket door** is a special type of sliding door that is suspended overhead on tracks and slides into a "pocket" in the wall when open.

Figure 3.6
This is an example of a reportable door deficiency. Note the rotting wood parts, poor fitting in frame, inoperable parts and tracks, visual damage or cracking.

Doors are rated for their energy efficiency or ability to keep heat within the structure. Since doors are opened, they can be a considerable source of air leakage into or out of the home. This can cause heating problems in the winter and cooling problems in the summer.

The home inspector should also be aware of the doors that go from the garage directly into the home. Fire codes require these doors to be fire-rated in the event of a fire in the garage. Inappropriate doors in these locations should be reported as a safety hazard.

For those homes that have an entrance to the basement that is below grade, make sure that the well is adequately drained, and the door frames are examined for signs of rot. Make sure that the wood casing around the door is painted and caulked properly.

The knobs and latches should operate without any sticking or binding. Check the operation of the locking mechanism as part of the inspection. **Sliding glass doors** should be made with tempered glass and should glide smoothly through the full range of travel. Inspect the door locks on sliders because they are often not strong enough to withstand continuous use.

Figure 3.7
Door styles

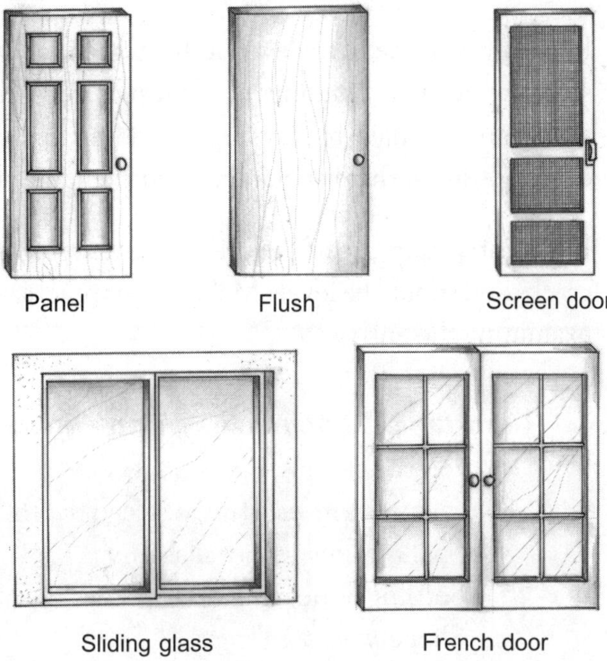

Reportable Deficiencies - Doors

- Air or water leakage
- Rotting wood parts
- Fitting improperly in frames
- Rusting metal either in doors or hinges
- Inoperable parts and tracks
- Visual damage or cracking
- Missing trim

- Missing or poorly functioning drip cap
- Cracked or broken glass
- Missing weather stripping
- Torn or missing screens
- Stained parts of doors

Entryway

The **entryway** itself should be examined for safety hazards. It should be large enough to accommodate an outward-swinging **storm door**. The stairs leading to the entryway should be full size and securely constructed. Stair treads should be of uniform dimensions and sturdy enough to support someone carrying a large item.

In most cases, the entry level of the home is above grade. In order to get in, steps are needed. Landings at the top of steps should be big enough to open a door and not have to step off the landing to do so. If there are more than a couple of steps, there should be a secure handrail.

If the entry stairs are of the pre-cast concrete variety, they should be free of cracks and should be level. Make it your practice to check the doorbell when examining the entryway.

Reportable Deficiencies - Entryway Steps and Landings

- Sloping stairs
- Inconsistent rise, run, or tread depth
- Spalling concrete or masonry
- Settling or heaving of steps
- Slippery or loose steps

Trim

Trim refers to the finish materials in a building, such as moldings applied around openings (window trim, door trim) or at the floor and ceiling of rooms (baseboard, cornice, and other moldings). Trim around windows is also referred to as **casing**. Trim is usually a different color or material than the adjacent wall. It can be installed either on the outside or inside of the building and covers the space between the window frame or jamb and the wall.

Figure 3.8
Trim is usually a different color.

Although largely cosmetic in nature, trim serves the purpose of protecting other more vital structural members. The inspector needs to make sure that all exposed trim is properly painted, caulked, and free of rot. Rotten trim will usually be hiding rotten wood behind it.

Shutters

Largely decorative in nature, **shutters** can often trap moisture behind them. This condition will promote rot, and the inspector should check this area when examining the exterior of the home.

Flashing

Flashing is the term given to the material used to prevent the intrusion of water at the place where dissimilar materials or surface planes intersect. Typically, flashing should be installed at any roof penetration where leaks may occur such as chimneys or vents, and any exterior wall openings such as windows or doors. Flashing seals the edge of membranes and is used to direct water away from the structure and its components. Flashing is by nature corrosion resistant and can be made of copper, stainless steel, galvanized steel, or various plastics. Flashing will be discussed in greater detail in Chapter 4.

Flashing Types

Cap flashings cover the upper edges of **base flashing**, which covers the edges of the membrane. It is also sometimes known as **counter flashing**.

Drip edges, or **eave flashings**, allow water to flow over decking and keeps it from getting into the fascia and cornice board.

Step flashing is used when the roof touches a vertical wall and prevents water intruding into underlying materials at the junction of the two areas.

Vapor Barriers

Vapor barriers are nonporous sheeting or coatings that prevent water vapor from saturating insulation. Polyethylene sheeting is used under concrete slabs and behind walls. This helps to control the moisture that accumulates when there is a temperature difference between two surfaces. The nature of concrete will allow the passage of water through it due to capillary action. The accumulation of moisture between the top surface of the slab and the bottom surface of the floor can cause substantial damage to finished flooring.

Figure 3.9
Drip edges with step flashing

1) Stucco walls
2) Rain gutter
3) Drip edge and step flashing
4) Spanish tile roof

Vapor barriers must be installed correctly to work properly. Those placed in walls must be fastened to the inner surface of the studs to allow accumulated condensation to drain to the exterior of the house. If accumulated moisture is not allowed to drain from the wall cavity, rot will destroy the structure.

Reportable Deficiencies - The Exterior

- Defects in wall construction
- Inadequate or insufficient fasteners
- Lack of proper vapor barriers
- Unsuitable materials

Building with Wood

A basic understanding of how a house is built is vital for the home inspector. A properly built home will offer protection against the weather and seismic stability of the structure. With the knowledge of basic materials used to build a house, the inspector is equipped to notice any abnormalities or deviations from standard practices.

Wood

Since wood is used to construct most homes, some knowledge of the various types and grades is essential to the inspector. The two main classifications of wood are softwood and hardwood. The terms hardwood and softwood refer to the types of trees that these woods come from. **Hardwood** comes from deciduous trees that lose their leaves in the fall like oak, maple, and cherry. **Softwood** comes from evergreens like pine and fir. Hardwood is stronger and more durable than softwood. It is also considerably more difficult to work with and therefore not as desirable for home construction. Typically, wood is used in construction as lumber or plywood. Lumber refers to the boards, planks, etc. cut from trees for use in construction. **Plywood** is a wood panel (frequently 4 feet by 8 feet) composed of an odd number of layers of wood veneer bonded together under pressure.

Lumber

Lumber that is sold as dimension lumber (such as 2 inches by 4 inches or 4 inches by 4 inches) is designed for residential construction and is used for studs, joists, and rafters. **Studs** are the vertical wood structural components of the house in wall framing that are usually spaced 16 inches apart and can be seen in the garage where walls are often unfinished. **Joists** are also structural components, laid out horizontally, which hold up floors or ceilings and are spaced 16 inches apart normally. **Rafters** are the structural components that support the roof. The actual dimensions of structural lumber are smaller than the size designation because the lumber has been "surfaced" to provide smooth uniform edges for ease of construction. Thus, the standard 2 inches by 4 inches is actually $1^5/_8$ inches by $3^1/_2$ inches. Wood destined for residential construction must be brought to a uniform moisture level by drying. Drying can be accomplished naturally by storing cut lumber in the yard for a period of time, or by using an oven or kiln. In either case, the maximum allowable moisture content for residential structural wood is no more than 19 percent. Wood with moisture content exceeding 19 percent is subject to fungal growth, rot, and inevitably loses strength.

Figure 3.10
Wall framing

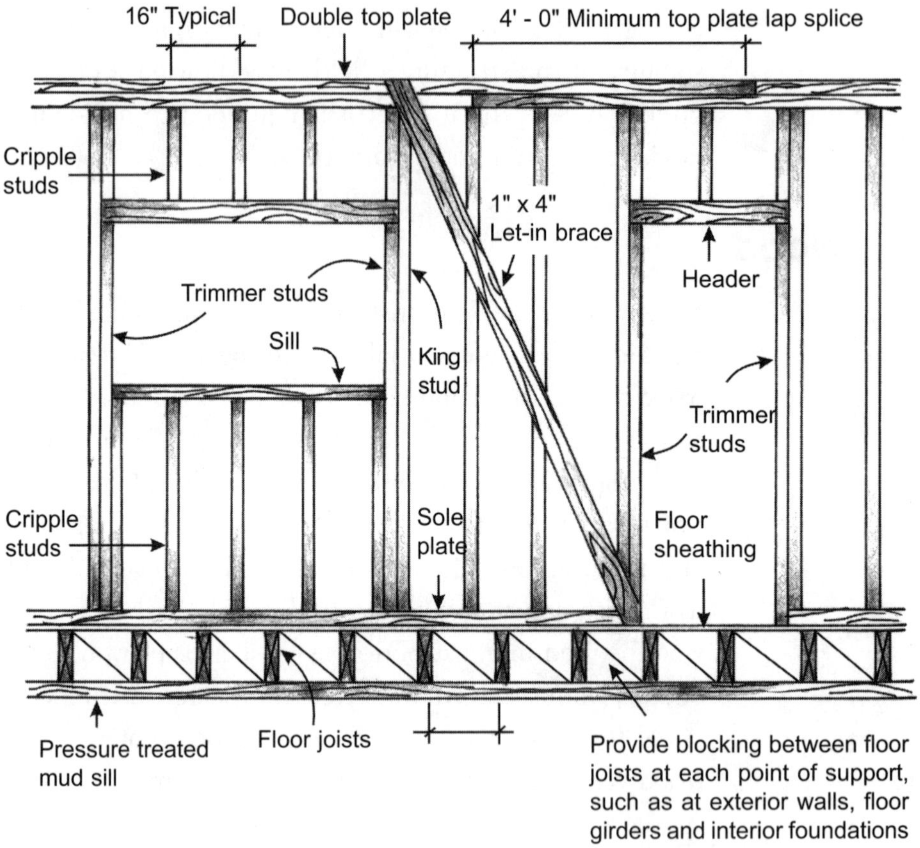

In order for lumber to be used in residential construction, it must meet the grading requirements of an approved agency. The grade stamp will show the type of wood and number of imperfections in the wood.

Figure 3.11
Lumber grading

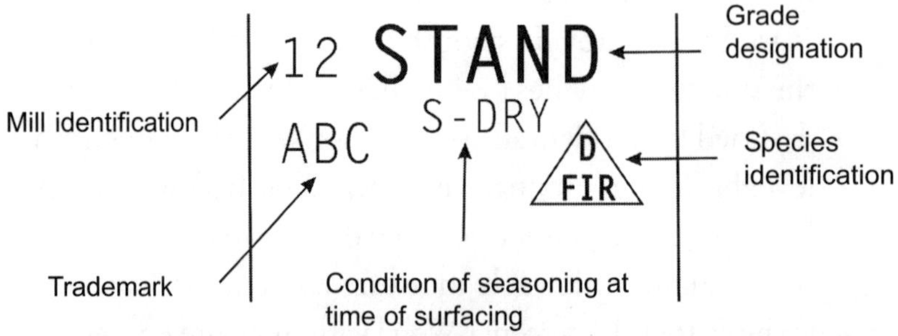

Plywood

Plywood is used extensively in the residential construction industry. Plywood carries its own unique rating system. The organization responsible for the rating of plywood is the American Plywood Association (A.P.A.). The A.P.A. uses a system of letter markings to designate the suitability of plywood for various applications. The highest grades are A and N. The surface irregularities increase through grades B, C, and D.

In addition to surface grading, plywood is also marked with an exposure-rating grade. This indicates the suitability for external or internal use. The grade stamp will also show the span rating as a pair of numbers separated by a slash. These numbers indicate the appropriate support distances depending on whether the plywood is being used for roof decking or flooring.

Wood Damage

The most prevalent form of damage to wood is **dry rot**, which surprisingly is caused by water. Other than the wrong grade of wood being used, the most important item for the home inspector to be aware of are signs of wood rot or insect infestation. Both of these conditions will lead to the failure of the structural member.

Mildew is a mold that can leave a dark stain on the surface. It will normally be found on those surfaces that are protected from adequate ventilation. Mildew requires a constant supply of moisture and can live on the dust adhering to and the organic material in the paint itself.

Figure 3.12
Dry rot

The one common requirement for both wood-destroying fungi and wood-destroying insects is moisture, and the inspector should be watchful in areas of the home where there is the smell of dampness, mold, or mildew. The inspector should leave the cause of insect damage to a specialist; however, any visible evidence should be reported. Any areas of poor drainage, particularly at sill plates or crawl spaces, should be thoroughly investigated.

Wood Damage Prevention

The most effective deterrent for both insect and moisture damage is the use of pressure-treated lumber. This lumber has preservative chemicals forced into the wood under pressure and should be used any time there is contact between wood and soil, posts that contact concrete, and sill plates. Other forms of wood preservatives include salt, borate, creosote, and oil.

4 Chapter

Roofs and Attics

Introduction

The major function of a roof is really to protect the home from the elements—rain, snow, sun, wind, etc. In order to perform this vital task, a roof must be appropriate for the climate and be well-maintained.

The attic, with its ability to ventilate and insulate the home, is a vital element to insure the integrity of the roof and the entire structure.

Roofs

Along with the obvious function of keeping weather out of the house, the roof serves several structural requirements. With its system of **rafters** (structural parts that support the load of the roof) and joists (boards laid perpendicular to rafters to which the ceiling is attached), the roof ties the house together at the top. This helps to keep the entire structure from racking and twisting during settling and shifting due to soil movement or seismic activity.

The condition of the roof is usually of prime importance to the prospective buyer due to its high replacement cost. There could be additional cost to repair any damage to the interior of the home if the roof leaks. Because of this, the home inspector should examine the roof very carefully. When inspecting a roof look for missing shingles, tiles, or even flashing, fastener problems, patching, too many layers of roofing, blistering, bulging, debris on the roof, rotting, mold, discoloration, openings, punctures, holes, leaks, movement, insufficient slope, or too much slope. In this chapter we will discuss roof types, roof construction, and elements frequently found on roofs such as chimneys, skylights, and gutters and downspouts.

Roof Types

The type of roof determines how easily rainwater, sleet, and snow are diverted. If water collects on the roof, the problem is probably with the slope. As well as determining drainage, slope also affects style. The slope of a roof affects its drainage and can determine the kind of roofing material used. The **slope** of the roof is also referred to as the **pitch**. The **roof pitch** describes how steep the roof is.

A roof's pitch, or slope, is determined by how much it rises for every horizontal foot it runs. For example, a roof pitch of 5/12 means that for every 12 horizontal inches the roof rises 5 vertical inches. A roof with a 7/12 slope means that for every 12 inches horizontally, it rises 7 inches. A roof with a larger fraction has a steeper roof. For example, a 12/12 pitch is steeper than a 5/12 pitch or a 7/12 pitch. A roof with a 12/12 pitch is a steep, 45-degree angle roof.

Based on the slope of the roof, there are two main categories: sloped and flat. A flat roof has a slope of 2/12 or less. A low slope roof is anywhere from 2/12 to 4/12. A conventional slope roof is 4/12, and anything more than 9/12 is considered steep. Roofs with steeper slopes are considered more visually pleasing and last longer. Steep sloped roofs can cost up to 50 percent more than 4/12 roofs because they require taller chimneys and more lumber for framing. However, the result may be worth it because it will require less maintenance and last up to 50 percent longer. Flat roofs pose their own unique drainage problems because they should be flat but not level. If there is insufficient pitch in a flat roof it will not drain, leaving standing water to damage parts below. The home inspector should report any evidence of standing water on a flat roof.

In rare instances, an architect will design a completely flat roof to collect water. The standing water reflects sunlight and the subsequent evaporation cools the home below.

Roof Styles

Residential roof styles include flat, gable, gambrel, hip, mansard, pyramid, saltbox, and shed.

Figure 4.1
Roof Styles

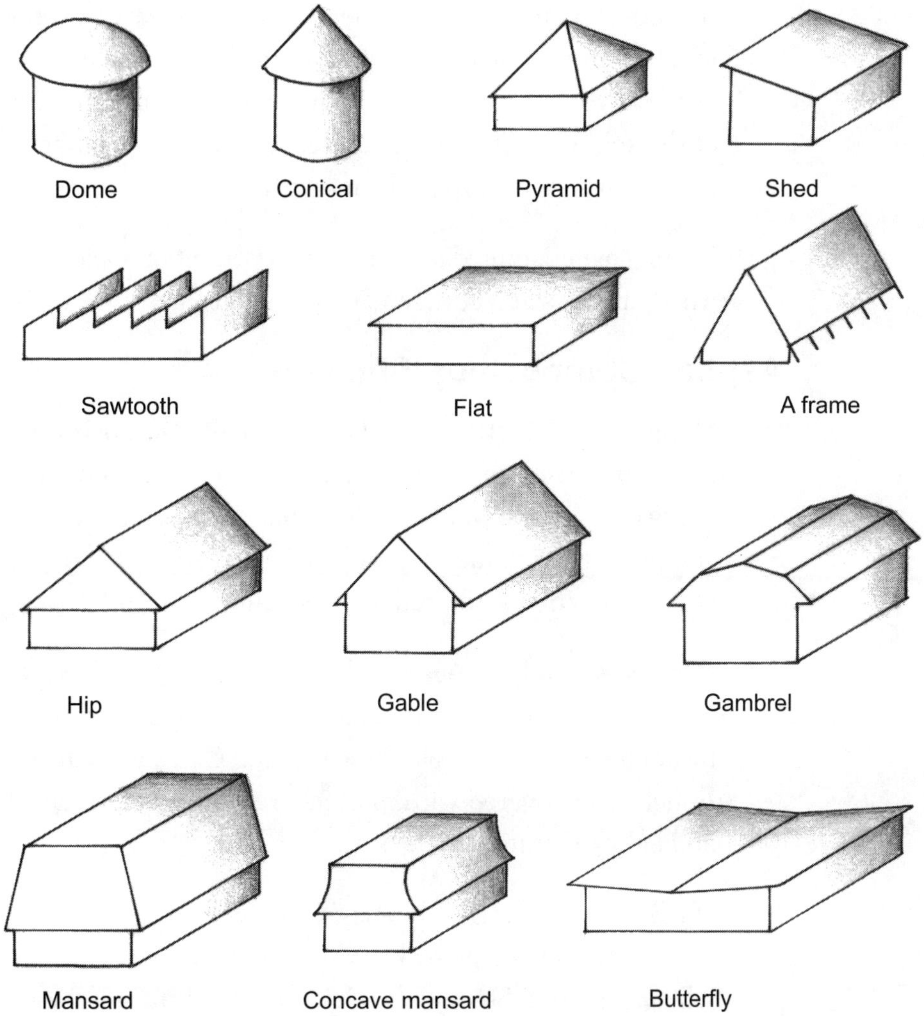

Roofing Coverings

Now that we have discussed the different types of roofs, we need to know the different components that make up a roof. The home inspector should be familiar with all the different types of roofing materials used in his or her market area. Materials used for roofing must be able to shed water and protect the interior of the home from the sun. In addition, they should be durable, aesthetically pleasing, easy to apply, reasonably priced, and not too heavy. The home inspector should be familiar with all the different types of roofing materials used in his or her market area. It is essential that the inspector assess the condition of the roof covering. This also includes making a determination if the roof covering is still within its reasonable life span and able to maintain its function.

Whenever prudent or safe, the inspector should use a ladder to gain access to the roof and literally "walk" the roof, or at the very least observe its condition up close from a ladder or window. Feeling the materials to see if they are brittle or loose can also assist in making the determination on the condition of the roof covering. Deficiencies noted on the surface of the roof will be important signposts to problems with the interior.

Roofing materials used in residential construction include asphalt composition, wood, metal, slate, concrete, clay, and bitumen.

Asphalt Composition Shingles

Shingles made of petroleum-based **asphalt composition** are one of the most commonly used materials for roof coverings. This material comes in a variety of colors, and is a durable, economical roof covering. Asphalt composition is made up of a layer of cellulose, or fiberglass particles in a mat, that is first saturated with asphalt.

Asphalt is a dark viscous petroleum-based product that provides the necessary water resistance. Certain additives are mixed with the asphalt to increase flexibility and reduce solubility in water. Since asphalt is naturally black, the shingles are covered with mineral granules to help reflect some of the heat and light generated by the sun.

Before attaching the shingles, the plywood deck is covered with roofing felt. This felt helps to keep the resins in the wood from degrading the shingles and enables the shingles to move a little as they expand and contract with the heat. Shingles should be installed from the lower part of the roof to the ridge and overlapped so that each new layer covers the nail holes of the previous one. The starter layer should actually be two layers with one facing down. It is sealed to the deck with roofing cement to prevent the wind from getting underneath and lifting the shingles. A drip molding, or runoff channel, should be installed to carry the runoff away from the trim.

Figure 4.2
Asphalt composition shingles

1) Asphalt composition shingles
2) Chimney cricket
3) Chimney
4) Chimney flashing

Shingles can become vulnerable and fail prematurely. Failure can be caused by deficiencies in the manufacturing or storage processes, insufficient penetration of the asphalt in the filler, or bubbles of asphalt boiling up through the filler and breaking at the surface.

Another cause of shingle failure is movement of the underlying deck surface. There is a recommended nailing or stapling pattern for each kind of shingle, and deviations will make the roof susceptible to leaks. Nail holes should never be visible on a properly installed roof. The first course of shingles should be a double course with the bottom layer face down. The slotted joints are staggered and the edge should be sealed with roofing cement.

In time, the protective granules will wear off the face of the shingles, leaving them vulnerable to damage from the sun. The loss of sun protection will increase the expansion and contraction of the shingles, leading to cracking. Eventually the entire shingle fails. Any evidence of cracking, curling, or separation of the shingles should be reported.

Reportable Deficiencies - Asphalt Composition Shingles

- Protective granules worn off shingles
- Visible nail holes
- Expansion of shingles and joints between them

- Cracking
- Curling
- Separation of shingles

Wood Shingles and Shakes

The major difference between shakes and shingles is that shakes are split and shingles are sawed. For this reason, shakes have an irregular appearance while shingles are flat and uniform. Beyond the cosmetic differences, the roofing material is similar.

Due to their irregular nature, shakes should be installed with a felt underlay. The underlay serves to compensate for the difference in thickness between the shakes.

Figure 4.3
Wood shingle roofs have more evenly cut and sized components than wood shake roofs

1) Chimney
2) Chimney cricket
3) Wood shingle roof
4) Rain gutter and downspout

The key to a successful application of wood roofing is to make sure that the pitch of the roof is at least 4/12, meaning at least 4 inches of rise per 12 horizontal feet. As with all roofing, the steeper the roof, the less likely it is to leak.

A wood-shingle roof has a life expectancy of twenty-to-forty years depending on quality of materials and installation. It is a good idea to install the shingles over spaced battens (reinforcements). The use of **battens** allows moisture to evaporate readily and minimizes curling and decay.

Figure 4.4
Wood shake roofs utilize wood parts that are split and are more uneven in shape and size than wood shingles.

Wood shakes and shingles must be laid with enough space between them to allow for the expansion that will occur when they become wet. The gap between the shingles should be offset slightly from course to course to prevent leaking. Cedar is the most common wood used for roof shingles or shakes due to its natural resistance to insect damage and dry rot. The natural oils that help cedar repel insects can sometimes provide a place for mold or mildew to grow. If you notice dark stains on the wood report it to your client. Cedar also contains natural elements that will react with copper and cause corrosion.

Reportable Deficiencies - Wood Shingles and Shakes

- Loose or missing shakes or shingles
- Damaged or worn shakes or shingles
- Gaps that line up between courses of shakes or shingles
- Moss or mildew present
- Debris on the roof
- Overhanging tree limbs that can scrape the roof in a storm
- Copper flashing corrosion
- Cedar corrosion in the form of dark stains

Tile Roofs

Tile made from clay or concrete is a very popular roofing material in the Southwest. **Tile roofs** are naturally fire resistant and are required by codes in many parts of the country where the danger of wildfire is high. It is costly to roof with tile, but its long life and low maintenance requirements make it attractive. As with many other types of roofing, the key to long life is proper installation and support. The average weight of a tile roof on a single family home is approximately 35,000 pounds. Therefore, it must be placed on a supporting structure designed to bear its weight properly and safely.

Figure 4.5
Clay tile
(Spanish or S-shaped tile)

It is not a good idea to walk a tile roof during a home inspection because the tiles are brittle and will break easily. Tile roofs are best observed from a ladder using binoculars to check for reportable conditions.

The inspector should look for broken, missing, or loose tiles. As usual, any evidence of repair should be reported to the client. Any indication of missing tiles should be followed up by checking the attic below for signs of leaking. As with other roofs, the inspector should report any debris on the roof as well as the proximity of overhanging tree limbs.

Reportable Deficiencies - Tile Roofing

- Broken or loose tiles
- Missing tiles
- Leaks
- Debris on the roof
- Evidence of repair (differing materials)
- Overhanging tree limbs

Built-Up Roofing

Built-up roofing is suitable for flat or nearly flat roofs. It consists of several layers of impregnated felt immersed in hot bitumen (a tarlike substance) and is covered with a protective layer of sand or gravel. The two main types of bitumen are petroleum and coal tar. They are too thick to flow through pipelines, so they are mined out by digging and steam heating. These compounds are incompatible and should not be used on the same roof.

A flat roof with insufficient pitch will have drainage problems. As water collects on the roof, its additional weight will cause the roof to sag and eventually collapse.

The nature of a built-up roof is such that leaks may appear some distance from the point of penetration. For this reason, it should be inspected frequently and properly maintained.

Reportable Deficiencies - Built-Up Roofing

- Cracks
- Areas where the protective minerals have eroded
- Holes
- Bubbles in the roofing material
- Improperly designed or poorly maintained drains
- Pooling or standing water

Metal Roofs

Metal roofs are durable and economical. Copper, stainless steel, and aluminum are the materials of choice for roofing because of their resistance to destructive corrosion. Galvanized steel is another popular metal roofing material. It is considerably less expensive than stainless steel but requires more maintenance.

Metal roofs are not without drawbacks. They can be very noisy if not properly insulated. Along with the characteristic drumming during a rainstorm, they are also prone to popping and snapping as they heat up and cool down during the day. Metal roofs also require periodic painting to resist corrosion unless they are made of stainless steel or copper.

Metal roofs are usually composed of corrugated sheets that are laid starting at the eaves and continuing up to the ridge line. This type of roof is attached with special nails that have a sealing gasket incorporated into the head. These nails are designed for use at the high point of the corrugation. Nailing at the low point will increase the likelihood of leakage.

Figure 4.6
A metal roof

Metal roofs are also constructed of flat sheets that are soldered together forming a single impervious sheet of metal across the entire roof. An expansion joint must be installed in this type of application. Another method of attaching adjacent sheets is by the use of folded seams. When folded seams are used, the nature of the process allows for the thermal expansion and contraction of adjacent sheets.

Reportable Deficiencies - Metal Roofs

- Leaks
- Corrosion
- Rust
- Paint peeling
- Missing pieces
- Exposed seams

Metal Shingles

Metal shingles made of galvanized steel or aluminum are used extensively in some parts of the country. Properly maintained, these shingles can last for fifty years or more. Aluminum shingles should be applied over plywood using a felt underlay.

Reportable Deficiencies - Metal Shingles

- Leaking
- Corrosion
- Rust
- Missing shingles
- Exposed seams

Slate

Slate is the king of roofing material, and can provide a high-quality roof lasting a hundred years. The key to making it last that long is to have slate of the correct thickness, and to have the roof installed by knowledgeable craftsmen. Only a few slate roofs are being built today due to the high construction expense.

Figure 4.7
Slate roofs are expensive and long lasting (100 years).

A slate roof is extremely heavy and must be installed on a structure designed to carry this load. A properly installed slate roof is maintenance free, but eventually even stone will succumb to the forces of sun and weather and will need to be replaced or repaired.

Reportable Deficiencies - Slate Roofing
- Sagging
- Missing or damaged pieces or parts
- Leaking
- Evidence of repair

Fire Ratings for Roofing Material

Roofing material is rated for its ability to resist the spread of fire. For common roofing materials, the fire ratings are as follows:

- **Class A** Resists severe exposure to fire. Roof coverings include slate, tile, concrete, cement, fiberglass, and similar fire resistant materials.
- **Class B** Resists moderate exposure to fire. Materials include corrugated steel, galvanized steel sheets, galvanized steel shingles, and copper sheeting.
- **Class C** Resists light exposure to fire. Materials include asphalt shingles, asphalt roll roofing, and pressure-treated cedar shingles and shakes.

Flashing

No area of the roof is more susceptible to leaks than where two different planes of the roof meet or where the roof is penetrated for vents. A special material called flashing is used at all of these junctions. Flashing is somewhat flexible and may be made of metal or plastic.

Figure 4.8
Roof flashing

1) Vent flashing
2) Asphalt composition roof
3) Plumbing vent flashing

Flashing must be attached in such a way that it seals against wind and water penetration but is still free to move to accommodate thermal expansion. Often more than one piece of flashing is used to ensure that the area is watertight. In this instance, the second piece of flashing is called counter-flashing. Pay particular attention to joints above windows and doors in order to detect any leaks. Many windows have drip caps or cap flashings that slope in towards the window instead of away from it to drain water.

The home inspector should perform a visual evaluation of the overall condition, remaining function, and probable life expectancy of all the flashing encountered during the inspection. Flashing must be periodically resealed in order for it to continue to remain an effective water barrier.

Figure 4.9
Counter or cap flashing of chimney and roof.

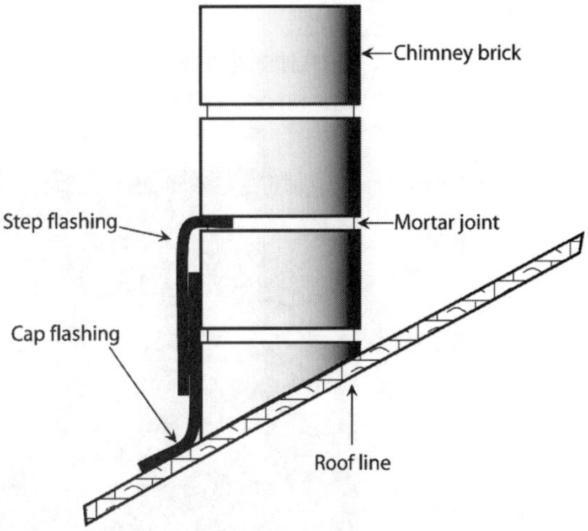

Aluminum flashings will corrode and leak if exposed directly to stucco. For this reason, a coating or another material to separate the two is needed to prevent the breakdown of the flashing and the eventual failure of the stucco itself.

Reportable Deficiencies - Flashing

- Worn-out flashing materials
- Water and air penetration
- Leaks
- Animal infestation of the home
- Rust
- Corrosion

Valleys

Valleys form at the intersection of two different roof lines. There are several different types of valleys used in roof construction. There are open, closed, and woven valleys. Each is suited to a different type of roof condition. Because most of the water drained from the roof flows down the valleys, special care must be taken to prevent leaking. In all cases, the flashing is installed before the valley is constructed.

Open Valleys

An open valley is composed of either metal or rolled composition roofing. The valley should have an end lap of 4 inches to 6 inches and a width of 12 inches to 36 inches, depending on the type of roof. When using rolled roofing for a valley, it is customary to install an underlay or to use two layers of roofing material.

Figure 4.10
Open roof valley

1) Shingle roof
2) Skylight
3) Open roof valley
4) Intersecting roof

Woven Valleys

A **woven valley**, as the name implies, consists of the shingle material interlaced at the valley to produce a weather-tight joint.

Figure 4.11
Woven valley

1) Asphalt shingle roof
2) Woven roof valley

The shingles used in a woven valley should extend at least 12 inches onto the adjacent roof plane. When properly executed the woven valley offers a neat appearance and excellent leak resistance.

Closed-Cut Valley

The **closed-cut valley** is constructed by laying the shingles along the eaves of one roof plane and across the valley. The shingles on the lower roof plane should extend at least 12 inches over the adjoining roof plane. All of the rest of the courses are laid the same way, pressing the shingles firmly down into the valley. In order to ensure the proper flow of water over the trimmed shingles, the corners should be trimmed at a 45-degree angle. The trimmed ends should be imbedded in roofing cement.

Roof Sheathing

The roof skeleton or framing is covered by some form of sheathing to provide a platform to which the roofing material is adhered. The most commonly used material for roof sheathing is plywood. Plywood is used because of its dimensional stability and excellent strength-to-weight ratio. Plywood sheathing should be placed over the rafter centers, and the joints should be staggered. In some cases, when wood shakes or shingles are the coverings of choice, they are nailed to 1 inch by 4 inch furring strips for increased ventilation.

It will be difficult for the home inspector to see the roof sheathing unless there are missing roof coverings. In any case, if the roof sheathing is seen, it should be reported.

Roof Framing

Normally the roof system uses joists and rafters spaced from 12 inches to 24 inches apart on center. Joists usually span one-half the width of the structure, and are supported in the middle by load-bearing walls. Inspectors should be familiar with local codes dealing with the acceptable span lengths and wood ratings for structural safety of roof framing.

Rafters and Joists

The rafters and joists support the dead loads of the sheathing, roofing material, and roof-mounted equipment. They also bear live loads from weather (snow, wind, rain) and people with their belongings. Rafters may also carry the ceiling loads below when cathedral ceilings are employed. Rafters and joists also create attic and ventilation space.

Figure 4.12
Rafter and joists in attic

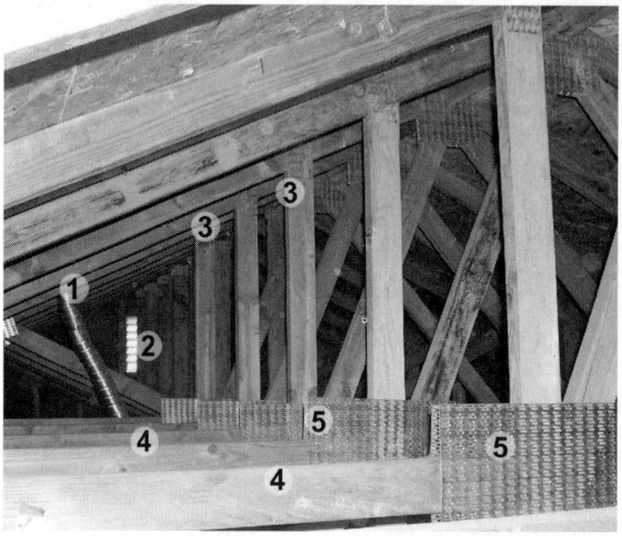

1) Plumbing vent
2) Attic vent
3) Attic rafters
4) Joist
5) Seismic bracing

Rafters tend to push the walls apart, and the joists (wooden framing members that run horizontally to rafters and have the ceiling nailed to them) contain this outward pressure and provide triangular rigidity to the roof system. **Purlins**, which are beams that run from the rafter to the joist and intersect the rafter at a 90-degree angle are used to reinforce the roof deck.

Reportable Deficiencies - Rafters and Joists

- Sagging due to the center of the rafters being lower than their ends
- Spreading apart due to the load on the rafters forcing them further apart than when they were installed
- Rot or water damage destroying the structural integrity of the wood
- Fire damage
- Poor connections on end bearings
- Splitting due to heavy loads that actually split the individual boards of the rafter

Roof Fasteners

Roofing systems are subject to extreme loads (weight bared by structural components) and environmental forces during high winds, storms, and seismic events. The home inspector should be familiar with the proper local codes for the specification of **roof fasteners** to be used to hold the roof on the home.

The roof has to be secured to the rest of the building to provide not only structural support, but to keep it from shaking off during high winds or jumping off during seismic events.

Bolts that are typically a 1/2 inch in diameter and 6 to 12 inches long are used to attach the roof structure to the walls and framing structure. They may be placed every 6 to 8 feet and sometimes closer depending on seismic or wind resistance requirements in certain areas.

The home inspector will most likely not be able to see these fasteners unless they are sticking up from roofing materials. The appearance of water spots or rotting in rafters will give the inspector clues to improper fastening of the roof structure.

Chimneys

Most homes have **chimneys** made of brick, stone, or a fire-resistant clay material. A masonry chimney may weigh several tons and must have proper support. The inspector should see that they are on solid footings and firmly attached to the home. Additionally, the chimney should be plumb (vertically straight).

In addition to being structurally safe, the chimney must be fireproof, gas tight, and resistant to the chemicals generated in the combustion process. Chimneys are required to extend 3 feet above the roof where they exit and 2 feet higher than any part of the structure within 10 feet. Chimneys less than 8 inches thick must be lined with a suitable fireclay material.

Chimneys that pass through a roof present a special challenge to the roofing installation. The roofing system of rafters and joists must be cut and boxed to allow the chimney to pass through. Where the chimney intersects the plane of the roof, a system of flashing and counterflashing must be installed to prevent rainwater from leaking into the attic.

In most cases, chimneys that penetrate the roof will have a "cricket" installed on the uphill slope of the roof. The **cricket** is a small peaked structure built perpendicular to the roof. The purpose of the cricket is to divert water and other debris around the chimney instead of allowing it to collect on the uphill side.

Figure 4.13
Chimney cricket and flashing

1) Asphalt composition roof
2) Cricket
3) Chimney
4) Chimney flashing

An important item for the inspector to observe is the flashing where the chimney penetrates the roof and joins the building. Missing or damaged flashing can lead to other problems in the home. All chimneys need to have a rain cap to keep water off the top face of the masonry and to keep water out of the flue itself. The chimney cap should also incorporate some form of spark arrestor to keep dangerous sparks from exiting the chimney. The home inspector should check for chimney caps or spark arrestors.

Some older homes have chimneys built without flue liners. Because the exhaust gases from a fireplace are toxic, and because masonry is porous, this is a potentially hazardous condition. The home inspector should check for a flue liner when applicable.

Reportable Deficiencies - Chimneys

- Leaking gases or backdraft
- Leaning or being out of plumb
- Cracking
- Spalling
- Efflorescence
- Missing parts or connections

- Being too short or too tall
- Improperly braced
- Missing or broken chimney liner
- Missing or broken chimney cap
- Soot build-up in chimney
- Non-functioning flue
- Missing or damaged spark arrestor

Skylights

A **skylight** is a glass opening in a roof that allows natural light to enter a home. These architectural accents can be found on steep and flat roofing. Skylights can be fixed or opened. Those that may be opened use either cranks or electric motors to do so. Skylights can be made of glass or plastic and can be clear or translucent. Glass used in skylights must meet local building code requirements.

Figure 4.14
A skylight allows natural light into a home.

In order for a skylight to function, the light from the outside must make its way from the roof to the interior of the home. To do this, light wells are installed leading from the roof through the attic and the ceiling into the interior of the room. Home inspectors should be aware that skylights could leak. A leaking skylight can be a greater problem than a leaking window. When rain falls directly on a skylight, it must flow against and around the skylight before flowing off the roof.

Another problem that skylights can cause is the creation of ice dams. A skylight-caused ice dam occurs when snow falling on the skylight melts, because the warmth from the house keeps the skylight above freezing and the melted snow refreezes when it flows down to a part of the roof that is below freezing. This refrozen snow builds up to form a wall of ice, called an **ice dam**, which can cause water to puddle on a pitched roof. If the water gets deep enough, it can back up under shingles and leak down into the attic. A substantial amount of damage from this cause can take place before it is apparent in the living area of the house. Although an inspector cannot always check for ice dams because the inspection is not done during the winter, he or she should look in the attic for damage that might have been caused by an ice dam.

Skylights have to be properly sealed and insulated. The inspector needs to know if the skylight uses the correct glazing. For example, a typical exterior window should not be used as a skylight window. Severe weather can penetrate skylights through improper seals, inadequate insulation, or incorrect glazing.

Reportable Deficiencies - Skylights

- Poor fastening
- Insufficient insulation or improper seals
- Wrong type of window used in skylight
- Water leaks
- Flashing damage or leaks
- Broken or cracked glass or glazing
- Patched skylights
- Mold or rot
- Ice dams

Antennas

Although the inspector is not responsible for inspecting a permanently attached television antenna or satellite dish, he or she must be aware of the problems that could be caused to the roof by these accessories. Antennas are usually anchored to both the chimney and other roof parts with guy wires. Damage can be caused to their connecting point on the roof and chimney when the guy wires are subjected to stress by high winds or weather. Satellite dishes can also cause damage to the roof when their fasteners become loose through aging or weathering. The inspector should note loose fasteners or guy wire connections.

This damage may include degradation of roofing materials and fasteners, loose connections of fasteners, and holes in the roof surface. In extreme cases, the roof structure can be damaged by these components. The inspector must be sure that the roof is sound, and the components atop it are not causing leaks or other damage.

Gutters and Downspouts

No matter what the design of the roof, it must have a system to drain the water. Water that simply pours off the roof during a storm will soon erode the foundation. Most homes are built with a system of gutters and downspouts to channel runoff safely away from the structure.

Exceptions to this are arid parts of the country such as the Southwest and heavy snow regions where the build-up of snow can then form ice dams and cause other problems. Ice dams can cause gutters to pull away from homes and cause exterior damage. There are even some homes with interior roof drainage systems where the water is directed through the house out to the sewer system.

Figure 4.15
Gutter and downspout system

Gutters are constructed of corrosion-resistant material such as aluminum or vinyl and need to be properly installed to do their job. Seams need to be sealed, joints should overlap in the direction of the water flow, and the pitch should be adequate. An upper-story downspout should not discharge directly onto a lower roof. It should be plumbed into a lower downspout or led into a gutter.

Reportable Deficiencies - Gutter and Downspouts

- Loose fasteners
- Dirt and debris build-up in gutters or downspouts
- Separated downspouts
- Corrosion, rust, or rot
- Missing parts
- Inadequate drainage where downspout terminates

Review - Reportable Deficiencies - Roofs

- Missing shingles, tiles, or even flashing
- Fastener problems
- Patching or replacement of some parts
- Too many layers of roofing
- Blistering
- Bulging
- Debris on the roof
- Rotting, mold, or discoloration
- Openings, puncturing, or holes
- Leaking
- Roof movement
- Insufficient or too much slope
- Damage caused by roof accessories

Re-Roofing

It is best to remove the old shingles before installing the new ones, but for cost reasons this is seldom done. Most codes limit the number of layers on a roof. Two layers are usually the maximum number of layers, but sometimes three are permitted when re-roofing.

As the number of layers of roofing increases, the weight bearing on the rafters increases. This added weight can cause sagging of the underlying roof structure and the inspector should look for this. In addition, the extra layers of roofing do not cool well and can cause premature failure. An experienced roofer will set the first course of the new roof at a different place than the first course of the old roof to keep the seams separated. If this is not done, the roof will have visible bulges where two seams meet. The inspector should notify the client if there appears to be too many layers of roofing installed.

Reportable Deficiencies of Re-Roofing

- Too many layers of roofing installed
- Cracking
- Seams exposed
- Leaking
- Sagging
- Same other deficiencies in a refinished roof as a new roof

Attics

The **attic** is the area of the home between the underside of the roof and the upper side of the ceiling of the top floor. It may be large enough to stand up in or just barely large enough to meet the definition. A large attic can often be accessed by a staircase or a built-in folding stairway in the ceiling located in an upstairs hallway or closet. The access panel, or hatch, may be difficult to remove.

Once opened, the inspector should note whether this hatch is properly insulated or if air was leaking down from the attic before it was removed. Some homes require a ladder to access the attic. If there is safe access to the attic, and the insulation is not higher than the joists, the inspector should enter to complete the roof inspection. There may be more than one attic space, so in the event one of them cannot be entered, the inspector should note this for the client.

Figure 4.16
Folding attic or "pull down" ladder

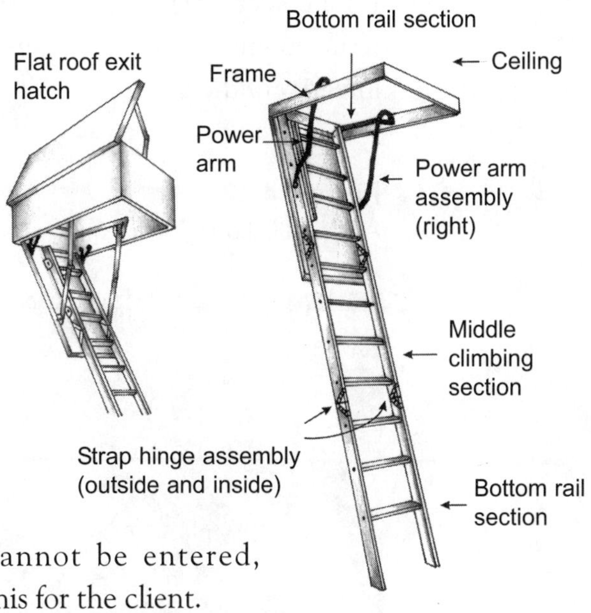

As a safety precaution, an inspector should be extremely careful when working in an unfinished attic to avoid stepping through the ceiling of the floor below. Additionally, the inspector should look for spiders or other pests that pose a serious risk.

Attics do not normally get a lot of traffic, so the inspector should be wary when climbing stairs or mounting built-in ladders. These features are often poorly maintained and unsafe. These features are potentially hazardous to the roof structure if the trusses are cut to make room for these fold-down stairways. Any safety defects or changing of the roof structure should be reported to the client and recommended for attention by a structural engineer.

While in the attic, the inspector should check to see if the insulation is adequate and that there is no evidence of water damage from roof leaks or condensation. The inspector should also check for any exposed wiring or breaks in the plumbing. Examine the attic area for any signs of unwanted pests such as mice, birds, or squirrels. Check to see that plumbing vents go through the roof and do not terminate in the attic.

Ventilation

Ventilation simply makes the insulation more effective. Investigate the **attic ventilation** system, including fans, turbines, and roof vents to make sure it is functioning.

There are two fundamental benefits of an effective attic ventilation system: (1) a cooler attic in summer and (2) a dryer attic in winter. Both benefits result in energy saving, greater homeowner comfort, and higher structural integrity of the home.

Figure 4.17
Attic ventilation

1) Rafters

2) Gusset

3) Attic vent

Adequate ventilation is essential to prolong the life of the roof covering as well as the building materials used in the roof structure. In addition to obtaining maximum life for the roof, proper ventilation can dramatically reduce the heating and cooling costs for the house.

During cold weather, adequate ventilation will prevent the condensation of moisture on the undersides of the roof deck. If unchecked, the condensation can rot the insulation and cause damage to the roof.

During summer months, the sun's heat can make surface temperatures rise to the point where the roofing material degrades. Asphalt shingles will curl and crack, and wood shingles will become distorted and brittle. An unventilated attic area can contribute to excessive thermal expansion of roof members, which will cause buckling and distortion of roofing material. This heat buildup can be reduced by ventilating the attic properly.

Roof Vents

To determine if adequate ventilation is in the attic, check for the number of vents. For example, if there is a vapor barrier, then there should be 1 square foot of opening (vent) per 300 square feet of attic floor. If there is no vapor barrier installed, homes in humid climates need the area to be doubled to 2 square feet of opening (vent) per 300 feet of attic floor. Since there is normally not enough vent area provided, the available amount should be split into at least two openings.

Figure 4.18
Roof vents

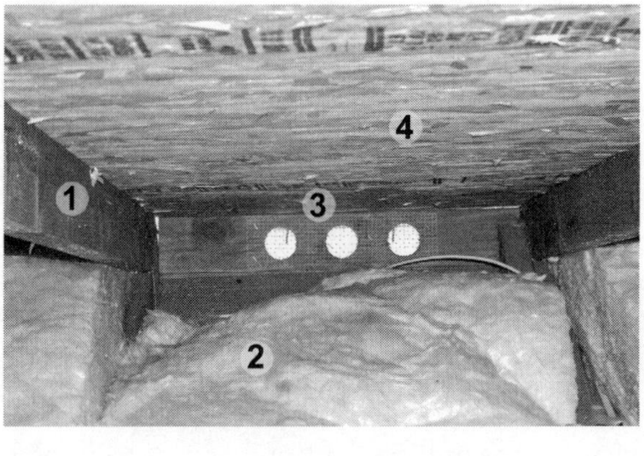

1) Rafter
2) Attic insulation
3) Roof vent
4) Underside roof sheathing

If one opening is placed higher than the other, the natural chimney effect will increase the efficiency of the system. Cross ventilation is not as effective as high low ventilation, because there is no ongoing motivation to ventilate. The most efficient flow of air is achieved when the vents are placed along the eaves and soffits. Soffits are the exposed undersides of the eaves. When the vents are located in this way, a current of air will flow along the base of the roof, helping to cool it off. Since warm air rises, this type of system takes advantage of thermal convection or a natural chimney effect, and air movement will be created through the attic, even when there is no wind. If the placement and size of the openings are adequate for summer heat removal, then they will be suitable for winter moisture control as well.

Attic Fans

In cases where the flow of air is inadequate, the condition can often be remedied with an **attic fan**. The fan should be sized to change the air in the attic once per minute. These fans can be thermostatically controlled or manually operated. If the inspector discovers the presence of attic fans, their operation should be checked by turning them on either manually or by programming the thermostat. There should be an adequate supply of makeup air for the fan or the whole point of having the attic fan is lost.

There are also large fans that are designed to change the air inside the living space as well. They are called whole house fans and are usually mounted in the attic or at the ceiling of an upper story hall.

Two factors determine if this type of fan will work well. They are (1) an adequate supply of makeup air, and (2) enough ventilation area to allow discharge air to exit the building. If the exit ventilation area is too small, a positive pressure zone will be created in the attic. This area of high pressure will cause dirt and dust from the attic to be blown into the rooms below.

Insulation

The concept of home **insulation** is a modern phenomenon arising from the increase in energy costs. As the costs of heating fuel increased, heat loss became both a comfort and economic issue. Products and systems were developed to deal with heat loss.

The dead-air space between walls is not an effective insulator. The convection currents that form between the warm inner wall and the cooler outer wall transfer the heat away from the living spaces. The installation of insulation in the wall cavity creates millions of tiny barriers to impede the convection flow and heat loss.

In a well-engineered home, insulation will be installed to surround the living space. When insulation is installed that has a built-in vapor barrier, the barrier should face the warm side. When the roof rafters have been insulated, the inspector will have difficulty examining the underside of the roof. If this is the case then this must be stated in the inspection report.

When the underside of the roof is insulated, it will often mask the signs of water penetration from roof leaks. A better way to insulate the area is to insulate the floor of the attic and leave the rafters bare. This effectively removes the attic from the heated area of the house and can reduce energy consumption and heating bills.

Types of Insulation

Domestic insulation is available in many forms. Some of the most common forms often encountered include batts (blankets), sheets, blocks, blowable pieces, and liquids that turn to foam.

Insulation thickness determines its **R-value**, or resistance-to-heat loss. The same R-value is required for insulation against both hot and cold temperatures.

One of the most popular insulating materials is rock or glass that has been extruded into fibers. This material is inherently fire resistant and has excellent insulating properties. Fibers created from this method will not rot, rust, or dissolve. Often these materials are coated with kraft paper or foil on one side to provide a vapor barrier and for ease of installation. When this style of insulation is used with a vapor barrier, some of the fire resistance may be lost.

Insulation batts and blankets are more stable in vertical applications compared to blown insulation because blown insulation has a tendency to settle. Cellulose insulation (made from ground up newspapers) is an excellent insulator, but it must be treated with fire retardant before it can be used safely in a home. Cellulose is only available as a blown-in product.

Another type of insulation is the chemical foam variety. Because it expands to fill the space where it is installed, it has the added advantage of being able to get into every nook and cranny of the area being insulated. The major drawback of chemical foam is the tendency for it to produce toxic fumes when ignited. Other than that, these foams are very effective and economical to install. Other less-popular types of insulation include cement foam, reflective foil, expanded mica, and perlite.

In colder parts of the country, the insulating qualities of storm doors and windows are used very effectively to reduce heating costs. In some parts of the country, dual-glazed windows are common. Having these dual-glazed windows is like having permanent storm windows as they provide the same insulating characteristics.

Inspecting the Insulation

The home inspector should be familiar with the different types of insulation used in home construction. The inspector should be able to make an informed judgment of the adequacy of the insulation as well.

To check the insulation on an outside wall, the cover plate from an electrical outlet must be removed. Probing around with a non-conductive instrument will often help determine the thickness of insulation in the wall. The effectiveness of a home's insulation falls dramatically if there are areas that have no insulation. The inspector should also examine all areas where pipe or electrical conduit is run, lapped joints, and heating and cooling registers where insulation is present.

Reportable Deficiencies - Insulation

- Areas with too little insulation
- Areas that have voids in the insulation
- Sagging insulation
- Missing insulation
- Moldy insulation (caused by roof leaks)

5

Chapter

Building Interior Finishes

Introduction

The interior of the house refers to the finishes of interior walls, ceilings, floors, doors and windows, counters and cabinets, and stairs and handrails. The condition of the house's interior finishes usually indicates the level of its maintenance and its overall quality. The interior of the house is the distribution place for the major systems of the house. Each room should have enough heat, air supply and electrical outlets for comfort and enjoyment.

It is not the job of home inspectors to judge style or taste of interiors. However, it is within their scope to evaluate the function of these components. The home inspector should inspect the interior of the house for clues to possible problems like water leaks and structural issues.

Walls and Ceilings

Both interior walls and ceilings serve a similar function in that they improve overall rigidity to help prevent racking and twisting of the structure and serve to strengthen the vapor barrier. In addition, they conceal the electrical, mechanical, and plumbing systems from the homeowner's view.

Interior Walls

Walls can be made of a variety of materials such as plaster, drywall, wood planks or panels, fiber cement panels, masonry, or concrete.

Plaster and drywall are the two most commonly used materials to finish interior walls. They are relatively inexpensive and are easy to paint or wall-paper. They are considered good materials at blocking sound and resisting fire and insect damage. Additionally, if damaged, they are easy to repair.

Figure 5.1
Drywall is a commonly used, inexpensive material for finishing interior walls.

Home inspectors use a few common techniques to check the interior walls of a home. The most prevalent way to check them is to push or tap on walls to determine if they are coming loose from their supports. An inspector should shine a flashlight parallel to a wall in order to see any blemishes of patching, material flaws, moisture, or other abnormalities. This will cause the abnormalities to stand out as a bulge or a depression compared to the otherwise normally flat wall.

The home inspector should also know common problems of interior walls so when they encounter them in the home, they can be reported. Stained or discolored paint or wallpaper can indicate water damage. This is important to note because the underlying structure of the wall may be damaged as well as the finish. Water damage is frequently found in many areas like bathrooms, below windows, chimneys, and vents. Cracks can be merely cosmetic or there can be a more serious underlying condition. Structural instability can cause walls to crack. Fresh paint or wallpaper should be reported as it may be used to hide flaws and other significant damage. Drywall and plaster walls can be loose, damaged, crumbling or powdery, bulging, or have nails sticking up. Wood wall problems to report include rot, cracking, splitting, loose, or even broken boards.

Reportable Deficiencies - Interior Walls

- Stained or discolored paint or wallpaper can indicate water damage
- Cracks caused by structural instability
- Fresh paint or wallpaper used to hide flaws
- Loose or bulging drywall
- Cracked, crumbling, or powdery plaster walls
- Cracked, split, broken, or loose wood
- Dry rot

Ceilings

Ceilings are made from the same basic types of material as interior walls. These include plaster, drywall, wood, or paneling. Occasionally, **acoustic tile** or metal ceilings may also be encountered in some homes. In addition to various materials that can be used, there are different types of ceilings such as textured and dropped.

Figure 5.2
Older homes may have decorative plaster ceilings.

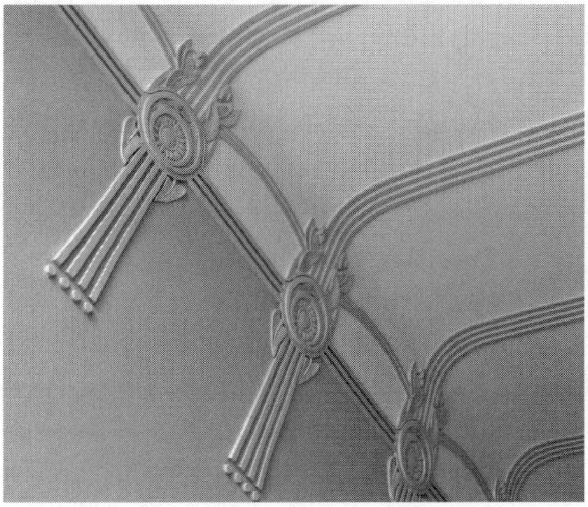

Textured ceilings are quick to apply and relatively inexpensive. The textured material is simply sprayed onto a drywall backing. Textured ceilings have a tendency to collect dirt and grease and should not be used in the kitchen or bathrooms. While they may be a pleasing finish to look at, they are very difficult to clean.

Suspended or **dropped ceilings** are made using acoustic tiles and a t-bar suspension. The **t-bars** (a framework of steel or metal channel suspended by wires) are filled with pre-cut acoustic tiles that are slipped into them. This type of ceiling was popular during the 1950s.

The home inspector should detect common problems with ceilings and report them. In general, these include water damage and cracking, loose, missing, or damaged materials. However, each ceiling material can have its own problems and preferred manner of inspection.

Suspended Ceilings. To find water damage in suspended ceilings a home inspector should lift the edges of the ceiling tiles to check them for signs of roof leaks or other problems. The home inspector should check for loose ceiling components that could fall and cause damage to the home or injury to the persons inside.

Plaster or Drywall Ceilings. The most common problems are sagging, bulging, crumbling or powdery areas, raised nails, missing parts, and textured ceilings in inappropriate areas like bathrooms and kitchens. The inspector should shine a flashlight at a slight angle to the ceiling to detect sagging or bulging.

Wood Ceilings. Typical problems include rot, damaged wood, cracked, split, or loose pieces.

Metal Ceilings. Rust and dents are the most common problem with metal ceilings.

Whenever possible, the roof joists that support the ceiling should also be checked for cracking, splitting, or compromise caused by improper cutting or notching of the truss. A condition known as **truss uplift** can occur during the winter months. It occurs when the center portion of a roof truss, connected to the ceiling, rises and creates a gap between the ceiling and an interior wall or partition.

Reportable Deficiencies of Ceilings

- Water damage
- Damaged, loose, or missing materials
- Sagging, bulging, crumbling, or powdery areas in plaster or drywall
- Cracked, split, or rot in wood
- Dents and rust in metal ceilings

Floors

There are usually two types of floors found in a house: (1) sub-floors and (2) finished floors. A **sub-floor** is a wood floor, typically unfinished plywood, which is attached to a room's floor joists and to which the finished floor is attached. The **finished floor** is the floor that is seen by residents and guests in the home. When just the term 'floor' is used, it usually refers to the finished floor.

Figure 5.3
Two types of floors found in a house are sub-floors and finished floors.

Floors are in homes to provide walking surfaces and to support furniture. Floors need to be level and smooth so occupants do not trip. They need to be very durable because they get more use than any other component of the interior.

Floors can be made of numerous materials, including concrete, wood, carpet, resilient tile, ceramic tile, and quarry tiles (stone, marble, granite, slate, etc.).

Concrete Flooring

Concrete floors are most often found in basements or crawlspaces. They can also be the main floor in a slab-on-grade home. However, in this type of home, the concrete flooring is more often used as the sub-floor that has finished or raised flooring installed on top of it. Concrete floors can have many of the same problems as foundations like cracking, heaving, settling, efflorescence, and water infiltration.

Wood Flooring

Wood can be used as a finished or sub-flooring material. Second stories of homes often use plywood as a sub-flooring on which the finished flooring is laid.

Figure 5.4
Hardwood planks are an example of finished wood flooring.

Types of finished **wood flooring** include softwood or hardwood planks and parquets. Common problems of wood floors include rotting, warping, staining, and squeaking. These problems can lead to the development of structural flaws, tripping hazards, and cosmetic blemishes.

Carpeting

Most **carpet** currently installed is made of synthetic fabrics, but occasionally wool carpeting will be found. Carpeting is usually attached to sub-flooring systems.

Figure 5.5
Carpeting is often found in bedrooms and the living room.

Common problems of carpeting include bunching, poor seam connections, protruding staples, rot, mildew, stains, and odors. Bunching carpet represents a tripping hazard to occupants. If carpet is rotting, it can be a sign of water leaking that can damage the structural parts of the home. There are also adverse health implications if mildew, mold, and odors are present in the carpet.

Resilient Flooring

Resilient flooring is a type of finished flooring that includes linoleum, vinyl tile, and asphalt tile. Bathrooms, kitchens, and basements are typical places where resilient flooring can be found. Splitting of the material or open and lifted seams are the most common problem with this type of flooring.

Figure 5.6
Linoleum is an example of resilient flooring which can be found in a kitchen, bathroom, or hallway.

Ceramic and Quarry Tile Flooring

Both ceramic and **quarried tile** (stone, marble, slate, etc.) flooring is set in a **wet bed** (a mud-like substance made of cement, sand, and lime mix) or a **thin set** (a highly sticky and powerful adhesive).

Typically, the wet bed system has problems associated with tiles cracking and becoming loose because the grout in between the tiles is damaged or missing. This can lead to an unstable floor and create tripping or slipping hazards. Cracks and damaged grout can also allow water to penetrate to the sub-flooring and cause other problems to the structure.

Figure 5.7
Ceramic tile can be found throughout a home.

Reportable Deficiencies - Flooring

Common flooring problems include tripping hazards, water damage, cracking, stains, or improper slope. Some problems can be found in many flooring materials, others are found in only one. Each type of flooring material with its deficiencies is listed below.

Concrete flooring

- Cracks, heaves, settling
- Efflorescence
- Water infiltration
- Stains

Wood flooring

- Rot
- Warp
- Stains, cracks
- Squeaks
- Missing or loose boards

Carpeting

- Bunching
- Poor seam connections
- Protruding staples or nails
- Rot (water damage)
- Mildew, stains, odors
- Rips and worn areas

Resilient flooring

- Open or lifted seams
- Stains

Ceramic tile, stone, and marble flooring

- Cracked tile, stones, or pieces of marble
- Damaged or missing grout

Doors and Windows

Doors provide access to rooms in a home for residents and guests. Windows light the interior and allow air to enter the home to heat or cool it. Both doors and windows provide security for the home by keeping intruders out. They are available in different styles for various uses and functions.

Doors

Exterior doors are used to enter and leave the home. They should also provide security and be weather-tight. Standard exterior front doors are usually hinged on one side and measure 6 feet 8 inches high, 36 inches wide, and $1^3/8$ inches thick. In homes with attached garages, the door between the house and the garage should also be fireproof or gas-proof.

Interior doors provide passageways between the different rooms of the home and privacy in the rooms as well. They are usually 27-to-32 inches wide and $1^3/8$ inches thick. While not as solid as exterior doors, they do provide some sound blocking and fire protection.

Although most doors are made of wood and hinged, they can be made of other materials and open in different ways. Rather than swing on hinges, doors can run on tracks to slide open and close, be attached at the top, both slide and fold, or even be flexible and roll up. In addition to wood, doors can be made of metal, vinyl, and even glass.

Wood doors come in solid, panel, and hollow variations and are used in exterior and interior applications like closets and rooms. Interior grade doors should not be used for exterior applications, as they are not weatherproof.

Metal doors are gaining popularity for their protective qualities. They can keep out intruders due to their superior strength, keep out the weather because they have better insulation, and provide better fire protection.

Vinyl doors can be used for either exterior or interior applications. They are usually very weather-resistant.

Glass doors are usually glass panes mounted in wood, metal, or vinyl frames that are then placed on tracks that slide to allow access.

In addition to knowing about doors, the inspector should be familiar with the parts that surround a door. Many of these terms are used when describing windows. The **door frame** is a general name that includes

Figure 5.8
Interior door components

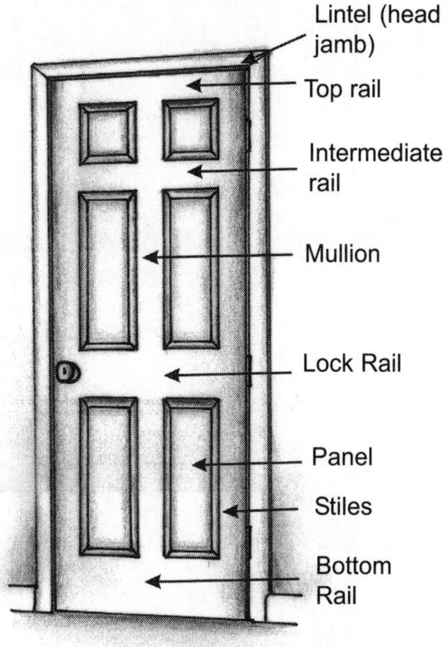

all the parts that surround a door. It can be made of wood or metal. The **header** is the horizontal piece of the doorframe that is above the door. Sometimes it is called the head jamb. **Jambs** are the vertical pieces of a doorframe. The hinges are attached to one jamb and the latch to the other. The jambs are sometimes called the door lining. Sometimes the header is called the head jamb. The **stop** is the name given to the pieces of molding that are nailed to the sides of the door jambs and header that face the door. The door closes against the stop and prevents the door from swinging through. The **sill** is a strip of wood or metal that is beveled on each edge and attached to the finished floor under an outside door. Its purpose is to keep water from entering the house. Interior doors have a **threshold** or **saddle** instead of a sill. The **casing** is the decorative wood finish trim that surrounds doors and windows. On exterior doors, some sort of **weather stripping** is attached to the jambs, header, and sill to prevent air from leaking into or out of the house. The weather stripping can take the form of metal flashing, a rubber or plastic gasket, or foam strips.

Figure 5.9
Exterior door components

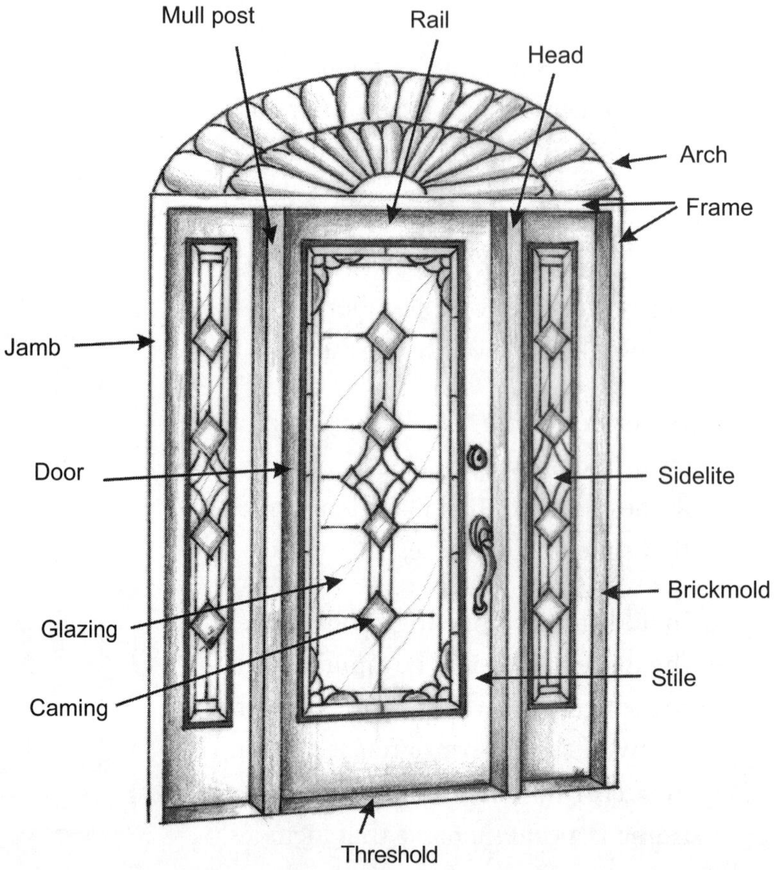

Doors usually provide good clues as to the overall condition of the home. Doors that do not fit into their frames may indicate an underlying problem. It could be as simple as a bad hinge, or as major as a settling foundation causing the doorframe to move. In either case, it is a good idea to open and close as many doors as possible to check for proper function and closure.

Jumping to conclusions when observing a door out of square is not a good idea, as further investigation is required. It merely points out a potential defect to the alert home inspector.

Reportable Deficiencies - Doors

- Air and water leaks
- Damaged or missing weather stripping
- Missing or damaged trim, flashings, or sills
- Not locking properly
- Not fitting into doorframes
- Opening and closing without being touched
- Cracked, chipped, or rusted parts
- De-lamination and peeling
- Insect infestation, rotting
- Improper use of door type

Windows

Windows allow for proper ventilation of a home and for light to enter. They can also serve as an exit in the event of an emergency.

Windows come in traditional glass but may also be laminated glass, tempered glass, and wired-safety glass. Acrylic is most common for skylights, and polycarbonates are used for strength and security applications. Windows are also typed by the material used to frame them. Common window frame and sash types include wood, vinyl, metal, or even fiberglass.

Additionally, windows are categorized by their function and movement. With **single-hung windows,** only the bottom sash can be raised or lowered, whereas **double-hung windows** can operate at both the top and bottom sash. **Casement** windows swing in or out on vertical hinges, like a door. Both awning windows and hopper windows open outward. **Awning windows** are hinged at the top of the sash, whereas **hopper windows** are hinged at the bottom. **Fixed windows** do not open, like those in high-rise buildings. A large fixed window is called a **picture window. Glass block**

windows are another type of fixed window. **Jalousie windows** are made up of overlapping horizontal slats of glass that open by rotating along their length via a single control. They are usually only found in warm climates, as they do not seal very tightly. **Slider windows** have sashes that slide horizontally to open.

In addition to categorizing windows by framing material, function, and movement, the inspector should be familiar with the parts that surround a window. The basic components of windows are the panes, frames, sashes, muntins, and mullions. The **pane** is the plate of glass itself. Panes are held in place by a putty-like substance called **glazing compound**. The **frame** holds the window system in place in the side of the building. The top of the frame is referred to as the head and bottom is called the **sill**. The **sash** is the part of the window that holds individual panes and is what moves when the window is opened or closed. **Muntins** divide individual panes within a sash, and **mullions** divide two or more windows within a frame. When inspecting a window's parts, an inspector should also examine the hardware on the window.

Figure 5.10
Window components

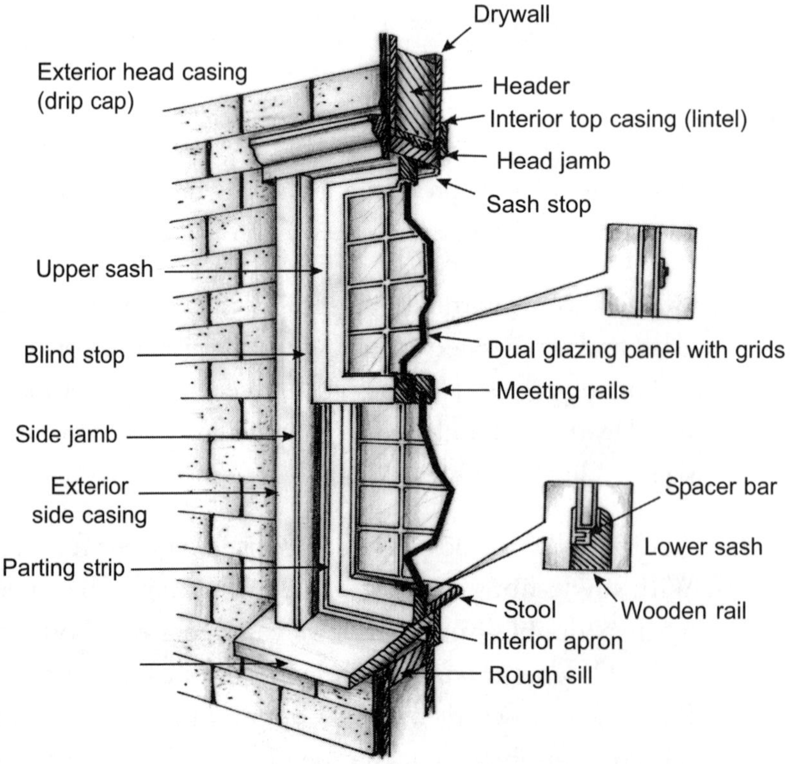

Safety Glazing

Safety glazing is defined as any glazing material that will prevent injury if it is broken. Tempered glass, laminated glass, wired glass, and rigid plastic meet safety standards. **Tempered glass** is a heat-treated glass that breaks into very small pieces when broken. **Laminated glass** is an assembly with clear plastic sandwiched between two pieces of glass, allowing the broken glass to stick to the plastic if broken. **Wired glass** is a thick glass with embedded metal wire. Areas in homes where safety glass must be used are determined by the Safety Glazing Materials Act of the Department of Labor and Industry. Some common places to find safety glazing in the home are the sliding glass doors, storm doors, shower doors, bathtub glass enclosures, or other glass panels near building entrances or exits. Usually, safety glazing materials are required to be labeled as such, and the labels must be visible after installation.

Security Bars

Security bars, or burglar bars, are often put on the outside of windows to protect the home from intrusion due to fears of becoming a crime victim. A problem arises when the security bars are installed without a quick-release mechanism. If a fire occurs, occupants can be trapped inside when they need to escape. All security bars, old and new, should have the quick-release safety mechanism.

Reportable Deficiencies - Windows

- Broken or cracked glass
- Air or water leakage
- Rotting or rusting of hardware and other components
- Missing exterior drip cap
- Missing or damaged window sill
- Damaged or ineffective glazing or safety glazing
- Damaged or missing caulking
- Inoperable or loose parts
- Loss of seal in between panes of glass
- Missing, rusted, or torn screens
- Missing safety release on security bar

Counters and Cabinets

Counters and cabinets provide workspace and storage in the kitchen, bathroom, and laundry areas of the home. A **counter** is like a table, whereas a **cabinet** has drawers, shelves, and doors.

Counters

Counters can be made from a number of materials such as wood, particleboard, plywood, or metal. Whichever covering is used for a countertop, it should be durable, waterproof, abrasion resistant, scorch proof, and non-porous. Typically, countertops are made from materials such as wood, laminate, ceramic tile, slate, granite, marble, and stainless steel.

Figure 5.11
Counters and cabinets are found in kitchens, bathrooms, and laundry areas.

Counters should be fixed securely to their base. The inspector should look for signs of scorching, dry rot, chipping, cracking, and delamination. Areas where the counter veneer has separated from the wall are likely spots for mold to form, which can present a serious health hazard.

Cabinets

Cabinets provide storage in kitchens and bathrooms. They can be located on the floor (base cabinets) or hung on the wall (wall cabinets). They are usually made from materials like solid wood, particleboard, or even metals. Cabinets made from particleboard are usually covered with a plastic laminate for protection as well as to improve their appearance.

The parts of the cabinet should be in working order. Hinges should operate smoothly as should drawer sliders. The usability of cabinets and drawers is important to home buyers.

Reportable Deficiencies - Counters and Cabinets

- Counters and cabinets not properly attached
- Loose countertops
- Scorched, chipped, cracked, or delaminated countertops
- Inoperable cabinet doors and drawers
- Broken glass or missing hardware

Staircases

Homes with basements or more than one floor will have a staircase connecting the different levels. A **staircase** is a flight of stairs including the stringers, steps, landings, and handrails or guardrails. Stairs in homes are usually made from wood but can also be concrete, brick, or even metal.

It is important for the home inspector to know the inspection guidelines for stairs as well as the handrails and guardrails attached to them. Staircases need to meet standard dimensions. One requirement is that there must be at least 6 foot 8 inches of clearance vertically between the top of the step and a ceiling. Another is that a stairwell or set of stairs has to be at least 36 inches wide.

Parts of a Staircase

The major components of a staircase are stringers, treads, risers, landings, handrails, and guardrails.

The **stringer** is the long, diagonal support that runs the length of stairs. There are usually two—one on each side of the stairs. Sometimes there is a third stringer in the center of the stairs. The minimum width of a stringer should be at least $3^1/2$ inches to provide stability to the stairs. The treads and risers are attached to the stringer.

Figure 5.12
Staircase

1) Tread
2) Run
3) Rise
4) Handrail
5) Ballusters
6) Stringer
7) Wood floor

The **tread** is the flat part of the stair that is stepped on. The width of the tread is called the **run**. The minimum width of each tread varies between $8^1/4$ inches to 9 inches. The tread should be as level as possible for safety. However, if it is not level, it should not slope more than 2 percent.

The riser is the vertical, solid part at the front of the tread. Open stairs do not have **risers**. The height of each step is called the **rise**, which should be no more than $8^1/4$ inches.

Figure 5.13
Parts of a staircase

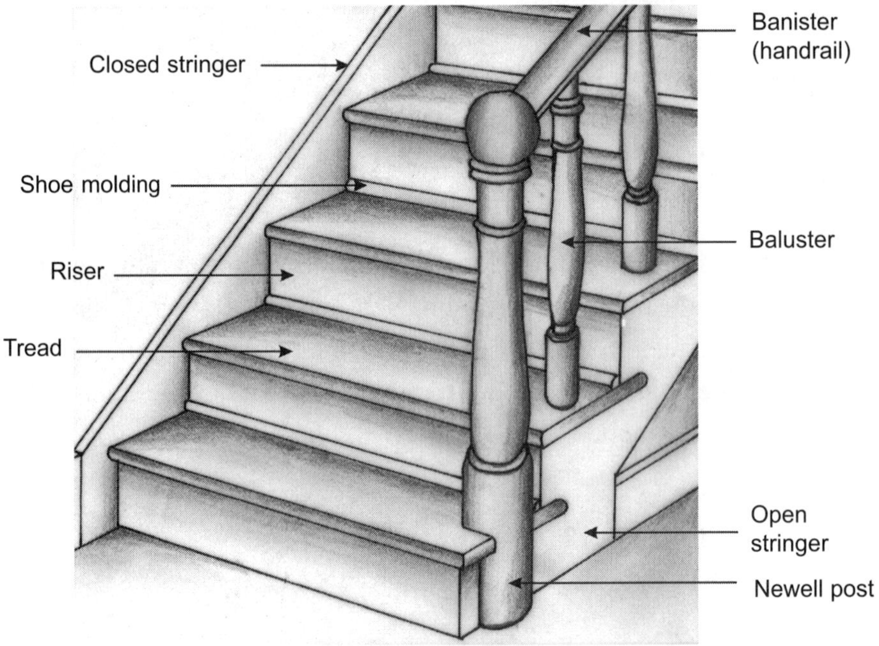

Landings provide safe standing areas in entryways and staircases. The first type of landing is a raised area on each side of a door when it is open or closed. The second type is a platform located at the top or bottom of a staircase or in between flights of stairs. Landings must be at least 3 feet by 3 feet for safety. Much like stairs, the maximum step down or step up is $8^1/4$ inches. The step up to a threshold or entry point must be 4 inches to 6 inches to prevent water intrusion.

Handrails are required on stairs with a height greater than 24 inches. This usually equates to two or three steps. **Balusters**, the vertical support bars of handrails, should not be spaced more than 4 inches apart to keep children from getting caught in them. The height from the first stair to the edge of the handrail cannot be less than 34 inches in height.

Guardrails are required on stoops and landings that are more than 24 inches above the ground or floor. They are also required to be at least 36 inches in height to prevent falls. Baluster or spindles must be no more than 4 inches apart to prevent children from getting stuck or squeezing through them.

Staircase Safety

The safest staircases are straight with all of the treads being the same depth and width and all of the risers being the same height. If a staircase changes direction, it should have a landing at the turn. Safe staircases are well lit. There should be a light switch at the top and the bottom of a staircase.

To make sure that no one slips on steps, wooden steps should have slip-resistant pads and carpeting on stairs must be attached securely. Handrails or guardrails should be installed on both sides of a staircase.

Reportable Deficiencies - Staircase

- Too narrow staircase or landings
- Incorrect size for rise, run, or tread
- Unstable, too much slope, slippery
- Bent, broken, or missing parts in handrails and guardrails

Chapter 6

Electrical Systems

Introduction

For most, living without electricity, or a power source in a home would be unimaginable. All the appliances that make lives more convenient would have no power source if not for the electricity pumped into homes. No lights at the push of a button or flip of a switch. No refrigerator making drinks cold or keeping food fresh. No radio, no television, and no computer for all the things it is needed for now.

With so much of the home affected by the electricity that runs through it, the home inspector needs to have a basic understanding of electricity. As always, safety is of paramount importance when dealing with this potentially dangerous form of power.

According to the basic laws of physics, energy can neither be created nor destroyed. It can only be changed from one form to another. Electricity starts as some form of energy, such as heat, kinetic, radiation, or chemical reaction. In most cases, this happens at the power station. Once the change to electrical energy has been accomplished, the power must be delivered to the home to do useful work.

Electrical Delivery

Electrical power is delivered to the home in two ways. In older communities, the power will come through an overhead transmission line hung from a power pole. In newer communities, the power will come from subterranean lines run to the home. In either case, the transmission lines serve as **conductors**, or materials that allow the flow of electricity from the power generation point or power plant to the home.

Figure 6.1
In older communities, electricity to homes is delivered through an overhead transmission line hung from a telephone pole.

Where either the overhead or underground supply wires end, there is a splice, or joining of two wires, that is sometimes known as the **service point.** Incoming service voltage can be calculated by counting the wires that join at the service point. Two wires indicate 115 volts available and three wires indicate that 230 volts are available. Most modern homes have three-wire service so that higher voltage appliances, such as air conditioning and electric stoves, can be run.

Elevated Power Delivery

In elevated power delivery, the conductors are led from the utility pole to the main supply panel of the home. This group of conductors or wires that connects to the supply panel of the home is known as the **supply drop**.

The municipally supplied power enters the system via a service entrance at a point called the **masthead** or **service cap**. A fitting called a **weather head** or **drip loop** is also located here and is designed to keep rainwater from running along the wires into the electrical service panel.

Figure 6.2
Electrical service entrance

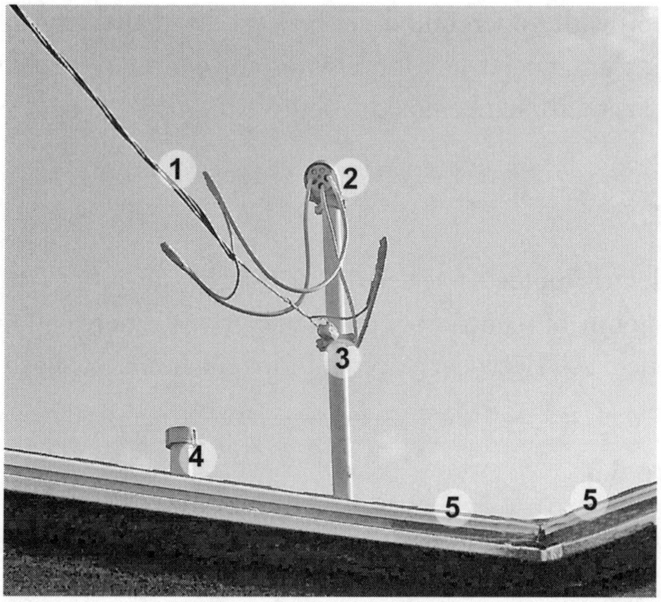

1) Service wires

2) Electrical mast

3) Service point

4) Plumbing vent

5) Gutters

When the conductors enter a home from above, there are certain restrictions that must be observed. The conductors must have drip loops incorporated into the connection. They must clear a flat roof by eight feet and a pitched roof by three feet. The conductors must not be lower than 12 feet above a driveway, 18 feet above a public street, 15 feet above an alley, or 10 feet above sidewalks, platforms, porches, or decks. In addition, service drops must be at least three feet away horizontally from windows, doors, fire escapes, decks, and porches. These restrictions help provide clearance against accidental contact and to reduce the risk of shock or electrocution.

Reportable Deficiencies of Elevated Power Delivery

- Trees or bushes interfering with wires
- Wires too high or too low from the ground, driveway or roof
- Damaged wires
- Wires too close to windows and doors
- Wires not secured to house
- Poor wire connections

Subterranean Power Delivery

Newer communities have utility lines underground. The electric power lines or conductors enter the home from below grade and are sometimes referred to as **service laterals**. Local regulations will mandate the kind of cable that is required for underground service. Modern homes will have at least 100 amps of power capacity and the conductor that supplies this power will be at least 8-gauge. The home inspector will most likely not be able to see problems with underground delivery except at the service entrance to the home. Deficiencies like loose wires and poor connections can still be a problem and should be noted if observed.

Electric Meter

The **electric meter** is a sealed device used by the utility company to measure the amount of electricity consumed by the electrical appliances in the residence. All electrical power entering the home passes through the meter.

Figure 6.3
Electric meter

Reportable Deficiencies of the Electric Meter

- Broken seals or tampering (to change readings)
- Meter not properly secured to the house
- Meter located in an area that will get damaged by cars or people
- Rusted or damaged meter box

Main Panel

The **main electrical panel** is where the electricity that enters the house gets divided and sent to different areas. It also contains the main disconnect and the individual circuit breakers. The **main disconnect** allows for all the electricity in the home to be shut off with one switch. Circuit breakers provide a method to turn off different areas of the electrical system for servicing. Sometimes the main panel and wiring has been repaired or upgraded to modernize the system or to rectify a serious design flaw. In any case, it should be reported.

Due to its importance, the main panel should be the focus of the home inspectors' evaluation of the residential electrical system.

Good business practice requires the removal of the main panel cover by the inspector. Before removing the attachment screws, the inspector should barely touch the panel cover as a safety precaution. If there is a "tingle," it means electricity is flowing to the panel cover (which it should not be doing). Therefore, do not remove the cover and contact a licensed electrician to look at this problem.

Figure 6.4
Electrical main panel

1) Electrical wires to house circuits
2) Circuit breakers
3) Circuit breakers
4) Main disconnect
5) Power in

With the panel cover removed, the inspector can determine what type of conductors or wires are being used, the size of the conductors relative to the breaker protection, and the adequacy of the installation (loose connections are a problem). Look for any evidence of overheating, such as burnt or discolored insulators, as well as evidence of arcing on the panel. No more than one wire should be connected to any terminal post. The individual breakers should be tightly connected to the bus bar without wiggle or slop. The electrical capacity for each circuit breaker will be found on the breaker itself and can be checked to see it is not being overdrawn by the wiring. The capacity of the main breaker will indicate the system capacity overall and may give clues as to why there are other electrical malfunctions in the home, like flickering lights and power surges.

Reportable Deficiencies of the Main Panel

- Main panel not accessible
- Main panel not secured
- Water or rust in the panel
- Use of a non-waterproof service box
- Damaged parts
- Evidence of overheating
- Burnt insulation
- Incorrect fuses
- Poor connections

Electrical Protection Devices

All homes are equipped with some form of protection devices built into the electrical circuits. In the event of a short circuit or serious overload, these devices will shut off the flow of power to the circuit.

Circuit Breakers

Newer homes have circuit breakers for protection. A **circuit breaker** is like a re-useable fuse. The breaker has a heat-sensitive switch in it that opens if too much heat is detected and shuts off the power to that circuit. Circuit breakers can be reset after the cause of the overload has been corrected.

Figure 6.5
Circuit breakers

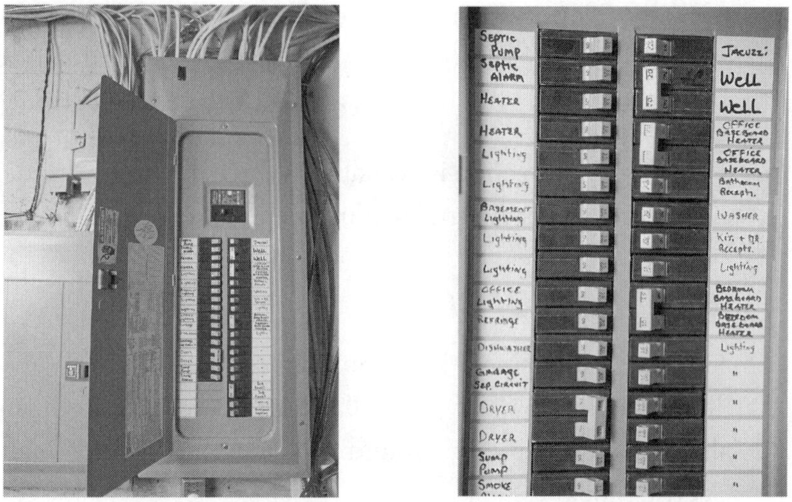

Fuses

Older homes use fuses to protect the electrical circuits. A fuse is a heat sensitive device that has a conductor designed to melt at a preset temperature. If the fuse becomes too hot because of an electrical malfunction or an overloaded circuit, the thermal link in the fuse melts and the flow of electricity is halted. Fuses are not reusable.

Figure 6.6
Fuse box and fuses

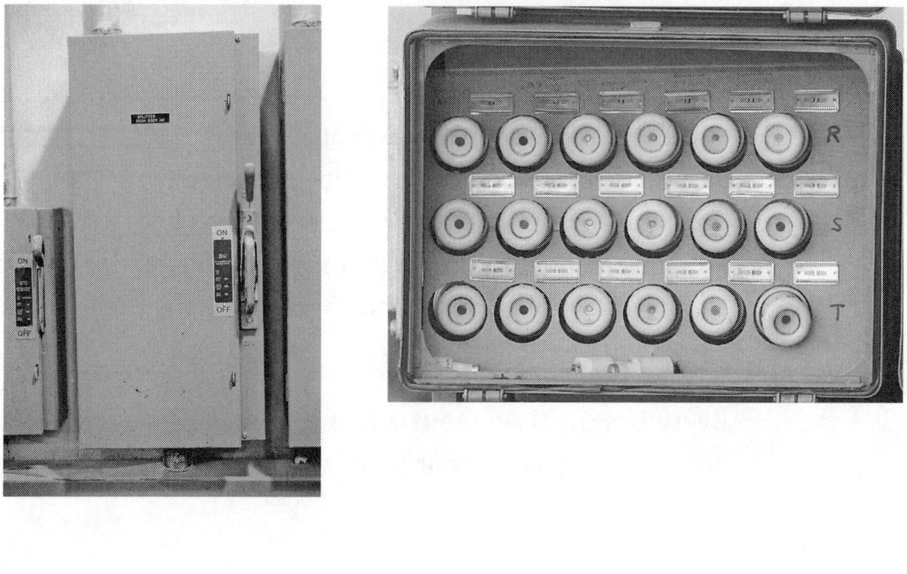

Ground Fault Circuit Interrupters

Another safety device found in the home is a **ground fault circuit interrupter (GFCI)**. Newer construction codes require GFCI protection on outdoor outlets, bathrooms, kitchen counters, wet bars, and garages. In addition, GFCI protection is required on any hot tub or pool lighting system.

This form of protection is available in three different varieties: a receptacle, a circuit breaker, or a portable plug in the unit.

Receptacle GFCI

The GFCI receptacle has a built-in detector that is sensitive to current fluctuations as low as 5 to 8 milliamps (thousandths of an amp). It can react almost instantly to any ground problem and therefore can protect against electric shock.

Circuit Breaker GFCI

The circuit breaker variety combines the overload protection of a conventional circuit breaker, with the added advantage of being able to detect a grounding problem.

Portable Plug GFCI

This type plugs into a standard receptacle and adds protection to the circuit.

Figures 6.7
Example of a ground fault circuit interrupter (GFCI). Color coded buttons make it easier to distinguish their function. All GFCIs have a black "Test" button and a red "Reset" button.

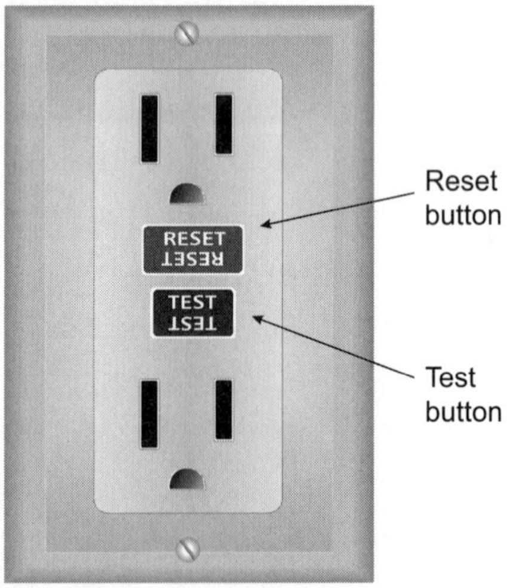

Basic Circuitry

In order for electricity to power an appliance, it must complete a circuit. A **circuit** is the path of an electric load from a source through a fixture or appliance and return to a grounding source. The **source** is where the alternate form of energy is transformed into electricity. This can be a storage battery, a power plant, or even the sun's rays.

Every electrical source has two terminals: a positive one and a negative one. The negatively charged electrons congregate at the negative terminal.

Because all these electrons have the same negative charge, they repel each other and generate electrical pressure at the negative terminal, which pushes the electric flow.

Figure 6.8
Electrical circuit path

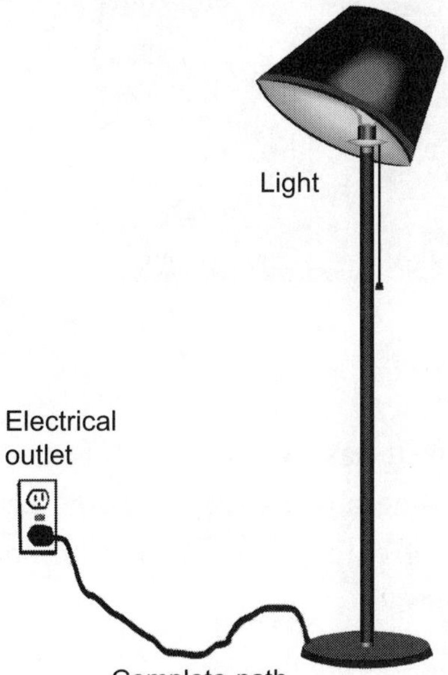

The **path** is the conductor. The negatively charged electrons are transported to the appliance via this path. This is the hot leg of the circuit. The load is where the work happens. A **load** is an area of electrical resistance where the energy of electricity is converted to another form of energy such as heat or light.

After doing the work, the electrons are transported back to the positive terminal via the neutral leg.

Electrical Circuits

An electrical circuit consists of a power source, connecting wires or conductors, and a device that uses the electrical energy. The device, such as an outlet, that uses the energy is called the load. The term circuit can also refer to the wires that make the flow possible by connecting the source and load and ground.

Electrical loads such as lamps or outlets can be wired in series or parallel. In a **series circuit**, the electrical current flows through all the loads sequentially. In this case, if one load fails, all the loads will be de-energized and the flow is cut off in the circuit.

In a **parallel circuit**, the individual loads are arranged like the rungs on a ladder. See the following graphic for an example. The current flows through all loads simultaneously and the failure of one load will not affect the others.

Figure 6.9
Loads (wired end-to-end)

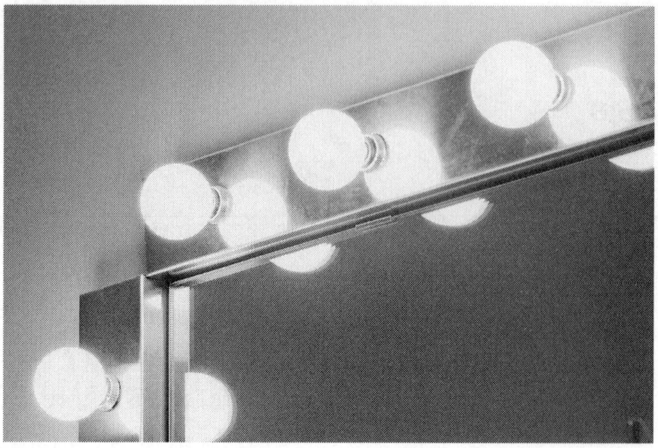

Grounding

In order for electricity to flow, it has to have a path to ground. When the grounding system is not working properly or is missing key parts, safety is compromised and there are greater risks for electric shocks, fires, and damage to electrical appliances.

Figure 6.10
Electrical grounding

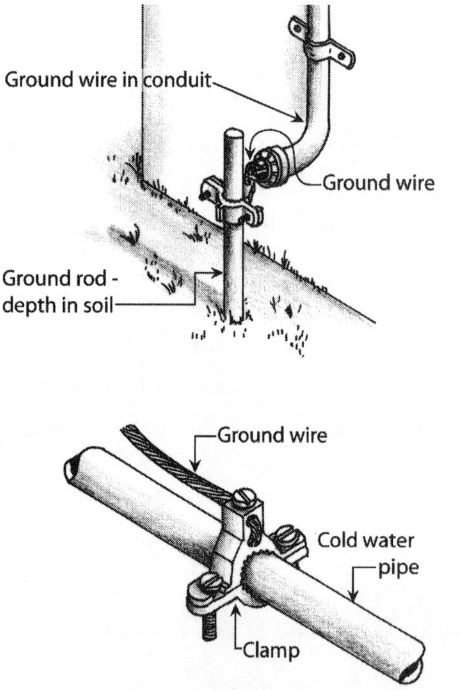

The part of an electrical circuit that allows electricity to flow to the ground is called the grounding or **ground**. Normally electricity will flow through its designated circuit, but sometimes it may flow elsewhere. Anyone who touches something that is conducting electricity may unintentionally become a ground and have the electricity flow through them. The grounding found in the home is there to protect the residents by giving the electricity a safe path by which to reach the ground. It is important for the home inspector to look for proper grounding systems.

The system ground electrically ties together the metal parts of the electrical installation—such as the service switch, the main panel box, the armored cable, and conduit —and leads from them to a safe ground. This diverts any dangerous overload to the ground and not into the home system.

There are two types of grounding employed in the home. One is the equipment grounding and the other is the earth grounding. The purpose of these grounds is to protect the electrical system in case of lightning strike, major overloads from the power company, static electricity, or other malfunction.

Equipment Grounding

The equipment or appliance grounding in the home is done by connecting to the neutral supply wire entering the home. This protects people from electricity being where it should not and allows fuses to blow and breakers to trip.

Earth Grounding

The actual ground connection is a heavy-duty cable that is either led to the water main serving the house, or to a grounding rod buried in the soil. This is used as a path for lighting or static electricity to flow away from items in the home and safely to the ground. When the water main is used as a ground conductor, the connection should be made at the street side of the meter. If the connection is made at the house side, then a jumper wire must be provided in case the meter has to be removed.

Reportable Deficiencies of Grounding

- Missing grounding
- Bad connections
- Spliced ground wires
- Attachment of the earth grounding wire to a plastic pipe
- Corroded wiring
- Grounding rod cut too short
- Not large enough gauge ground wire
- Ground wire being attached to the house side of the meters or valves

Bonding

Bonding is sometimes confused with grounding, where electrical wires are connected to the earth. **Bonding** describes the permanent connection of two electrical conductors. The result of bonding is that each wire has the same electrical potential as the other and current cannot flow between them. Unlike grounding, bonding alone cannot protect anything.

In most places, gas-piping systems are required to be bonded to electrical grounding systems and are not allowed to be used as a grounding source for the electrical.

Conductors

The flow of electricity through a conductor is often compared to the flow of water through a pipe. Certain materials are better conductors of electricity than others. Metal is a much better conductor than wood. Certain metals offer almost no resistance to the flow of electrons and are the preferred materials used to make electrical wire. The two most popular choices for residential wiring are copper and aluminum.

Of these two choices, copper is by far the better conductor, but it is heavier and more expensive.

A popular brand of conductor for residential applications is Romex® cable. This brand, like most wiring, consists of three separate wires wrapped in a protective plastic sleeve containing a white neutral wire, a black hot wire, and a bare ground wire.

Wire Sizes

Like water in a pipe, the electrical wire must be the proper size (diameter) for the load it is required to transport. **Wire size** is measured in numerical gauges, the lower the gauge number, the larger the wire. Wire used in residential applications ranges from 14 to 8 gauges.

Wire size is based on the number of amps of electricity that need to be run through a given wire. The larger the gauge number of the wire, the smaller its actual size is. Every size of wire has a corresponding number of amps it can move safely and a fuse or breaker that goes with it.

The following are common sizes in copper wiring:

- 8-gauge copper wire needs 40-amp fuses or breaker
- 10-gauge copper wire needs 30-amp fuses or breaker
- 12-gauge copper wire needs 20-amp fuse or breaker
- 14-gauge copper wire needs 10-amp fuses or breaker

Aluminum wire sizes and the fuses required are different in that a larger gauge wire is used with a smaller fuse.

- 6-gauge aluminum wire needs 40-amp fuses or breaker
- 8-gauge aluminum wire needs 30-amps fuses or breaker
- 10-gauge aluminum wire needs 20-amp fuses or breaker
- 12-gauge aluminum wire needs 15-amp fuses or breaker

Home electrical circuits for receptacles (plugs) and lights use 14-gauge copper wires or 12-gauge aluminum wires and are on 120-volt circuits. 240-volt circuits usually employ larger wires like 10 gauge copper or 8-gauge aluminum wires for powering dryers, air conditioners, water heaters, stoves, and ovens.

The use of appropriate sizes of fuses or breakers is important in homes. If a fuse or breaker is too small, it will shut off the power too soon even though there is no danger to harm the electrical circuit. This becomes very inconvenient as the homeowner needs to reset the circuit or replace the fuse each time this happens. If a breaker or fuse is too big (**overfusing**), it will not shut down the power before the wires overheat and possibly cause a fire or other serious damage.

Wire Types

Aluminum Electrical Wire

Aluminum is light and inexpensive, but it has a large rate of **thermal expansion**. This expansion and contraction due to an increase or decrease in heat can cause electrical connections to become loose and fail. For this reason, **aluminum wire** should only be used with connectors that are designed for it. Terminals designed for aluminum wire bear the legend CO/ALR.

Homes built after 1965 may have aluminum wire and the home inspector should be familiar with the problems associated with it. Aluminum wire, when exposed to the atmosphere, is subject to a form of corrosion or film called aluminum oxide. This film acts as an insulator rather than a conductor and will decrease its ability to conduct electrical current.

When inspecting a home that has aluminum wiring, the inspector should look for cover plates that are warm to the touch. Another major problem with aluminum wiring is that connections become loose over time. The wire literally backs away from connectors. This can be seen at junctions but can also be diagnosed by flickering lights. The larger aluminum wires, without insulation, should have grease to prevent oxidation when exposed to air. Overheated cover plates and flickering lights are symptoms of loose connections or overloaded circuits.

Reportable Deficiencies of Aluminum Wiring

- Overheating of aluminum wiring
- Loose connections
- Missing antioxidant grease

Copper Electrical Wire

Copper is one of the best conductors of electricity and is used widely for wiring in houses. The oxide produced when copper corrodes is as good a conductor as the copper itself. In addition to the effects of corrosion, copper has a low coefficient of expansion that reduces the risk of connections loosening over time.

Reportable Deficiencies of Copper Wire

- Loose connections
- Splicing
- Fraying

Knob-and-Tube Wiring

Homes built before 1950 may have a form of wiring called **knob and tube.** In knob-and-tube wiring, the wires are supported by a porcelain or glass insulator when installed along a flat surface. This insulator is the knob. When the wire passes through a stud or joist, it does so through a tube. Since knob-and-tube wiring is an old method, the wires, insulation, and sheathing tend to get dried out and brittle. Additionally, knob-and-tube wiring was often buried within insulation in attics or walls and should be reported if found as it is a safety hazard.

Knob-and-tube wiring does not have grounded circuits or receptacles where one prong is larger than the other to prevent reverse polarization. This is a safety hazard and many insurance companies will not insure homes with this type of wiring. It is now obsolete and should be replaced. If the inspector encounters this type of installation, it should be reported to the client with a recommendation for an electrician's evaluation.

Reportable Deficiencies of Knob-and-Tube Wiring
- Brittle wires, sheathing, and insulation

Insulators

In order to prevent **short circuits** where a fuse blows or a circuit breaker trips after a hot and neutral wire touch one another, wire must be surrounded with a nonconducting material called an insulator. An **insulator** is a material that does not conduct electricity.

Some excellent insulators are rubber, glass, and plastic. The use of an insulating coating around the wire keeps the flow of electricity confined to the desired path. If a wire is properly insulated, an accidental contact by a person will not cause harm.

In addition to restricting the flow of electricity, a good insulator should be resistant to corrosion, chemicals, moisture, heat, and pests.

The color of the insulation around a wire indicates its intended use. Black, red, or blue indicate a hot wire; green indicates a ground wire; and white indicates a neutral wire.

Insulators are coded for their composition and for intended application, using letters as well as colors.

Four basic types of insulators

1. Rubber (R)
2. Mineral (M)
3. Asbestos (A)
4. Plastic (T)

In addition to these designations, we find U (underground), H (heat resistant), and W (water resistant).

There is a great deal of information contained in the codes printed on the insulators or cable jacket. By knowing what these letters mean, the inspector can easily determine if the proper gauge wire was used and if the insulator is correct for the conditions. For example, wire that runs underground should have a U coded on it.

Sheathing

Sheathing covers the insulation of wires and cables and makes up the rest of wiring. It serves as another layer of insulation and protection for the wire. It is what can be touched in unfinished parts of the home. On older wire, sheathing used to be rubber. Now most sheathing on wiring is plastic.

Conduit

In areas where additional protection is required or desired, wiring is enclosed in either rigid or flexible tubing called **conduit**. Conduit can be made of any one of several materials, including aluminum and plastic. Different wall thicknesses are available and the one chosen will depend on the application.

The conduit should be sized so the wire bundle does not fill more than 40% of the volume. Inadequately sized conduit is a deficiency. There should be no more than 360 degrees of bend in the length of conduit that runs from one enclosure to the next. See the graphic below for examples of acceptable and unacceptable amount of bending. This is to prevent damage to the insulation when wires are pulled through.

Reportable Deficiencies of Conduit

- Inadequately supported conduit
- Crimped or sagging conduit
- Loose couplings

Electrical Fixtures

There are numerous fixtures within the electrical system, which must also be checked by the home inspector. These include switches, lights, receptacles, ceiling fans, smoke detectors, and doorbells.

Switches

A **switch** opens and closes the electrical circuit by interrupting the flow. When the switch is open, the circuit is not complete and therefore no electricity will flow. When the switch is closed, electricity can flow through it. Switches are located on the hot legs of circuits and are used to isolate loads.

The home inspector should turn on all the switches in the home to make sure they are working and sending electricity to the circuit to power appliances. Switches that do not work should be reported.

Figure 6.11
Four different types of electrical switches

Lights

The home probably will be wired with many different types of **lights** such as recessed lighting, fluorescent lighting, and low voltage lighting. Lights can also be in each room of the home, hallways, or stairways and all must get checked to see if they work. The home inspector must also be able to determine if the bulbs in the lights are faulty or if the fixtures themselves need to be looked at by an electrician. Damage to electrical fixtures and their coverings are also items the home inspector must report. All of the light fixtures must also be properly attached and connected. Loose connections or hanging parts must be noted.

Inspectors must also make sure the clearance between lights and combustibles meets basic requirements. In closets, lights must be mounted at least 18 inches from combustibles. There must be six inches between flush mounted light fixtures and combustibles. Recessed lighting will be most likely inspected from the attic but also has clearances that must be verified. There needs to be one-half inch spacing between the recessed lighting fixture and combustible materials and three inches of thermal insulation between recessed light fixtures and combustible materials.

Reportable Deficiencies - Lights

- Inoperable lights
- Do not stay on or flicker when switched on
- Make buzzing sound when switched on

Receptacles

Electrical **receptacles** or outlets are an integral part of the home wiring system because they deliver current to the plug of an appliance such as a lamp or a toaster. Receptacles are mounted in a metal junction box inside a wall. Receptacles that are on the outside of the house must be mounted in a weatherproof box to prevent moisture from shorting out the circuit. Receptacles have faceplates mounted to them to cover the gap between the receptacle and the wall.

Receptacles should be tested to make sure they still are providing power. This can be done easily with an electric gauge available at any building supply outlet. Additionally, the home inspector should test them to make sure the polarity has not been switched to the opposite sides of the plugs in the receptacles. This can cause appliances to malfunction. The inspector should also feel the outside of the receptacles to make sure they are not hot. Even a receptacle with nothing plugged into it may run hot if it is passing current through to other outlets on the same current. Hot receptacles indicate an improper connection and should be reported.

Figure 6.12

Interior receptacle

Exterior receptacle with cover

Reportable Deficiencies of Receptacles

- Receptacle visibly damaged or broken
- Receptacle loose in the wall
- Receptacle not working
- Receptacle hot or warm to the touch
- Receptacle has a broken plug in it

- Receptacle not at least three feet away from bathtubs or showers
- Receptacle missing the GFCI
- Improper voltage and incorrect polarity at the receptacle
- Outdoor receptacle or switch not mounted in special weatherproof boxes
- Switches, receptacles, and splices not housed in a junction box that is anchored to a stud or joist
- Junction boxes not covered with an appropriate faceplate
- Faceplate that feels warm to the touch

Ceiling Fans

Ceiling fans are often found in homes during a home inspection. The fan should have all of its parts and work properly. The inspector must make sure the fan is securely fastened to the ceiling and does not sag. The fan should also be checked to make sure it works at all speeds and that the reverse switch operates properly. Loose wiring near a ceiling fan is a defect that must be reported. Ceiling fans must also have GFCI protection on them for safety.

Reportable Deficiencies - Ceiling Fans

- Missing parts
- Inoperable or malfunctioning controls
- Sagging or loose parts
- Sagging or loose wiring
- Missing GFCI protection

Figure 6.13
Ceiling fan with defective wiring

Smoke Detectors

Smoke detectors help occupants get out of a home in the event of a fire. The National Fire Protection Association (NFPA) estimates that having operable smoke detectors reduce the possibility of dying in a home fire by 50%. The NFPA also estimates that fully 1/3 of all home smoke detectors do not operate properly nor are they properly maintained.

Traditionally, smoke detectors were battery-operated devices. Modern homes are often built with smoke detectors wired right into the home's **electrical system** for increased safety and performance. The home inspector must check the wiring to make sure it is connected and not loose. The battery back-up of these modern smoke detectors should also be verified as working. The detector should be checked for dust or dirt build-up near the sensors.

Figure 6.14
Smoke detector

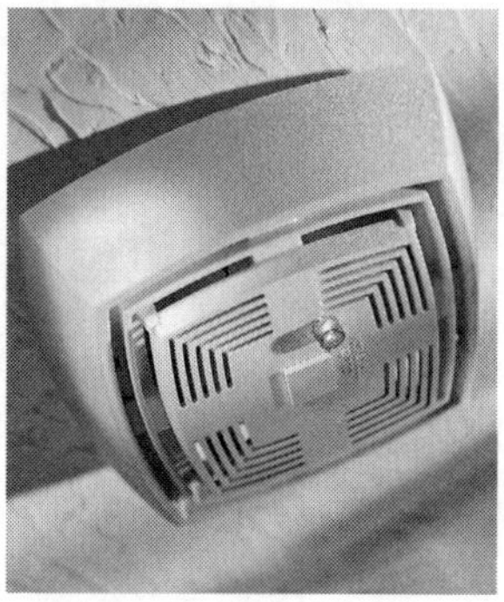

Reportable Deficiencies - Smoke Detectors

- Inoperable or dirty sensors
- Missing batteries
- Loose wiring connections

Doorbells

Doorbells allow visitors to signal the occupant they are at the door. The inspector should verify that the chime rings when the doorbell is pushed and that the parts of the doorbell are indeed intact.

Electrical Measurement

In order to control the amount of electricity available to do various forms of work, some terms of measurement were created.

Voltage is the amount of pressure at which electricity is delivered. This pressure is similar to the water pressure in a hose. Electricity will not move through a circuit unless it is pressured or forced to do so.

Amperage is the measurement of the quantity of electricity in an electrical circuit available to do a given job. This is similar to the concept that two pipes may both be full of water at 50 pounds of pressure, but if one pipe is twice the size of the other, it will deliver a lot more water.

Watts are the measurement of the actual amount of electrical force available to do work. It is a function of both amperage (quantity) and voltage (pressure). The mathematical formula for calculating wattage is Volts x Amps. A fifteen-amp circuit at 120 volts will produce 1,800 watts of power.

Resistance is what restricts electricity from flowing in a circuit. The greater the resistance restricting the flow of electricity, the more heat that will be generated. When this resistance becomes excessive, it can create enough heat to causes fires.

Ohms are the unit of measurement given to the resistance in the circuit. This resistance is normally associated with the load that the current is acting upon. A complete electrical circuit will always have three components: (1) voltage, (2) amperage, and (3) resistance. According to Ohm's law: Amperage=Voltage/Resistance; if any two values are known, the third can be determined.

Electricity comes in two types: (1) **AC** (alternating current) and (2) **DC** (direct current). A battery delivers DC in which the current produced flows constantly in one direction, from negative to positive.

Power plants produce AC current by reversing the flow of electricity every $^{1}/_{120}{}^{th}$ of a second. The advantage of AC power is its ability to change voltage by use of a **transformer**. This allows the power plant to ship the electricity at extremely high voltage that is efficient for transmission, and then step the voltage down at the residence to a safe practical level for home use. When AC current completes one cycle by changing direction, it is known as a **hertz** (Hz).

Chapter 7

Plumbing

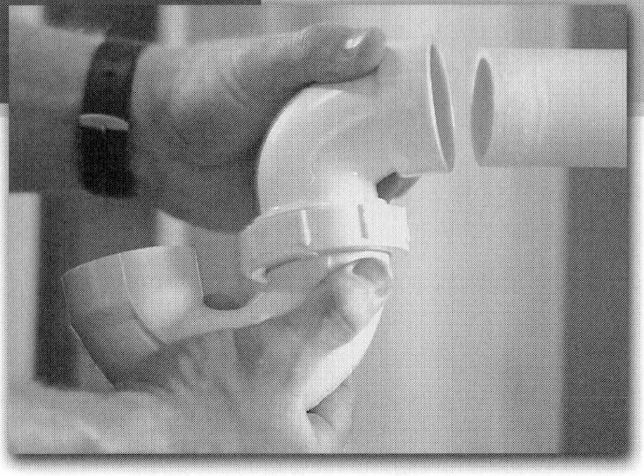

Introduction

A house's **plumbing** is the system of pipes with its connected fixtures that enables clean water to enter the house and used water and sewage to exit the house. Residential plumbing can be broken up into two separate systems: 1) the aseptic system and 2) the septic system.

The Aseptic System

The **aseptic system** is the potable or "clean water" system. **Potable water** meets the requirements set forth by local health departments for human consumption and use. That means that it does not have enough impurities to cause health problems.

The aseptic system starts with the pipes or lines that originate at the **supply**, or source of the water (such as a municipal water main or a domestic well). It also includes all the associated **valves** (devices which control liquid flow) and **taps** (fixtures where liquid comes out of lines) in the home. In addition to the piping, the potable system includes the water heater and any kind of water softening device.

Supply

Water from a municipal supply is the source for water used in 84% of the homes in the United States. It provides a constant source of clean water at a relatively steady pressure. Each home connected to this municipal water supply has a **water meter**, which measures the quantity of water used. There is a valve or "stop" on each side of the meter to isolate the system for installation and repairs.

The alternative to municipal water supply is a private well. Although water quality testing is beyond the scope of the home inspector, the inspector will need to have an understanding of the basic plumbing requirements for well water also.

The well must be located at least 100 feet from any potential contamination such as a septic tank, or other fuel or liquid storage tank. If possible, the well should be located on high ground to prevent the possibility of surface-water contamination. The deeper the well, the more natural filtration will have a chance to act on the water supply.

A private well system requires a pump to remove the water from the well and a pressurized storage facility to be able to supply the residence with instantly available water. Both tanks and pump should be adequately sized with enough capacity for use and needs of the household.

Supply Piping

Potable water is supplied and distributed throughout a home by a system of pipes and valves known as **supply piping**.

For efficient operation, piping should be as direct and straight as the architecture will allow. Piping should also be supported by hangers installed at regular distances. Piping that is not properly supported can sag or bend and can cause interruptions in the lines or problems with the water pressure in the home.

Since most homes are electrically grounded through the water piping, builders must provide an alternate ground path if the continuity of this piping is broken for any reason.

The size of the service line piping or water supply is determined by the anticipated flow of water required for the home. Most modern houses use a

$^3/_4$ inch line from the water meter into the home. This line is reduced to a $^1/_2$ inch for appliances and further reduced to $^3/_8$ inch for faucets.

Local codes will specify the depth to bury the incoming water service line. In most areas, water supply piping must be buried at least 12 inches underground and in colder areas where the ground freezes, it must be buried 12 inches below the frost line. Therefore, it probably will not be seen by the inspector except where it enters the building or out at the water meter. If the water supply line is visible other than where it enters the building or connects to the water meter, it should be noted.

Types of Supply Piping

There are several different types of materials used for residential water supply and waste piping. These include copper, galvanized steel, and plastic.

Copper Pipe

Copper pipe is durable, flexible, and corrosion free when used as water piping. However, it is relatively expensive and must be wrapped when passing through concrete to avoid corrosion.

Gas Piping

Black iron pipe is used to deliver natural gas because copper will react with certain compounds in gas and form corrosion.

Galvanized Steel Pipe

Galvanized steel piping is no longer installed in new homes being built. It commonly rusts or oxidizes from the inside out and reduces the interior of the pipe. This restricts the water flow and causes leaks at threaded joints. Ferrous (metal that contains iron) piping is economical but is subject to corrosion and mineral buildup.

Plastic Pipe

There are also a number of different kinds of **plastic pipes** used to carry supply and wastewater to and from homes:

- Polyvinyl chloride (PVC)
- Chlorinated polyvinyl chloride (CPVC)
- Acrylonitrile butadiene styrene (ABS)
- Polybutylene (PB)

PVC pipe should only be used for cold-water service because it will become soft when heated. CPVC pipe can be used for either hot or cold applications. ABS pipe is mainly used for waste, drains, and vent piping. Polybutylene (PB) is a form of plastic resin that was used extensively in the manufacture of water supply piping from 1978 until 1995. PB pipe can be used for either hot or cold service and has the ability to expand should freezing conditions be encountered. However, it has been discovered that PB pipe can degrade and leak as it ages and reacts with water-soluble oxidants. Because the oxidants are carried in the water, the pipe deteriorates from the inside, which makes it very difficult for a home inspector to determine the condition of poly piping. However, an inspector generally can determine if there is poly piping installed in the home. Typically, PB piping is blue, gray, or black in color and is 1/2" to 1" in diameter.

Problems in Supply Piping

All piping is subject to various forms of deterioration and corrosion over time, and the home inspector should be aware of the symptoms of these problems. The most obvious sign of pipe deterioration is leaking. Reduced water flow or pressure and strange odors are also signs of problem in the piping. This is sometimes expressed as a lack of water volume or flow. In any case, this should be reported.

Figure 7.1
Main water shut-off valve

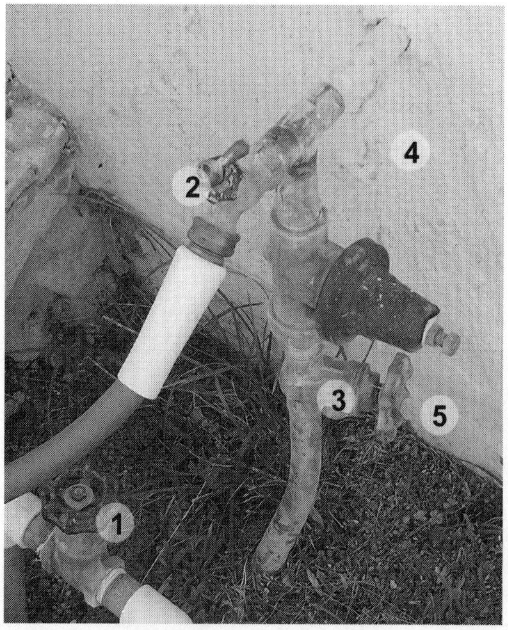

1) Sprinkler shut-off
2) Hose bibb
3) Main water shut-off
4) Stucco exterior
5) Stucco screed

In time, the chemicals, such as chlorine, used to render water safe to drink will form deposits on the walls of the supply piping. If not properly treated, these deposits will eventually restrict the flow of water throughout the house.

Rust on piping is also a sign of a problem and should be noted. In some cases, rust can cause the eventual failure of the pipe. Pipes can also be damaged, crushed, crimped, and cracked which will cause their performance to deteriorate. Another problem found in piping is a lack of support. Piping that lacks support will probably leak and eventually fail. This is a problem that should be noted if seen.

Cross connections occur when the non-potable water gets into the potable water system. This raises the possibility of serious illness or even death so it is important to note signs of possible cross connection in the water system. An example would be where a sink has a low hanging faucet that could end up being cross-contaminated if the water level is raised too high. This puts the supply water in contact with the drain or wastewater and makes a cross connection. Areas where cross connections can occur should be reported.

Reportable Deficiencies - Supply Piping

- Deteriorated, corroded, or rusted pipes
- Broken, damaged, crushed, crimped, or cracked pipes
- Leaking pipes or valves
- Reduced water flow or pressure
- Strange odors
- Lack of support for the piping
- Cross connections between potable and non-potable water

Valves

Every home plumbing system should have one shutoff valve that allows all the water coming into the home to be turned off.

Valve Types

There are three types of valves used in residential plumbing: gate valves, globe valves, and check valves.

Gate Valves

Gate valves use a wedge-shaped disc, which fits against a smooth surface, to control the flow of water.

Globe Valves

Globe valves use a ring seat and disc to regulate the water flow. The globe valve is durable, and easy to fix.

Check Valve

A **check valve** is an automatic device that allows water to flow in only one direction. Check valves are installed wherever it is necessary to prevent backflow contamination. Examples where check valves are needed are pools, spas, and sprinkler systems.

The Septic System

The **septic system** is the waste removal system. The septic system includes all the pipes, traps, drains, vents, and pumps that together allow waste to move from a home to the sanitary sewer or septic system. The pipes carry water, solid wastes, and methane gas (a by-product of decomposition). In order to avoid health risks and to reduce odor, the system is sized to remove the waste and by-products quickly.

Drain Piping

Drain piping, like supply piping, can consist of different materials. These include copper, plastic, cast iron, lead or galvanized steel. Brass is a common material used for fittings for these pipes.

The drain piping must be carefully engineered to handle the projected flow of wastewater. **Wastewater** is the spent or used water from individual homes, a community, a farm, or an industry that often contains dissolved or suspended matter. The system should be adequate so that the waste flows while the pipe is half-full. This size insures adequate scouring while preventing solid-waste deposit in the pipe.

The pitch or angle of waste discharge piping is critical. If there is too much pitch, the wastewater will move too fast to allow the solids to float out with it. If the pitch is too little then the wastewater will not be able to transport the solids. The recommended pitch for drainage should be $^1/_4$ of an inch for every foot of pipe run. Directional changes should be kept to a minimum and there should be a clean-out at every change of direction.

The individual drain pipes for each appliance are connected in tree fashion with horizontal and vertical runs until they terminate at the building drain. This drain is at the lowest part of the system.

A critical fault to be aware of is the possibility of cross connections. A cross connection allows wastewater to be siphoned into the potable water supply.

A common area for this to occur is at a sink where the spray nozzle extends below the level of the standing water, or where a garden hose is submerged in pooling water. Check valves or backflow preventers should be used to keep this potential health hazard from occurring.

Plumbing Traps

A key ingredient in the waste management system is the **plumbing trap.** The purpose of the trap is to prevent the entrance of sewer gases into the home without impeding the flow of waste. There should be a trap installed at every plumbing fixture except toilets, which have their own integral traps.

The **"P trap"** is commonly used for all fixtures that do not flow a great deal of water. For larger flows such as tubs, the **drum trap** is used. **"S traps"** should not be used in residential plumbing. The "S trap" is difficult to vent properly and as such creates a perfect siphon.

Figure 7.2
P-Trap

1) Inlet
2) 2" Water seal
3) Top dip
4) Bottom dip
5) Crown
6) Outlet
7) Dishwasher line

Plumbing traps operate by containing a small amount of water in the pipe. This water creates a barrier that keeps sewer gas from entering the house.

This barrier or water seal can be lost in several ways such as the siphoning effect of one fixture on another (allowing gas to break containment) and evaporation (which can occur if a fixture has not been used for a long period of time and the seal evaporates). In multi-story structures, trap seals can be lost by **back pressure**, which is created when water completely fills the drain stack. Air pressure generated by the column of water is sufficient to blow the water out of the trap. In rare occasions, the capillary action generated by some foreign material in the line will wick the water out of the trap.

Figure 7.3
Drum traps

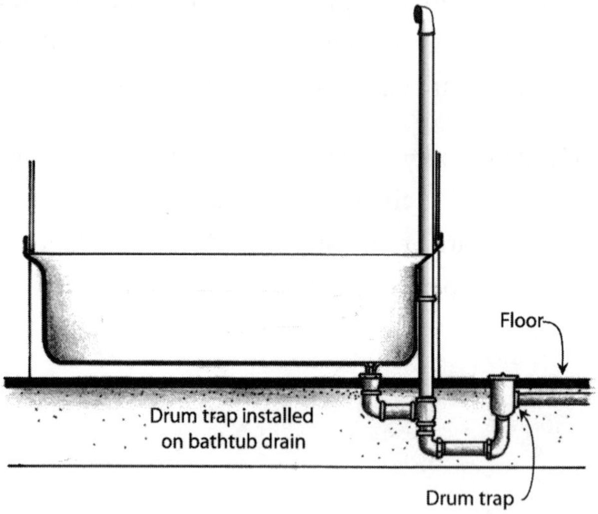

Plumbing Venting

In addition to the pipes that carry the waste, there are additional pipes attached to the septic system called **vent piping**. This system discharges gases and equalizes atmospheric pressure. These vents terminate above the roofline.

The purpose of plumbing vents is to equalize air pressure in the system. If these vents are not properly installed, the ability of the waste system to function properly is severely limited. Proper venting is essential to the operation of the sewer line traps. These traps must operate properly in order to keep harmful sewer gas from entering the living areas of the home.

Reportable Deficiencies - Drain Piping, Traps, and Vents

- Water leaks
- Waste leaks

- Gas leaks (if the water seal is broken)
- Rust on the pipes
- Clogged pipes
- Pipes that are noisy when used
- Damaged pipes
- Missing parts
- Lack of proper supports
- Crimped or pinched pipes
- Damaged traps
- Poorly functioning (slow) drains.

Figure 7.4
Plumbing vents and other roof penetrations

1) Chimney
2) Chimney flashing
3) Attic vent
4) Plumbing vent

Sewer Systems and Septic Tanks

Waste and wastewater generated by residential indoor plumbing systems are disposed of by municipal sanitary sewer systems or septic tanks.

Sewer Systems

Many municipalities have both a sanitary sewer system and a storm water system. When there are two systems employed, they must be kept separate. **Storm water systems** carry storm water runoff out of the city to prevent or minimize flooding and soil erosion. Public **sanitary sewer systems** take wastewater generated from residential, commercial, and industrial properties and channel it to sewer treatment plants.

Septic Tanks

There are many neighborhoods not served by municipal sewer systems in both rural and suburban areas. For these homes, the septic tank is the most-often-used way to rid the home of and treat waste (liquid, solid or gas).

A **septic tank** is a watertight vessel designed to accommodate liquid and solid waste. It is located on the property and buried beneath the ground.

Figure 7.5
A septic tank is a watertight vessel designed to treat and rid the home of waste. They are located on the property and buried beneath the ground.

A typical system includes a tank and a drain field. A **drain field** is the area into which the liquid from the septic tank drains. This area is prepared to receive the effluent by digging trenches and filling them with gravel, rocks, or sand to help drainage. The **effluent** or treated sewage is accumulated in the tank and then dispersed through the drain field using a system of perforated pipes. The tank itself is designed to separate the solids from the liquids, allow for partial decomposition of the organic material, and let the clarified liquid discharge to the drain field.

In those situations where the drain field is higher than the septic tank or the property is below the city sewer line, then a sewage ejector must be used. This device is a pump capable of moving both solid and liquid waste. It must be equipped with proper venting and a series of check valves to prevent the re-entry of gas and sewage into the house. For storm or ground water removal, a sump pump connected to a float valve can be used.

Figure 7.6
Septic system

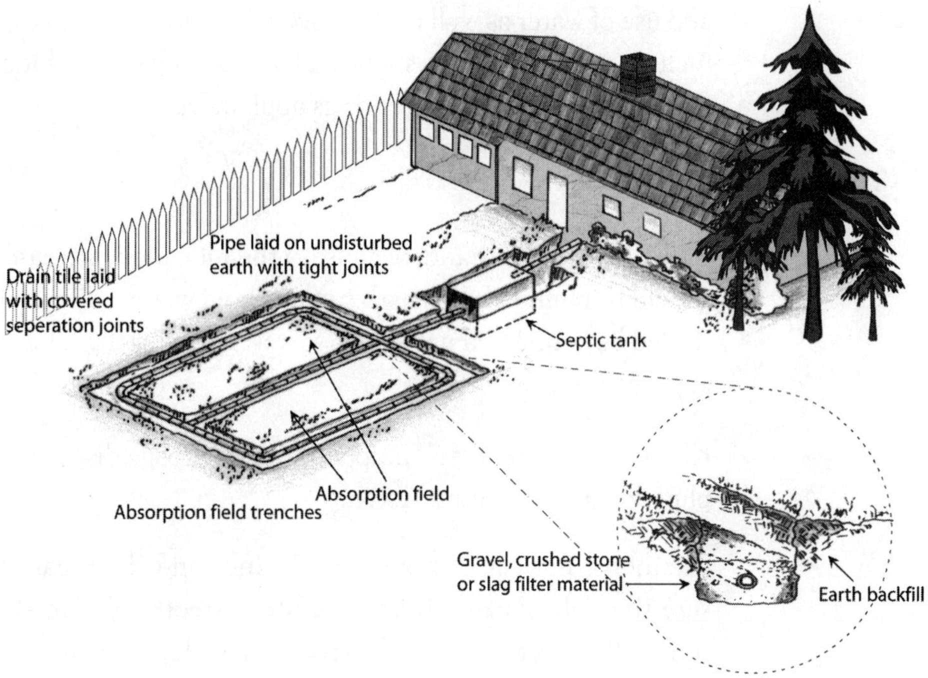

Statistics show that most septic tanks fail within ten to twenty years. The principle cause of septic tank problems is the failure to have the contents pumped out regularly. The septic tank should be pumped out every three years.

The home inspector should determine the location of the tank and obtain a pump-out schedule from the current owner. In cold weather, the location of the tank may be revealed by lack of snow covering or early greening of the lawn. This is caused by the warmer temperature of the contents of the tank.

The actual inspection of the tank should be left to a professional but the home inspector should be able to spot any major deficiencies.

Reportable Deficiencies - the Aseptic System

- Discolored water may indicate cross connection
- Leaks in the system such as dripping faucet or a broken pipe
- Lack of water pressure

Fixtures

Plumbing fixtures are attached to the plumbing system for the distribution and use of water as well as the disposal of waste. Typically, plumbing fixtures include sinks, bathtubs, showers, faucets, toilets, and bidets. Water heaters may be classified as fixtures or as appliances.

Sinks

Sinks are used daily and, because of their location, are easily inspected. They should be plumbed with both hot and cold water. All fixtures and appliances should be connected with the hot water on the left. The drain must have an approved trap.

Kitchen sinks are often equipped with a garbage disposal. These devices are plumbed into the drain system.

The home inspector should check sinks and the areas around them to be sure that faucets and drains operate correctly. There should be no visible surface flaws in the sinks or basins, such as chips in porcelain coatings. Always check under the sink to check for any leaks from the basins or fittings.

Reportable Deficiencies - Sinks

- Faucets not operating correctly with hot and cold on wrong side
- Drains not operating correctly
- Chips in porcelain coatings
- Other visible surface flaws
- Leaks of basins (check the under sink areas)
- Rust (check under sink area)
- Fixtures are not tightly connected to the sink
- Fixtures are off balance
- Fixtures are at a level where a cross connection could occur

Bathtubs and Showers

Bathtubs are not always combined with a shower. Many homes have separate tubs and showers. Bathtubs are heavy, especially when filled with water, and should be well supported underneath. Seeing under bathtubs is not always possible, so the real area to be aware of is that they are secured in place.

Newer homes often have one-piece fiberglass tub and shower enclosures. While it is rare that the fiberglass itself leaks, it is not uncommon for the area surrounding the enclosure, including the floors and walls, to become waterlogged. The tub enclosure should be tightly sealed and secured to the surrounding area in order to prevent water from accumulating behind or beneath the tub. The entrance over the sill into the bathtub must be 18"tall.

Many homes have **showers** stalls and they often leak. The problem is that leaks behind fiberglass or tiled shower stalls are nearly impossible to detect until components fail due to water damage. This means the inspector has to be diligent in spotting signs of component failure such as falling or loose tiles, water-stained drywall, raised flooring, missing seals or gaskets, and rust.

The inspector should know a few basic design features for all shower stalls in order to detect their problems. In order for the shower to drain properly, all shower stall floors should slant toward the drain at a rate of 1/4 inch per foot. Drains should not be at high points. There should be no standing water on the floor of the shower stall while it is running. The entrance over the sill must be at least 22 inches wide.

Figure 7.7
Bathtub & Shower

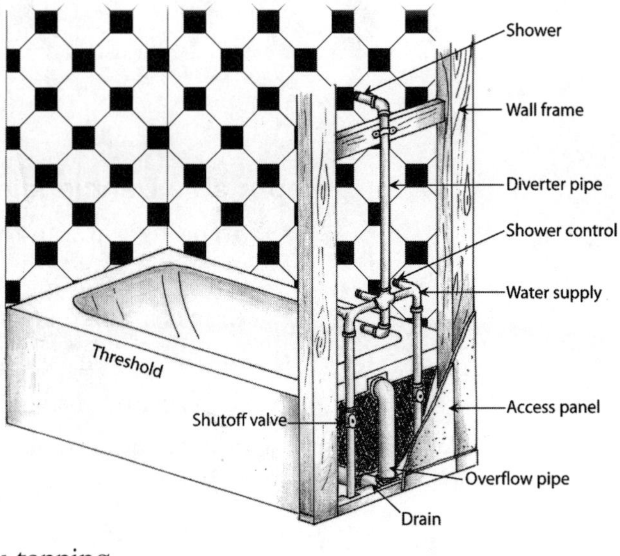

Fiberglass tubs and shower stalls need to be inspected for cracks. To do this, the inspector should remove his/her shoes and step into the tub to examine the walls.

In tiled tubs and showers, the inspector must check to make sure that there are no loose tiles and that the joints are properly grouted (fill in). Check for loose tiles by tapping gently with a screwdriver handle. A loose tile will make a hollow noise.

If the shower enclosure is glass, the inspector should check to be sure it is tempered or safety glass. If it cannot be determined that safety glass was used, it should be noted on the inspection report.

In all styles of tubs, the overflow device is particularly prone to leaking. Look for evidence of leakage on adjacent walls, downstairs ceilings, and nearby areas.

Figure 7.8
A tiled bathtub and shower enclosed in glass

Figure 7.9
Bathtub

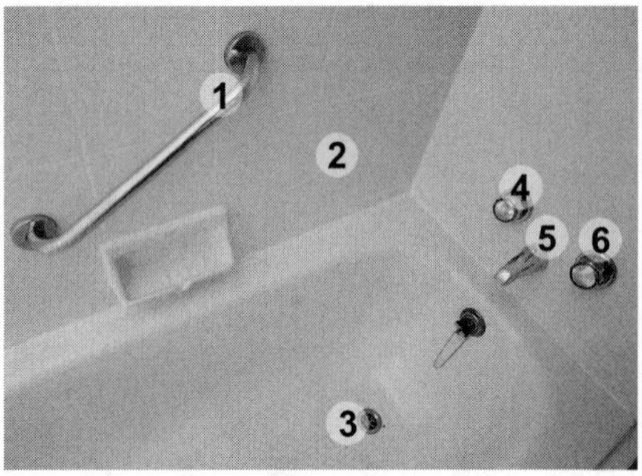

1) Tub with grip bar
2) Tile
3) Drain
4) Hot water control
5) Faucet
4) Cold water control

Reportable Deficiencies - Tubs and Showers

- Standing water in the tub or shower stall
- Slow drains
- Cracks in fiberglass or tiles
- Missing, loose, or discolored grout
- Rust on any surface
- Cross connections
- Instability of tub or shower stall

Whirlpool Tubs

A **whirlpool tub** uses a pump powered by an electric motor to create a pressurized and therapeutic stream of water in the tub. This stream is discharged via holes called jets, from various locations in the tub.

Figure 7.10
Whirlpool tub

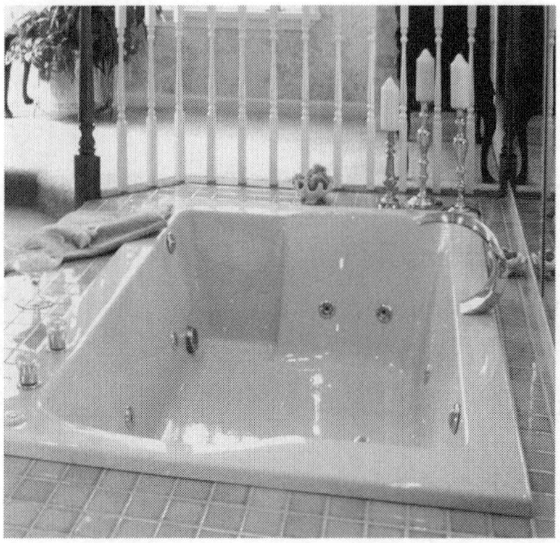

When inspecting a whirlpool tub, the inspector should make sure that the pump is connected to a GFCI (ground fault circuit interrupter) protected outlet. Another area to inspect is the control switch. This switch should be located so it cannot be reached by someone in the tub, unless it is an air-operated remote switch. This is mandatory so that the user of the tub will not electrocute him or herself.

The whirlpool tub system should be designed to drain completely, including the pump and all lines, when the tub is emptied. If water is allowed to remain in the system for any length of time, bacteria will grow. Before operating the pump, the inspector should make sure that the discharge and inlet ports are covered with several inches of water. Failure to do this can cause serious damage to the pump.

After filling the tub so that the intake and outlet ports are covered with water, the inspector should turn on the jets to make sure they work. The inspector should also note and report if there is any discolored water discharged when the pump starts.

Reportable Deficiencies - Whirlpool Tub

- Mold, mildew, or discoloration on the tub or fixtures
- Discolored water discharged when the pump starts
- Pump not plugged into a GFCI protected circuit
- Electrical switch less than three feet from the tub
- Plumbing cross-connection

Faucets

A **faucet** is a water valve located in a sink. These devices normally use a neoprene washer to control the flow of water. In certain cases, two faucets will terminate in a single spigot spout to mix hot and cold water. Faucets are available in compression and non-compression models.

Compression Faucets

Compression faucets are used primarily on the outside hose bibbs. A **hose bibb** is a water faucet that has its tip threaded to accept a hose.

Compression faucets employ a series of neoprene washers to control water leakage. These compression models are also used in bathrooms, laundry rooms, and some kitchen sinks.

Figure 7.11
Hose bib

Non-Compression Faucets

Non-compression faucets require less maintenance because they are "washerless" and do not have moveable discs to regulate water flow. One disc is stationary in the body of the valve while the other is free to rotate with the handle. Holes drilled in the discs line up when the handle is moved allowing water to flow.

Figure 7.12
Compression faucet

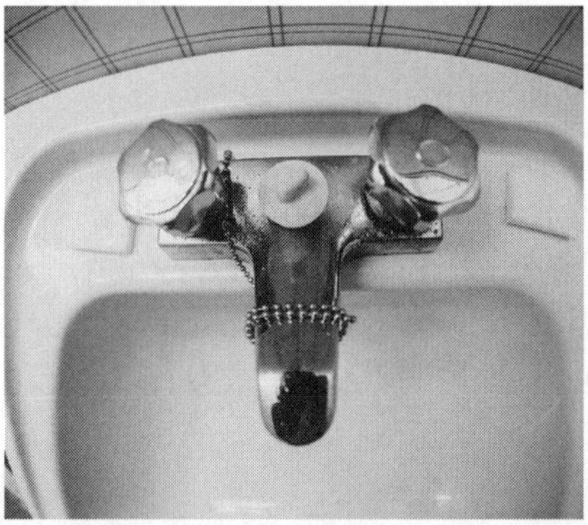

Another popular type of faucet is the single lever variety. This device controls both the flow and temperature of the water with a single operating arm.

Reportable Deficiencies - Faucets

- Leaks
- Dripping
- Stiff controls
- Inoperable controls
- Loose connections
- Cross connections
- Missing or damaged parts
- Reversed hot and cold installation
- Noisy operation

Toilets

Toilets or commodes use water to dispose of waste into the sewer or septic system and prevent sewer gases from entering the house. They are usually described by their flushing mechanisms, such as the direct flush using water pressure or the tank type using gravity.

Direct Flush Toilets

The **direct flush** system uses no storage tank. When the toilet is flushed, a valve opens allowing water to flow directly into the bowl. This system requires high volume water for a very brief time. Since it is used for only a short duration, very little water is used. Therefore, direct flush makes the most efficient use of water because it uses the water at full pressure and full volume for a short time.

Gravity Toilets

Traditional **gravity toilets** depend on gravity to pull the water and waste through the toilet bowl and into the drain. The storage tank for gravity systems is usually attached to the bowl. The bowl is designed so that the flow of water running through it performs a scouring action each time it is flushed. As the toilet is flushed, water from the tank swirls through the bowl, carrying the waste with it.

Gravity forces the water through the trap and into the sewer line. As the water flows through the trap, it generates suction that helps to move the waste through the system. As the flow of water and waste diminishes, the reduced pressure allows air to enter the trap and equalize the pressure. This causes the trap to reseal.

Figure 7.13
Gravity toilet components

1) Toilet or commode
2) Resilient flooring
3) Cabinets
4) Sink
5) Faucet
4) Counter top

The toilet is connected to the drain by a flange and bolts anchored to the floor. A unique wax seal is used at the connection to prevent leakage. The inspector should make sure the toilet is securely fastened to the bathroom floor. One way to do this is to grasp the bowl between ones knees and rock slowly from side to side. The toilet should not move.

The inspector should check the flushing mechanism by removing the tank cover. The float should be set so the tank fills without overflowing or running continuously. The flapper should seal properly (free from leaks) and be free of deterioration (degraded surfaces). The area around the toilet should be checked for any evidence of water leakage.

Reportable Deficiencies - Toilets

- Does not flush completely
- Toilet runs continuously or overflows
- Water leaking around the toilet
- Toilet loose and moves
- Noisy high-pitched whine when filling

Bidets

The **bidet** is not a common bathroom fixture in most homes, however, if one is encountered it should be inspected. The bidet is similar to a sink in that it utilizes hot and cold water and is used for personal hygiene.

Similar to a commode or toilet in design, the bidet should be securely mounted to a wall or bolted to the floor. It does not use a wax seal to connect to the floor like a toilet. The inspector should make sure the bidet is not leaking, is stable and well connected to the wall or floor, has both hot and cold water, and does not overflow when flushed.

Figure 7.14
A bidet

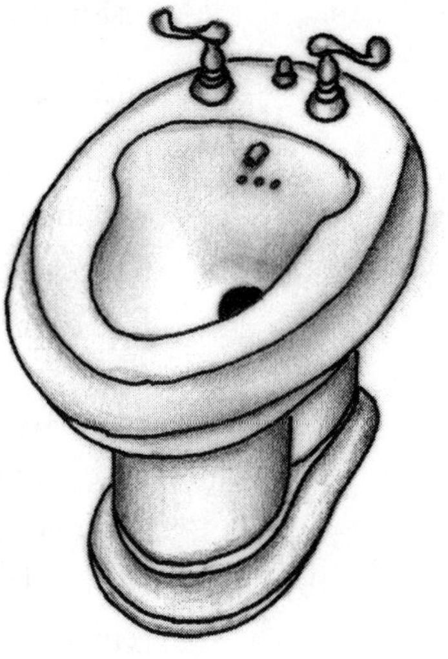

Water Heaters

The **water heater** is an essential part of the residential plumbing system. As the name suggests, it is a device to make water hot as it passes through it and in some cases store it as well. The residential water heater can be fueled by natural gas, electricity, fuel oil, or solar energy.

Figure 7.15
Water heater with unsulation blanket and seismic bracing

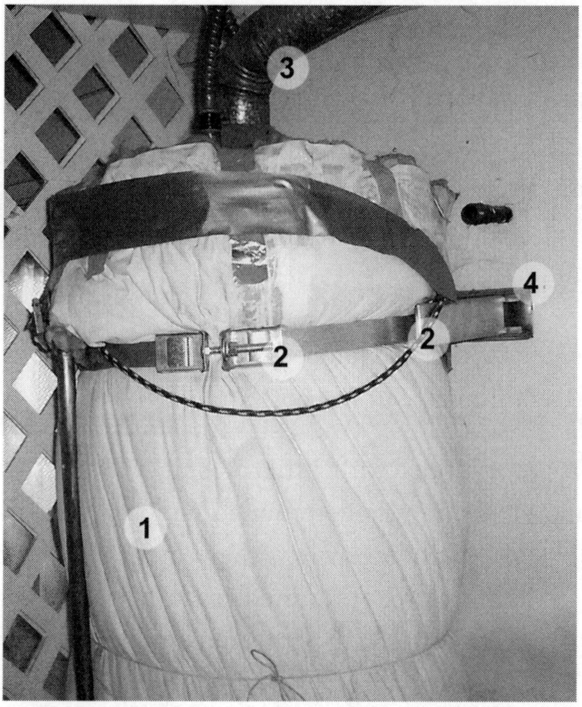

1) Insulation blanket
2) Seismic bracing
3) Water heater vent pipe
4) Wall anchor

The home inspector should treat water heaters with caution during the inspection. The water heater is under tremendous pressure and severe damage and injury can result from a malfunction. The inspector should note and report any dents or unusual stains on the heater jacket or insulting blanket surrounding the heater itself. If the heater is not covered with an insulating blanket, the manufacturer's identification plate will tell you when the unit was built, the capacity in gallons, and the output in BTUs. This can aid in assessing the viability of the water heater for future use. Keep in mind the average life expectancy for a residential water heater is seven-to-ten years.

Water heaters are rated using a standard called **recovery rate**. This is the rate at which water can be heated from 50° F to 140° F (or 90° temperature variance taking into account starting temperature and maximum allowable temperature for the water). The current standard for hot water is now 120° F to eliminate scalding and heat-related burn injuries from hot water.

All water heaters are equipped with both a **high-temperature shutoff** and a temperature/pressure relief valve. The high-temperature shutoff automatically shuts off the heating of the water when it reaches its maximum allowable temperature. It can be reset on electric water heaters, but must be replaced on gas water heaters if it is used.

The **temperature pressure relief valve** should be located within six inches of the top of the heater. It is designed to open if the preset limits are exceeded and reduce the pressure in the water heater. This valve will operate without warning and release scalding water and steam. For this reason, the valve must be plumbed away from the heater to a discharge point outside the building. The plumbing used to carry the scalding water and steam by the temperature pressure relief valve should be the same size as the valve and have as few bends as possible. The pipe should terminate between six and 24 inches from the ground and be face down. No other valves or restrictions may be placed in the line.

The water heater should be equipped with a cold water shut off valve on the inlet side and a drain valve at the bottom.

Water heaters are equipped with a **thermostat,** which is an electrical circuit that opens and closes at a predetermined temperature. A thermostat will automatically start the heater when the temperature of the water in the storage tank falls to a predetermined level. A good temperature for a residential water heater is 120° F with a maximum of 140° F.

In normal operation, the pilot flame acting on a thermo-couple will induce a current in the **solenoid** (coil of wire). This energizes the solenoid, which allows the main gas valve to open. There are a number of fail-safe mechanisms built into the system that automatically shut off the gas supply if any failure of the heater is detected.

An important part of every water heater with a tank is the **sacrificial anode**. This is a metal bar, usually made of magnesium, which is installed in the water heater's tank by the manufacturer and attracts the minerals in the water. This allows the anode to be degraded by the minerals instead of the water tank.

The cold water is delivered to the water-heating element by the dip tube. The **dip tube** conducts the cold water to the bottom of the tank and does not allow it to mix with the already heated water on top. The dip tube has a small hole located near the top that prevents the hot water from siphoning back during long periods of inactivity. If the water heater is idle for a protracted period, it may develop hydrogen sulfide gas that will give the water a "rotten egg" smell. The solution for this problem is to use the heater more actively or replace the sacrificial magnesium anode with an aluminum one.

Figure 7.16
Gas water heater near flammable materials

1) Wall anchor
2) Water heater tank
3) Gas line in
4) Seismic bracing
5) Flammable materials

Water heaters located in a garage must be installed on a platform with their ignition source at least 18 inches above the garage floor. Those heaters located in an attic or on a second story must be installed in a drain pan that is plumbed to the exterior.

(Note: Some states, such as California, require the water heater to be strapped, braced, or anchored to the wall. This will prevent the water heater from falling over and possibly starting a fire during an earthquake. Some states will also require water heaters to be wrapped in an energy saving blanket, so checking state or local codes is imperative before the inspection.)

Gas-Fired Water Heaters

Gas-fired or older oil-fired water heaters use a burner at the bottom of the tank core to create the heat needed to warm the water. The exhaust from the burner travels up a central cylinder of the core, or heat exchanger, giving off the heat to warm the water in the tank. The exhaust then travels to and out the top of the water heater tank to vent connectors that carry the exhaust out of the home.

Gas-fired water heaters, like all other gas-fired appliances, need an uninterrupted supply of combustion air. **Combustion air** is the air that is combined with natural gas to produce a flame and heat the water in a water heater. Water heaters located in a confined space such as a closet must have a vent that is big enough to allow in the proper amount of combustion air. The minimum requirement for this vent is 1 square inch of opening per each 1,000 BTU's (British Thermal Units) per hour of water heating capacity.

All gas-fired water heaters will develop condensation when the tank is filled with cold water and the burner is on. This condensation will drip onto the burner causing a sizzling sound. This condensation sizzle is often mistaken for a leaky water heater. If poor venting causes excessive condensation, it can contribute to other problems. Some of these problems include frequent extinguishing of the pilot light and premature corrosion of the burner area.

Figure 7.17
Large homes may have more than one water heater and furnace

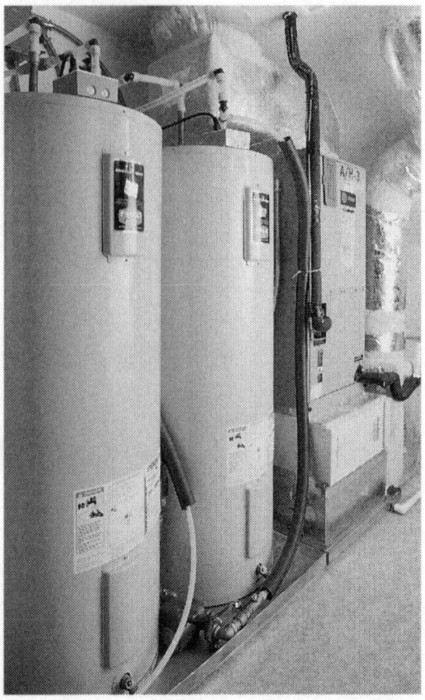

Water heaters that use a burner fueled by either gas or oil must be adequately vented to the outside air. Failure to provide sufficient exhaust ducting can result in carbon monoxide gas being introduced into the living space. For efficient operation, the exhaust flue should be as short and bend-free as possible. Since most water heaters are located in the garage or lower floor of the house, the exhaust gas is usually vented to an outside wall rather than the roof. Horizontal duct runs should pitch up at the rate of ¼ inch per foot. If the water heater vent is connected to the furnace exhaust system, there should be a Y-connection and not a T-connection.

Care should be exercised in determining where the flue terminates outside the building. The flue should not be easily blocked by ice, snow, or falling leaves or other debris. It should not be placed where it can be reached by small children either. Inspection of the water heater's exhaust pipe is a critical item for the home inspector.

The inspector should verify that the flue is properly constructed, installed, and free from obstructions and corrosion.

If the demand venting needs to be changed, a power vent is installed on the water heater's vent pipe. This type of vent uses 110 volt of electric power to open or close the vent depending on the demand of the water heater. The power vent should be located within five feet of the water heater and the flue must be dedicated to the water heater only.

Figure 7.18
Electric water heater

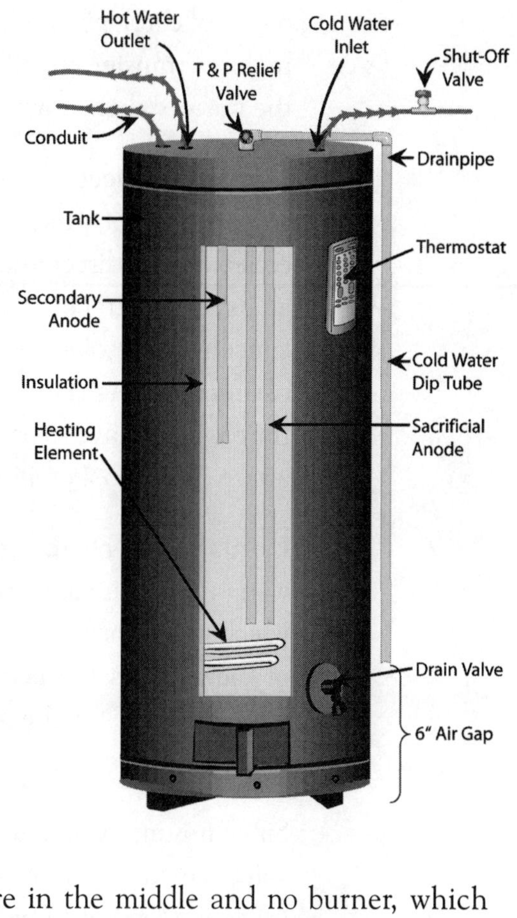

Electric Water Heaters

Many water heaters use electricity to heat water. An **electric water heater** generally has an upper and lower heating element and each is controlled by a separate thermostat. For efficient operation, these thermostats should be set to the same temperature.

Electric water heaters have no core in the middle and no burner, which means no heat exchanger or venting is needed either. Instead, two heating elements, controlled by a thermostat, are immersed at the top and bottom of the water heater tank. Usually, the two elements are not running at the same time but this is not absolute. Some units are simple and have temperature settings to make both elements run concurrently.

Solar-Powered Water Heaters

In certain parts of the country, solar energy is finding increased acceptance as a way to generate hot water. While the initial equipment expense is considerably greater, there is no monthly fuel bill to contend with after the original installation.

The basic parts of a solar water heating system are a heat collector, a storage tank, a pumping system to move the water from collector to storage tank. There are two types of solar energy collectors available: (1) concentrating collectors and (2) flat plate collectors.

The **concentrating collector** uses concave mirrors to focus the sun's energy on a collector pipe. This system can generate very high temperatures but requires transfer chemicals and an expensive tracking mechanism to keep the mirrors aligned with the sun.

Flat-plate collectors are fixed facing south and often mounted at the same angle as the roof, which is often within the recommended angle of tilt. Flat-plate collectors use direct and reflected solar energy, and since they do not require an expensive tracking device, they are considerably less expensive than the concentrating solar systems. Flat-plate collectors are available in a wide range of sizes and weigh between 100 and 200 pounds each. Because of this weight, the roof may have to be reinforced to carry the load. The inspector should be aware of any roof sagging due to the weight of solar panels.

In solar water heaters, the heat energy of the sun is used to heat either the water itself as it passes through pipes located on the roof or a glycol solution, which in turn heats water in a heat exchanger. All systems use an arrangement of **thermistors** (semiconductors with electrical resistance that varies with temperature) and check valves to prevent siphoning hot water back to the roof during cooler temperatures.

Since it is impossible to regulate the sun's energy at the source, a tempering valve is used to introduce cold water into the system to prevent the water from becoming too hot. The key to an efficient installation is adequate insulation of all the piping used to transport the heated water or the glycol solution.

Although the home inspector does not need to be familiar with the engineering requirements of a solar heating system, he or she should be able to identify the basic parts, check for leaks, check for adequate insulation, and check for the delivery of a reliable supply of hot water at the tap.

Tankless Water Heaters

In some cases, instant or tankless water heaters may be encountered. Tankless water heaters warm water only when there is a demand for hot water. Larger tankless units may be centrally located and service the entire home. Smaller units can be installed near the use of the hot water. Tankless water heaters do not waste the energy that water heaters with tanks do in keeping large volumes of water heated as a standby measure. The drawback to this type of water heater is that it cannot supply enough hot water for two major hot water uses at once (like a washing machine and a shower). For this reason, these heaters are normally used in low volume applications such as campers and guest quarters.

Reportable Deficiencies - Water Heaters

- Not producing hot water
- Taking too long to heat or a slow recovery rate
- Leaking, rusting, or tank damage
- Not enough clearance from potentially combustible materials
- Poor insulation
- Instability
- Missing or damaged pressure release valves
- Poor placement within the home
- Missing earthquake bracing, when required

8

Chapter

Built-In Appliances and Systems

Introduction

The advent of cheap dependable electrical power spawned a host of labor-saving household appliances. An **appliance** is a machine or device that completes one or a number of household jobs. Those appliances that are a permanent part of the home, such as stoves and garbage disposals, should be evaluated in a home inspection.

Freestanding items, such as refrigerators or washing machines, are considered personal property and do not need to be included in the inspection. The exception is that any appliances included in the sale of the home must be evaluated and reported.

Permanent Appliances and Systems

When inspecting appliances, the home inspector should always operate them to make sure they work. Appliances that are permanently attached to or are an integral part of the home include items such as garbage disposals, dishwashers, stoves, ovens, microwaves, and exhaust vents.

Disposals

The **disposal**, or **garbage disposal**, is designed to chop up food wastes to send down the drain line. The motor in the disposal turns a steel blade at a high speed much like a blender. It is mounted under the sink and connected to the drain.

Figure 8.1
Garbage disposal construction

1) Garbage disposal
2) Power cord
3) Dishwasher
4) "P" trap

Cold water is flushed through the disposal while it is operating, and it carries the liquefied waste down the drain. The reason for using cold water instead of hot water is to congeal the grease and keep it in suspension until it enters the sewer system. If hot water is used, the grease may redeposit on the walls of the drain line and eventually cause a stoppage.

Garbage disposals occasionally jam, and for this reason, there is usually a fitting for inserting a hex wrench to manually turn the blades and release the jam. Disposals are also equipped with overload protection to keep the motor from burning out during a jam.

Disposals are available as batch feed or continuous models. The batch feed variety has a plastic cap for the top that activates the start switch when rotated. The continuous feed model has its start switch mounted on the wall near the unit and a rubber splashguard to keep debris from flying out the top during operation. This type is more common in homes. The inspector should operate the disposal for a few seconds to verify that it is in good order.

Reportable Deficiencies - Disposals

- Disposal does not work
- Too much vibration and excessive noise
- Leaks or missing splashguard

Dishwashers

Modern **dishwashers** are designed to scrub, rinse, and dry dishes, pots, and utensils. They need a supply of hot water at 140^0 F or hotter to operate efficiently. Some models have an electric water heater to boost the temperature if the supply is not adequate.

Figure 8.2
Dishwasher

The operation is accomplished by the use of an electric pump that circulates hot soapy water throughout the cabinet via a rotating spray arm. After washing, an electric heating element mounted in the base of the cabinet facilitates the drying process. The cycle can take anywhere from 30 to 90 minutes.

The various operations of the washing cycle are controlled by an electric timer. Always stop the dishwasher by unlocking the door before adjusting the timer. The pump and motor are operated by the timer. The dishwasher is designed to leave a small amount of water in the cabinet at the end of the cycle. This water keeps the shaft seals from drying out. If there is a substantial amount of water remaining after the cycle is completed, the dishwasher has a deficiency and should be reported.

The solenoid-operated soap dispenser opens at a predetermined time to add soap to the circulating water. A rotating spray arm directs a jet of high-pressure, hot, soapy water at the dishes. The inspector should make sure that the arm rotates freely and the tiny orifices are not clogged with deposits.

The washer drain is plumbed through the disposal and should have an air gap to prevent contamination. An electric heater serves to dry the dishes and preheat the water when necessary. The door of the dishwasher should be counterweighted or sprung so it does not fall open. The rubber seal should be intact, and the latch should work smoothly.

Reportable Deficiencies - Dishwashers

- Dishwasher does not work
- Loud, noisy operation
- Does not produce hot water
- Door has bad seals or does not open and close properly
- Racks not properly protected
- Does not drain properly

Cooking Surfaces

Cooking surfaces may be either built-in or drop-in cook tops or freestanding ranges. They are powered by gas (natural or propane) and/or electricity. Natural and propane gas will be discussed in Chapter 9.

Gas Cook Tops

A gas appliance will have burners controlled by valves located at the front of the unit. In order to light the burner, there will be either a standing pilot light or an electronic igniter. When lit, the flame should be bright blue in color and about $^3/_4$ of an inch high.

The inspector should light each burner and observe the flame. The flame should be steady and modulate properly with the control knob.

Modern burners are very efficient in transferring the heat of the flame to the food being cooked. There will be a grate above each burner to maintain the proper distance between pot and flame.

Reportable Deficiencies - Gas Cook Tops

- Noisy or gusting flame, overly large flame height
- Smoking or soot build-up
- Gas smell
- Failure to light or burner controls do not working properly

Electric Cook Tops

Electric cook tops use either single or dual element heaters, which are operated by infinite control knobs or by predetermined push-button selectors.

The electric cook top is 75% more efficient than the gas version as the cooking utensil sits directly on the electric heating elements versus being elevated above it like a gas cook top.

The cooking system can be radiant heat like traditional electric coil cook tops, conducted heat like traditional cast-iron coil cook tops, or induction heat as found in electric coils under ceramic glass cook tops. Single element burners use an infinite control knob to adjust the heat. Dual burners use a push button or step system to control heat.

The low settings use the inner element with no color, the medium settings use the inner element with some coloration, and the high settings use both elements with cherry red coloration.

Reportable Deficiencies - Electric Cook Tops

- Heating elements that do not work, get too hot, or are damaged
- Controls that do not work properly
- Damaged cook tops

Magnetic Cook Tops

Induction cook tops use an electric coil that induces a magnetic field. This field acts upon the iron or steel in the cookware, which causes the pan to heat up. This form of energy is extremely efficient, since there is no heat loss from stove to burner.

The advantage of this system is efficiency and safety. There is no open flame or hot coil. A disadvantage is that the cookware must contain iron. Pyrex and ceramic utensils cannot be used on an induction stove.

Ovens

Ovens can be either electric or gas powered; although, electric is much more common. The oven may be integral with the stove or a separate unit in a cabinet. Most ovens use radiant heat to cook.

An oven needs to have a thermostatically controlled heat source. Ovens should be tested and the temperature should be within 15^0-20^0 of the dial reading. Most ovens contain timers that will turn the oven on and off at predetermined times.

Some ovens are equipped with a self-cleaning feature. In this mode, the oven is locked and heats to a very high temperature (approximately $1{,}000^0$ F). This high temperature turns all spills and stains to a fine ash that is easily removed when the cycle is over.

Figure 8.3

Electric cook top and oven

Gas cook top, microwave, and oven

State-of-the-art ovens are also equipped with a convection fan system that circulates hot air around the food. This provides a very even cooking temperature throughout the oven, which cooks foods more evenly and quickly. Some units incorporate the heating element into the circulating fan, which prevents hot spots. Convection ovens use a selector switch in conjunction with a thermostat, so that you can turn off the convection feature when you do not want to use it.

Reportable Deficiencies - Ovens

- Oven does not heat or does not heat to the required temperature
- Inaccurate temperature control

- Oven light non-operational
- Broken oven lock, if installed, or intact door seals

Microwave Ovens

Microwave ovens operate on a very simple premise. They warm foods and liquids using microwave frequency sound (radio waves) rather than a gas burner or an electric heating element.

Figure 8.4
A microwave

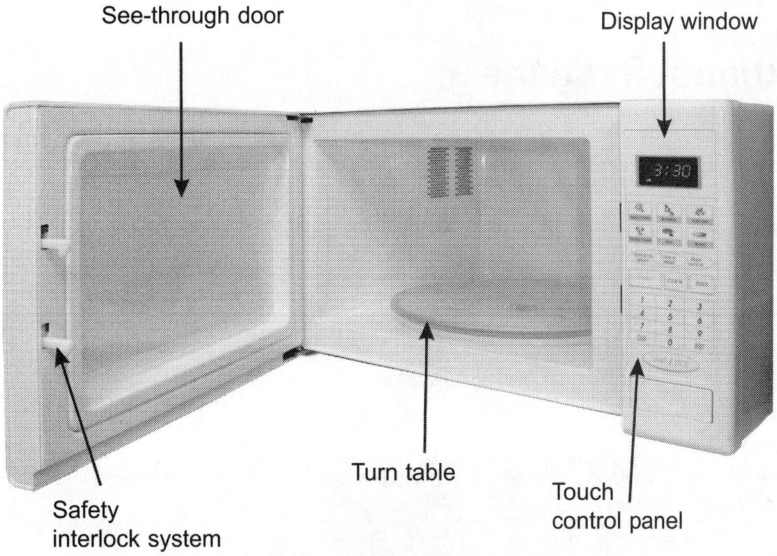

All microwave ovens operate on the same electromagnetic principle, which converts electrical energy to microwaves by the use of a magnetron tube. The magnetron is a cylindrical cathode that is heated by a filament; the resulting electrons are attracted to the anode. There is an electromagnetic field between the cathode and anode. This field deflects the normally straight path of the electrons and causes the anode to resonate. This resonance creates the microwave. The generated microwave energy responds differently to various materials. Metal causes the microwaves to be reflected. There is no heat produced, but there might be sparks and arcing. Glass, plastic, and paper products will allow the passage of microwave energy without heating.

The molecules of sugar, fat, and water contained in most food products absorb the microwaves. This causes the molecules to oscillate, producing heat by friction.

The microwave can be inspected by moistening a business card with water and placing it in the oven. Turn the microwave on and check the card in 30 seconds. If the oven is working, the card will be warm and dry.

Reportable Deficiencies - Microwave

- Not turning on, cooking or reaching proper temperatures
- Light or timer not working
- Turntable not working
- Door not opening or shutting properly

Exhaust Systems

The cooking area of the home produces a great deal of water vapor, heat, odor, and grease particles. In order to maintain a safe and healthy environment in the home, these bi-products of cooking should be removed from the air.

Figure 8.5
A kitchen exhaust system.

1) Outside vent flue

2) Vent hood

To facilitate this process, most kitchens are equipped with some sort of exhaust system. In order to be effective, this exhaust system needs to be vented to the outside.

The removal of these airborne pollutants is a three-step process. The offensive materials must first be collected, then removed from the kitchen, and finally delivered to the outside.

Exhaust systems are available as updraft or downdraft installations. The requirements of the kitchen design will dictate which one is used. Installations using an exhaust blower are generally more efficient than systems using a fan.

Updraft Exhaust

In this system, exhaust vapors travel from the cooking surface upward and are trapped in a vent hood. The vent hood should cover all burners and be no further than 30" above the cooking surface. These vapors and odors are then removed by a blower or fan. The exhaust products are vented by a ducting system to the outside-either under the home or above the roof.

As in most plumbing installations, the ducting runs should be as straight as possible and adequately sized for the load. Exhaust ducts smaller than 10 inches in diameter will not be able to handle the requirements. There should also be no blockages of the ducting, and filters should be replaced at regular intervals.

Downdraft Exhaust

This type of system has an air-receiving chamber, a filter, and a blower to create a high-speed exhaust pattern, which efficiently eliminates cooking odors, water vapor, and smoke.

Non-Vented Exhaust

In some cases, it is impossible to vent kitchen fumes to the outside. When this occurs, the alternative is a non-vented exhaust system. This system employs a charcoal filter to trap the grease and odor-causing particles. It cannot trap or remove heat or steam however. Charcoal filters cannot be cleaned and must be replaced periodically.

Whether cooking on a updraft or downdraft cook top in the kitchen, it can add more than five pints of water to the air in a house each day. Ventilation is needed to help eliminate the chance for mold or mildew resulting from this excess water in the air. The home inspector should make sure there is a means of eliminating this excess water from cook tops in the home.

Figure 8.6
Hoodless venting

1) Faucet
2) Downdraft gas cook top
3) Built-in microwave
4) Built-in oven
5) Side-by-side refrigerator/freezer

Optional Appliances and Systems

Sometimes there are optional appliances or home systems that are included in the home inspection and therefore become the realm of the home inspector.

Refrigerator and Freezer

Figure 8.7
Refrigerator/freezer

The fundamental reason for having a **refrigerator** is to slow down the activity of bacteria in order to help food stay fresh longer. Normal operating temperature for a refrigerator is between 34^0 and 38^0 F and 0^0 F for the **freezer**.

The inspector can easily check this using a simple dial thermometer. The doors should open and close easily and the door gasket should seal completely. Since most refrigerators are frost-free, any sign of frost usually indicates bad doors seals or air leaks.

If the refrigerator is equipped with an automatic icemaker, it will probably cycle during the inspection and its operation can be verified. There will be a connection to a water supply and a valve to shut this off in an emergency. Some refrigerators are equipped with ice and water dispensers in the door. For these models, the inspector should check to see that the dispensers work properly. The supply line and shutoff valves should also be inspected for leaks and damage. When evaluating a refrigerator, the inspector should note the condition of the inside racks and storage bins.

Reportable Deficiencies - Refrigerators and Freezers

- Inaccurate thermostat in the refrigerator or freezer
- Automatic water/ice dispensers and/or ice makers not working
- Broken, cracked door seals
- Doors do not open and close properly
- Frost in the refrigerator
- Broken compressor, evaporator coil, or fan
- Signs of leaks on the floor around the appliance

Trash Compactors

A **trash compactor** compresses trash, which reduces the volume of trash that is sent to landfills. A trash compactor uses a mechanical ram to reduce the volume of the trash to approximately 25% of its original size. Since the reduced volume means that the trash will be in the compactor for a longer period of time, compactors have some means of odor suppression installed.

Figure 8.8
Trash compactor

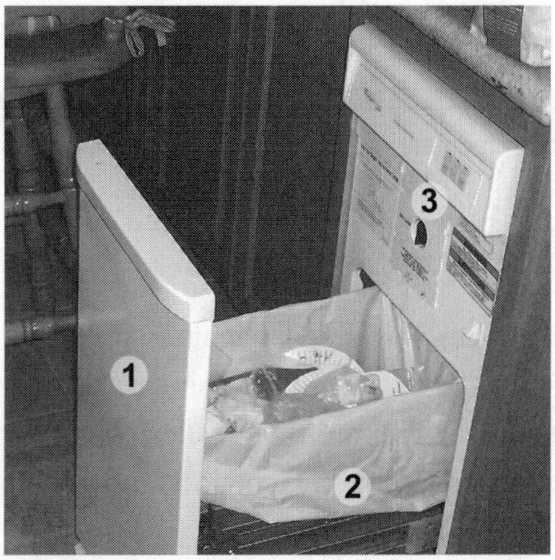

1) Trash compactor

2) Trash bin

3) Controls

Reportable Deficiencies - Trash Compactors

- Broken safety interlock switch which permits the appliance to operate with the door open
- Door does not close completely
- Trash not properly compacted
- No odor control

Washers and Dryers

Clothes washers and dryers can be purchased separately or as a matched set. Most are side by side, but some are stackable units with the dryer above the washing machine. There are even washer/dryer combos that wash and dry clothes in a single unit. These single units are ideal for small spaces, or homes that do not have dryer vents.

Figure 8.9
Two types of washing machines and dryers

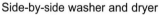

Side-by-side washer and dryer

Stacked washer and dryer

Washers

There are two common types of washing machines available: (1) front loaders and (2) top loaders. Both types of washers come as high capacity and have many available features, such as multiple cycles, water temperatures, and automatic dispensers for detergent, bleach, and fabric conditioner.

Front loaders are the most common type of machine with the front door that opens to the right or to the left. Front-loading washers do not have an agitator, but use a tumble action. They fill to just below the door opening and the clothes tumble in and out of the water to be cleaned. Then they are spun to remove the detergent and water, rinsed, and spun dry. Front-loading washers use less detergent, electricity, and water (typically 20 to 28 gallons in a regular front-loading wash cycle, compared to 45 gallons in a regular top-loading wash cycle).

As the name implies, **top loader**s have the main door on the top of the machine that lifts up. Top-loading washing machines have an agitator that moves the clothes in the water and detergent to get them clean. After washing, the basket spins at a high speed to remove the detergent and water. The washer fills with water again, the agitator moves the items to remove any remaining detergent, and then it spins the items until they are dry enough to put into the dryer or hang on a clothes line. Typically, about 45 gallons of water are used in a regular wash cycle.

The inspector should run a normal washing cycle and check for leaks at the inlet and discharge hoses. The lint filter should be in place and working. The agitator, if there is one, should be moving while cycled on. The control of the washer should be intact and working properly as well.

Reportable Deficiencies - Washing Machines

- Washer moves or "creeps" during the spin cycle
- Washer needs leveling
- Agitator does not move
- Tub does not fill or drain
- Tub is leaking
- Lid or door does not close

Clothes Dryers

The major difference in dryers is how they are powered—either by natural gas or electricity. The dryer produces heat and dries clothes while tumbling them. The inspector should check for signs of worn bearings or slipping belts. These conditions will be evidenced by a squealing noise when the dryer starts. The controls, whether electronic, dials, or push buttons should work. The dryer should be equipped with a functional lint screen. All dryers should be vented to the outside because interior venting is a fire hazard.

Reportable Deficiencies - Clothes Dryers

- Dryer not vented to the exterior of the home
- Inadequate heat in the dryer
- Tumbler is not working
- Missing lint trap
- Dryer door not closing tightly
- Missing, broken, or cracked seals

Central Vacuum Systems

Central vacuum systems have the advantage of less noise, more power, and no heavy machine to drag around the house. These systems are usually located in the garage or basement and consist of a suction motor and a receptacle to catch soil and dust. From this location, a series of tubes connects to wall inlets conveniently located throughout the home. The tubing can be run behind the walls, under the floor, through the attic, or in the cold air returns in the house. These systems have exhaust filters to catch soil and dust and are vented to the outside of the home.

To use the vacuum system, the operator simply plugs the lightweight vacuum hose into any inlet. There is a switch at the inlet that starts the remotely located suction motor. The dirt is carried through the tubing to the dirt receptacle. Periodically the dirt receptacle must be emptied and the filter must be changed.

These systems are designed for dry pickup only and should never be used for water or other liquid spills.

Reportable Deficiencies - Central Vacuum Systems

- Little or no suction due to clogged filter
- Blocked exhaust venting

Automatic Garage Doors

These devices have become increasingly popular since the advent of two-car garages. The automatic garage door opener consists of an electric motor to raise and lower the door, and an electronic transmitter/receiver to tell it when to do so. The motor of the door opener should be checked for proper function and if it does not raise the door in a timely fashion, it should be reported.

The transmitter is a small battery-powered device that is usually carried in the car. The receiver, which is programmed to a matching code, is mounted on the door assembly in the garage.

A significant safety feature of these installations is the automatic reversing function. If the downward travel of the door is impeded for any reason, the reversing switch immediately stops the door and raises it. Some door systems incorporate an electric eye that will reverse the door if the beam is broken. The inspector must verify that the auto-reverse function is working properly.

Reportable Deficiencies - Garage Door Openers

- Electric eye beam is broken
- Auto-reverse function not working properly
- Inoperable motor for the door opener

Chapter 9 Heating Systems

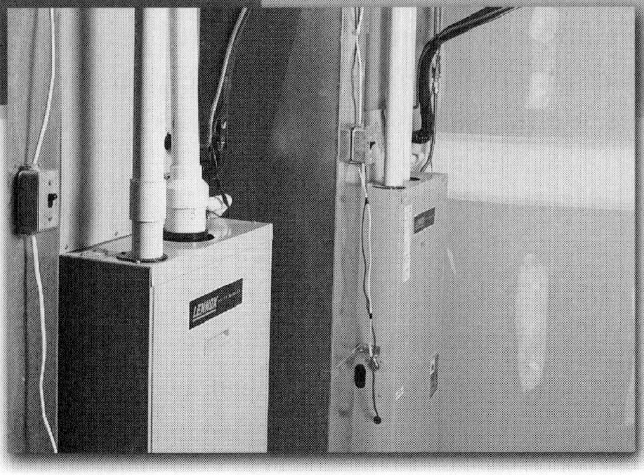

Introduction

Heat is a form of energy and is transferred from place to place according to the laws of physics. Heat always flows from a higher temperature to a cooler one. Cold is the absence of heat. Cold cannot be created. Heat can only be removed.

Transferring Heat Energy

There are three ways to transfer heat energy: (1) conduction, (2) convection, and (3) radiation.

Conduction

Conduction describes the transfer of heat from one molecule to another and only happens in solid materials. When a metal rod is placed in a flame, the heat travels from one end to the other by conduction.

Convection

Convection describes the transfer of heat via a moving fluid. Common fluid media for the convection of heat are air and water. Convection occurs when a hot pan is rinsed under cold water. The heat from the pan is transferred to the running water.

Radiation

A third type of heat transfer is called **radiation**. Radiation takes place when certain energy waves strike an object, are absorbed, and turn to heat. Some items, such as the sun or microwave ovens, produce electromagnetic radiation. Still other items, like a fire or a person, produce infrared radiation. When this energy strikes objects, it is turned to heat. When a person stands in the sun and becomes warm, it is the warmth created by radiation.

Heating Systems

In modern homes, central heating is taken for granted. Prior to 1900, fireplaces were commonly used to supply heat on an area-by-area basis. All heating systems that depend on combustion to generate heat must have a:

- supply or source of fuel.
- container in which to burn or combust the fuel.
- supply of air.
- means to discharge or vent the exhaust gases.
- distribution system to deliver the heat produced to the home's habitable areas.

Since most heating systems involve the controlled burning of fuel inside the home, safety becomes a primary consideration for the home inspector.

Heating systems are frequently described by the source of the fuel to create the heat. They are natural gas, oil, electricity, hydronic, and wood.

Natural Gas Heating System

The gas furnace is one of the most common heating systems in homes. In this system, natural gas is piped in as the fuel source and burned to heat air that is distributed throughout the home. There are two common distribution systems: gravity and forced-air.

Early central heating systems depended on gravity and convection currents to transport heated air to various locations in the home. In this type of system, called a **gravity system**, the furnace is located at the lowest point of the habitable area. There is no blower or fan to move the air. This system distributes the heated air based on the difference in specific gravity of warm air and cold air. Warm air is lighter and rises to higher points of a building as cooler, more dense air settles at lower levels, where it is then heated. This creates airflow.

Figure 9.1
Gravity heating furnace

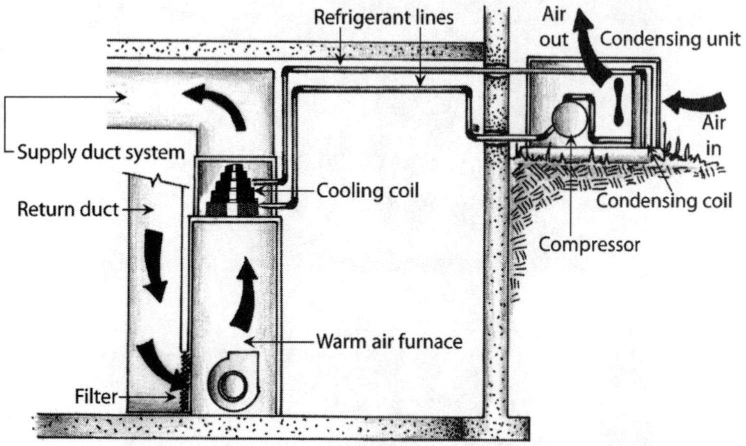

Currently, the forced-air system is commonly used in residential construction. A **forced-air system** uses blowers or fans to force the heated air through the home using a ducting system with return and supply registers.

The Fuel Source - Gas

Natural gas usually is delivered to homes from a utility provider via underground pipe systems. When this pipe enters the home, it is called the **gas supply line.**

The other source for gas heating systems is **bottled propane**. In this case, propane can be stored on site and does not need to be obtained or piped in from a municipality.

Individual lines that run to appliances in the home are known as **branch lines**. Different areas have varying requirements for what type of gas pipe should be used. The inspector should know these local requirements.

The most common type for gas piping is black steel. Steel tubing, brass, and copper are also used. Flexible connectors are allowed to connect appliances to the gas piping but must also have shut off valves and be in the same area as the appliance. The connectors are usually limited to less than six feet in length.

Figure 9.2
Two examples of gas furnace reportable deficiencies.

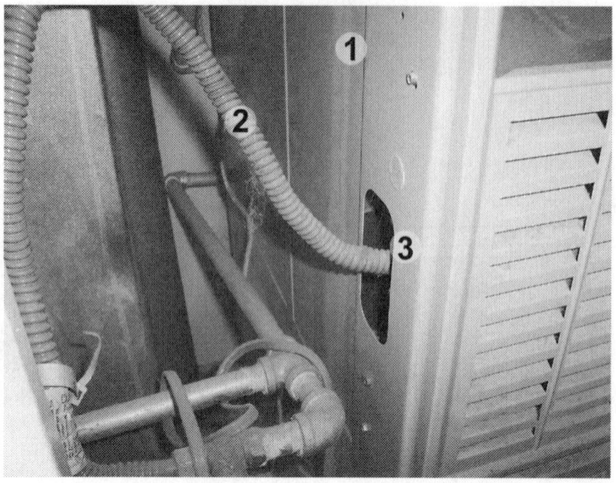

1) Furnace cabinet
2) Flexible hose gas line
3) Gas line into cabinet is flexible hose and therefore a reportable deficiency.

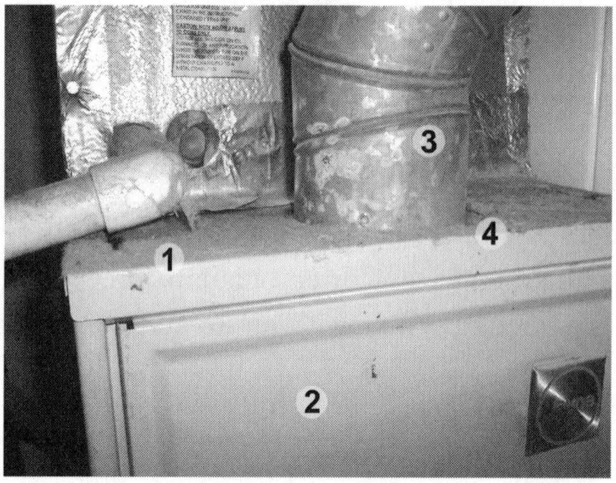

1) Furnace cabinet
2) Furnace door
3) Vent pipe corrosion
4) Vent pipe is not over furnace opening

Reportable Deficiencies - Gas Piping

- Leaks
- Missing shut off valve
- Improper installation
- Improper support
- Wrong materials used
- Rust
- Bad connections
- Piping in chimneys or ducts

Air Supply

In order for a gas furnace to work, it needs a supply of air to ignite the gas and to get rid of the exhaust products of the burning. The air that helps to get rid of exhaust gases is sometimes referred to as **dilution air.** Gas furnaces use about 30 cubic feet of air for every cubic foot of gas burned. When the furnace is located in an interior closet, it is essential that sufficient air supply is available.

There can be serious consequences if there is not enough air to burn the gas properly or completely. If there is not enough air, the complete burning will not take place and the result can be **carbon monoxide**, a poisonous gas.

The lack of air can also result in a **back draft**, where the exhaust cannot be expelled out of vents but instead is pumped back into the living space. The inspector can check for this potentially fatal condition by placing a hand near the base of the draft hood and feeling for warm exhaust gas coming back down. In addition, moisture is a bi-product of burning and can build up if a back draft occurs, causing rust and corrosion. These are indicators of a back draft and should be noted.

The Burner

In gas burners, the natural gas is mixed with air in two areas of the furnace. First, the air is mixed with the gas before combustion takes place. This is called the **primary air.** Second, the air is mixed with gas when the gas is exposed to the pilot, which ignites it. This is called **secondary air.**

The **pilot flame** or **pilot light** is a flame that is used to ignite the main burner. The pilot has its own mini-burner that also uses primary and secondary air for burning. In some older furnaces, the pilot flame burned continuously. Wasted gas resulted from keeping the system ready for use. To increase energy efficiency, the pilot flame is now electronically lit when it is needed.

The Flame

The **flame of a burner** should be blue and stable. It should not be wavering, fluttering, or drifting to the edges of the burner. The reason the inspector should check for a normal flame is that it indicates a complete burning or combustion of the gas.

Reportable Deficiencies - Gas-Fueled Furnace Flames

- Ignition of the flame is delayed at start-up
- Flame wavers horizontally
- Flame is yellow at the tip
- Flame lifts from the burner

- Flame rolls out of or exits the burner chamber
- Flame puts itself out

The Gas Valve

This valve controls the flow of gas to the burner. When it is closed, there is no gas flow, no ignition, and no flame on the burner. When it is open, gas flows, ignition occurs, and there is flame on the burner.

Figure 9.3
Globe valve (main gas shut-off)

1) Globe valve
2) Main gas shut-off
3) Gas line

The Thermostat

Modern systems use electronic thermostats to control the furnace. A **thermostat** is a device that will switch the furnace on and off in response to temperature changes in the room where it is mounted. When the temperature falls below a pre-set limit, the thermostat opens the gas valves and turns on the furnace by completing the circuits that control these items.

The **thermocouple** is a safety device for the thermostat. It senses if the pilot light is lit when the thermostat seeks to open the gas valves and allow gas to feed the main burner. If the pilot light is lit, the thermocouple allows electric current to flow to the gas valve and open it. If the pilot light is not lit, the thermocouple will not allow electricity to flow through the gas valve, thus keeping gas from entering the burner.

The Heat Exchanger

The **heat exchanger** is referred to as the heart of the furnace. It separates the two sides of the air in the furnace and moves heat from the burning air side to the home air side.

One side is the home air side and is composed of the return-air duct system, the blower, the filter, the supply-air plenum and duct system. The other is the burning air side and is composed of the burner, the flame, the draft hood, the vent, and exhaust chimney.

Reportable Deficiencies - Heat Exchanger

- Rust
- Cracks
- Holes

The Blower

The **blower** is a wheel with scoops that moves air through the heat exchanger to the living spaces being heated. There are two types of blowers. One is the belt-driven blower and the other is the direct drive blower. The blower is located on the house side of the heat exchanger.

Figure 9.4
Heating system fan with pulley

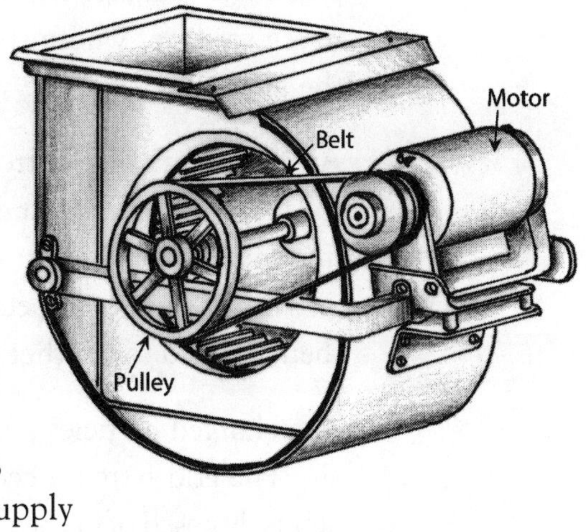

Air enters and leaves the heat exchanger in a continuous cycle. The cycle begins when the blower pulls cool air from the house into the return ducts on its way to the furnace. Once in the furnace, the blower pulls the cool air over the heated steel walls of the heat exchanger where it gets heated. Then the air passes through the blower, which pushes it through the supply ducts into the rooms of the home. The warmed air heats the living spaces. Cool air is pulled back into the return ducts to begin the process again. Before doing the next part of the furnace inspection, the inspector should turn off the power to the furnace and its blower for safety. The inspector should move the fan of the blower and associated pulleys by hand if possible to check for proper alignment and possible binding. In a properly operating blower system, the noise you hear should be the air moving—not the machinery.

The belts that transfer power from the motor to the fan should be in good condition, aligned properly, and adjusted to the correct tension. A loose belt will slip and be noisy; a tight belt will wear prematurely and can cause bearing failure. A variable speed pulley that is set to run the fan at high speed may be an indication of an undersized heating system.

Filters

All forced-air heating systems should have provisions for air filtration. The removal of dust and other debris from the air not only makes the home more comfortable but also increases the life of the heating system. The accumulation of dust over time can coat heat exchangers like an insulating blanket, drastically reducing their efficiency.

The **filter** in a forced air heating system screens out impurities from the air like dust, dirt, and lint. Filters are found where the air enters into the furnace. The filter removes impurities from the air before it passes over the heat exchanger and is recycled into the living spaces.

The two basic types of air filters used in house furnaces are mechanical filters and electrostatic filters. A **mechanical filter** made of fiberglass is able to passively trap and remove large particles that are in the air and could potentially damage the furnace. This is done by moving air through the fiberglass filter where the bigger particles are trapped and removed from the air.

An **electronic** or **electrostatic filter** removes much smaller particles than the mechanical filter. It does this by moving the air stream through a grid of fine wires that are electrically charged. The minute particles of matter that pass through this grid become similarly charged. These charged particles are then directed to another wire grid, which carries an opposite charge.

The charged particles stick to the second wire grid, taking them out of the air. The grid system needs to be cleaned periodically and the accumulated debris disposed of in the trash. The inspector should do a visual examination of the filter grid and report on its condition. The electrostatic filter screens and removes particles larger than 0.1 micron like dust, lint, pollen, fungus spores, bacteria, smoke, and organic odors. They cannot remove odors caused by vapors like cigarette smoke however.

Reportable Deficiencies - Air Filters
- Loose fitting filters in their frames
- Accumulation of dust and dirt
- Noisy filter when under air flow
- Missing filter
- Clogged filter

A clogged filter may restrict the airflow enough to cause a dramatic increase in air temperature. The hot air may trigger the high temperature, which shuts down the system to fail prematurely.

Venting

In order to prevent asphyxiation and carbon monoxide poisoning, all fuel-burning systems must be adequately vented. **Venting** contains the products of combustion and routes them outside the building. Without proper venting, a house can become **depressurized** (negative pressure). When this happens, carbon monoxide can exhaust into the home resulting in sickness and even death. Lack of proper venting is a serious safety issue and needs careful inspection.

The venting must be maintained so that it is clean and unobstructed in order to efficiently and safely remove the waste gases from the home.

The two methods used to vent a home of exhaust gases are natural draft and power venting. **Natural draft** venting allows the hot combustion gases to rise up through a vent and draw cooler air into the burning chamber by convection. **Power venting** utilizes blowers and fans to move air through the burner and vent system.

Another feature of the modern venting system that has increased energy efficiency is the **automatic vent damper**. This device automatically opens when the furnace is on to allow combustion gases to escape. When the furnace stops, the automatic vent damper closes to keep the warm air of the home from rising up and out of the vents.

Reportable Deficiencies - Venting
- Blockage in the vent system
- Leaks in vent system

Ducting

Air is delivered via a system of tubes called **ducts**. These ducts can be made of a variety of materials such as sheet metal, plastic, wood, fiberboard, or aluminum. Since the air is not pressurized, the duct need only be thick enough to be self-supporting. The duct can be made with any shape cross section, but it needs to be sized properly to carry the required amount of air.

Figure 9.5
Attic ducting

1) Rafters
2) Ducting
3) Vent pipe
4) Insulation

Reportable Deficiencies - Ducting

- Lack of or not enough support for ducting
- Inadequate or improper joining of duct sections together
- Ducting that has been pulled loose from the supply register
- Ducting crushed under foot in the attic
- Missing insulation from ducting installed in unheated areas

Balance

Proper airflow balance is essential to maintain heating efficiency. In ideal conditions, there should be a matching return for each supply register. Since running a return for each supply duct is not cost effective, builders resort to undercutting the doors so that there is enough space at the bottom of each door to allow air to flow back to a central return grille.

For efficient operation, return air volume should be at least 80% of supplied air volume. It does not get to operate at 100% because the return air is cooler and denser.

Registers

The grill that is mounted at the end of the supply duct where it enters the room is called a **register.** The register will have a pattern of grillwork designed into it to aid even distribution of conditioned air in the room. This grillwork may be fixed or moveable, to allow the air to be aimed towards or away from a particular part of the room. Modern forced air heating systems can have the registers mounted anywhere in the room that is architecturally pleasing.

The inspector should be aware of any changes in the house that will affect the performance of the heating system. In some cases, air registers are closed off or carpeted over. Other air sources may have been reduced in size or eliminated. These changes would reduce the efficiency of the system and could impose safety hazards.

Airflow through the register can be checked with an infrared thermometer or a simple smoke generator. You can also use a piece of tissue paper fastened to the end of a ¼-inch dowel and hold the tissue paper to the register to check the airflow.

Figure 9.6
A register can be mounted anywhere in the room that is visually pleasing.

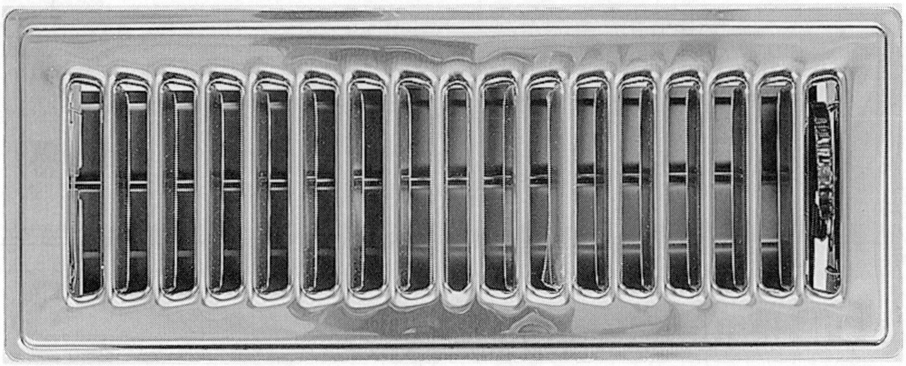

Reportable Deficiencies - Registers

- Not securely fastened or loose
- Covered with soot or dust
- Not working properly

Humidifiers

In some cases, a humidifying system is incorporated into the forced-air heating system. This system re-introduces moisture into the warmed air to make it more comfortable for the residents. The **humidifier** is controlled by a **humidistat,** which is a device that turns the humidifier on and off based on the amount of humidity in the air, just as a thermostat turns the heater and air conditioner on and off to regulate the temperature.

There are two major potential drawbacks to running a humidification system. The first is the potential for corrosion and rot caused by the water into the air. The second is that moisture is a prime requirement for the growth of mold.

The dark dusty interior of the ductwork is a prime breeding ground for this potentially serious hazard. A home humidification system should be monitored regularly for leaks.

Reportable Deficiencies - Gas Heating System

- Improper installation, connection, and support for all ductwork
- Registers that are not securely attached to the ductwork
- Fuel leaks
- Exhaust problems
- Blowers and fans not securely mounted, not balanced, or without adequately lubricated bearings

Location of Gas Furnace

When furnaces are located in the garage, there are special safety considerations. Because of the possibility of leaking gasoline from an automobile, a special installation technique is mandated. Gasoline vapors are heavier than air and will tend to accumulate along the floor of the garage. Building codes require that furnace burners be located at least 18 inches above the floor when located in a garage. If the furnace burner is not at least this high, it should be reported.

Oil Heating System

Some heating systems in homes use heating oil as fuel. Oil is a thick liquid and has to be converted to a vapor in order to be burned for heat. Older furnaces use a process called **vaporization** to do this, and newer ones use the process called **atomization**.

Commercial fuel oil comes in grades #1 through #6. Grade #1 is the lightest, and grade #6 is the heaviest. The grade most commonly used for household heating is #2, which will not ignite spontaneously in normal conditions and therefore is relatively safe as a residential fuel.

The Fuel Source - Oil

Fuel oil is normally stored on the homeowner's property in a large tank. This gives homeowners who use oil for heat the advantage of not being dependent on piped-in delivery of fuel from municipalities. This makes an oil-heating system a good choice for more remote homes that cannot be supplied in other ways.

Oil Storage Tanks

Oil storage tanks to supply home heating can be made from steel or fiberglass. They are typically located outside the house, although they can be inside. They can be above or below ground. They range in size from 275 gallons to over 500 gallons for the ones underground. Underground storage tanks are beyond the scope of the home inspector. The normal life expectancy for a fuel oil storage tank is 20 to 30 years. The date of manufacture can be obtained from the plate located near the fill opening. A leaking tank can cause environmental concerns. Oil storage tanks should be at least ten feet from any ignition sources unless separated by a masonry wall.

Tanks mounted indoors must be vented to the outside. The vent system should be at least two feet higher than the fill port, and have some sort of rain cap.

Most often, storage tanks that are located outdoors and above ground are cylindrical in shape to keep from blowing over in high winds. Outdoor tanks are also required to have containment booms around them to control spillage in the event of a tip-over or leak. Some rust and corrosion on an outside oil storage tank is to be expected. If it is excessive, it can cause the tank to fail or fall over and it should be reported. The location of the tank, fill pipe, and vent should be noted on your inspection report.

Oil storage tanks should never be allowed to get totally empty. This can cause problems with the heating of a home and the freezing of plumbing pipes.

Reportable Deficiencies - Above Ground Oil Storage Tanks

- Leaks or cracks
- Age of the tank should be noted
- Location less than ten feet from ignition source
- Excessive rust or corrosion
- Oil tank is empty

The Supply Lines

Oil supply lines carry oil from the storage tank to the burner, where it is ignited. Provision is made for the return of unburned oil to the storage tank. These pipes contain fuel and therefore must be protected from damage. The lines are usually made of copper, steel, or even brass piping and are buried in a bed of mortar. Shutoff valves are required at the tank on the supply line or where the line enters the home.

Reportable Deficiencies - Oil Supply Lines

- Leakage
- Rust
- Corrosion
- Exposed when they should be covered
- Crushed
- Too small for the demand

Air Supply

In order for oil to continue to burn, a supply of air is needed. To make sure the oil gets enough air, an **air blower** is built into the oil burner. This is a key difference compared to a gas-burning heating system, which relies on secondary combustion air.

For each pint of grade #2 oil, 14 pounds of air is needed for the oil to burn completely. If the oil is still not burning completely for some reason, excess air is added. As air is added, the result is less carbon dioxide gas. If the exhaust of an oil-burning furnace is measured and has 10% or less of carbon dioxide gas, it is considered to be burning completely.

Combustion Chamber

Oil burns at a much higher temperature than gas. To keep the metal of the heat exchanger, furnace cabinet or other components from being burned through, a **combustion chamber** or **refractory** (fire pot) is needed. This is where the oil is actually burned.

A combustion chamber is typically made of steel, cast-iron or brick and is lined with other materials to protect it from the extreme temperatures of the burning oil. Viewing the combustion chamber is not easy but can be done by removing the cover or opening the door on the furnace. Glowing hot metal of the furnace cabinet or a warped frame or cabinet are indicators of a failing refractory.

Reportable Deficiencies - Combustion Chamber

- Combustion chamber cracks
- Crumbling structure
- Oil saturation
- Spalling brick within the chamber

The Burner

The **oil burner** is comprised of a burner motor, air blower, oil pump, spark igniter, and the gun assembly. In order for fuel oil to burn, it must be vaporized. This is accomplished by using a gun-type burner. Pumps force the fuel oil through the orifice of the burner under pressure. This breaks the oil up into tiny droplets that are mixed with air into a vapor. This vapor is ignited by an electric spark.

The oil heating system should contain filters and strainers to insure a clean supply of oil to the burner head.

A home inspector should view the oil burner while it is operating. The first clues to efficient and safe operation are noise and odor. A properly adjusted oil burner should be odor free and relatively quiet in operation.

Figure 9.7
Fuel oil burner pumps

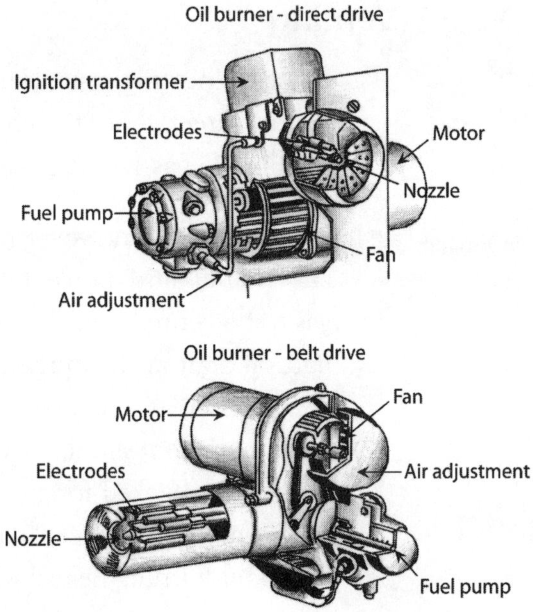

There will be an inspection plate to view the flame. This flame should be symmetrical and range in color from orange to bright yellow. No matter what the color of the flame, it should be free of sooty edges. Soot indicates incomplete combustion. Incomplete combustion wastes fuel and generates deadly carbon monoxide gas.

Reportable Deficiencies - Fuel Oil Burners

- Heavy fuel oil smells
- Puff back conditions when the burner fires up
- No heat coming from the burner
- Burner does not ignite immediately
- Leaking fuel oil (stains or pools observed under the burner)
- Black tipped flame or smoke

The Heat Exchanger

Just like in gas furnaces, there are heat exchangers in oil furnaces. In oil furnaces there are two heating surfaces that warm up the air that is supplied to the living space.

The primary heating surface surrounds the flame where the oil is burning. The secondary heating surface is a group of steel sections that the hot exhaust gas must pass over on the way out of the heat exchanger. The air that will heat the home passes over both of these surfaces to be warmed before it is pushed towards individual rooms.

Venting

Since oil-heating systems are supplied with a blower in the burner, they are vented directly into the chimney without a draft hood or diverter like those required in gas-heating systems.

Oil furnaces do however have a **barometric damper**, which automatically allows draft air to move inward into the chimney but does not allow exhaust gas to be vented into the living space. This damper controls the amount of natural draft at the burner. If natural draft is insufficient to support proper combustion, a fan may be used to provide positive air pressure at the burner. This equipment should be well lubricated and vibration free. These dampers should be checked for signs of corrosion or rust, improper adjustment and function. Check to see if dampers are present or missing. The venting system for an oil-burning heat system also includes the **vent connector**. This steel piping connects the burning chamber to the vertical vent or flue. It also moves the exhaust gases and products from the burner to the chimney for outside venting.

Vents should be located more than one foot above the ground, more than three feet from an oil tank or other vent pipe, and not above the gas service meter. They should be more than six feet from doors, windows or other air intakes, more than seven feet above a driveway or sidewalk, and not be below a porch or deck.

In addition, venting should be done so the hot exhaust gases dissipate into the air and not back into the home. The home inspector should check local codes for exact rules governing venting of exhaust gases.

Reportable Deficiencies - Venting

- Rust
- Corrosion
- Improper length
- Improper supports
- Improper connections
- Improper size
- Improper material type
- Obstructions
- Improper clearance from combustible materials
- Poor slope

Safety Controls

All fuel oil burners are equipped with a mechanism that will shut off the fuel supply if the flame goes out or the burner fails to light. This device, often called the **primary controller**, must be located remotely from the burner so that it can be shut down from a safe distance in the event of a fire or malfunction. These devices are sensitive to either light or heat.

Oil-fired furnaces also have **flame detectors**. If they do not detect the presence of a flame in a predetermined amount of time, they close the fuel supply by means of a solenoid valve. The inspector should check these shut-off switches for proper operation.

Electricity

Electricity is the cleanest and safest fuel for heating but it is also the most expensive. Electricity can be the sole source of heat in the home or it can be used in conjunction with another system to supplement the heating capability of the home.

Electric-generated heat systems have advantages and disadvantages over the other fuel sources for heating.

Advantages of Electric Heating Systems

- Less expensive to buy and install
- Quicker to respond to need
- Safer for the homeowner because they have no exhaust gases
- No exhaust vents or chimneys
- No spark and no combustion
- Quieter
- Fewer moving parts than other systems

Disadvantages of Electric Heating Systems

- More expensive to run (can cost twice as much to run as a natural gas heating system)
- Larger electrical service and the associated cost to install it
- Space heaters or radiant heating do not have central filtration or humidification

The Fuel Source - Electricity

Electricity is supplied by a municipality or privately by solar heating.

Municipal Supply

Normally, electricity is supplied by a municipality and to the home via transmission lines and a service drop. The specifics of this are discussed in the chapter on electrical considerations of the home.

Electric Heating Systems

Electricity can be used to run furnaces, room and space heaters, boilers, and radiant heating systems. Each of these different types of systems creates heat, using electricity to heat all or part of a home.

Furnaces

The electric furnace is similar to gas and oil furnaces in that it is enclosed in a cabinet and has a thermostat, a high temperature limit, a fan to circulate the heat, and a ducting system to deliver the heat.

The electric furnace produces heat with banks of resistors, which are similar to the elements in a toaster. As the thermostat calls for heat, the resistors heat up sequentially instead of all at once. The reason they do not all come on at the same time is because the current drain would cause the house lights to dim.

As in the other styles of furnaces, the circulating fan is electronically delayed to insure warm air is delivered to the house. A similar delay at the end of the cycle exhausts all the heat from the system.

If the temperatures in an electric furnace get too high, the consequences can be overheating of the unit, its elements, and other components. The home inspector may have a difficult time checking the heating elements in an electric furnace. Sometimes a furnace has as many as six elements. Therefore, a normal heat cycle may not detect if any of them are not working properly. An amp meter can be used to see if the wires or elements have electricity running through them.

Reportable Deficiencies - Electric Furnaces

- Damaged cabinet
- Rusting cabinet
- Improperly located thermostat
- Malfunctioning thermostat
- Dirty air filter
- Missing air filters
- Dirty ducts
- Disconnected ducts
- Leaky ducts
- Faulty controls
- Temperatures rise too much
- Heating elements, sequencers, or relays are not working properly

Room and Space Heaters

Room and space heaters are designed only to heat the room in which they are placed. Because of this, they do not have ducts or piping systems and may or may not have blowers to force out heated air. These heaters are individually adjustable and provide for almost infinite flexibility in comfort settings. They can also be controlled by a room thermostat as well. Common types of room and space heaters include baseboard heaters, wall-mounted heaters, ceiling-mounted heaters, and floor heaters.

Reportable Deficiencies - Room and Space Heaters

- Room or space heater is not working
- Room or space heater is blocked or covered improperly
- Room or space heater has electrical outlets above it
- Room or space heater has bent or damaged parts
- Room or space heater has rust on it
- Room or space heater is missing parts

Electric Boilers

Electricity can also be used to heat water in boilers. Electrical elements heat up water, which is then distributed through the home for heating. **Electric boilers** have similar problems to other boilers such as leaking, rusting, getting damaged, and being poorly insulated.

Radiant Heating

Electric **radiant heating** is typically found embedded in ceilings and floors. There are advantages of electric radiant heating. It does not take up much space, is not connected to a boiler, and weighs little. It also produces very even heat.

The disadvantage for this type of heating system is that it is easy to damage by adding light fixtures or fans to ceilings. Once the embedded radiant heating system is damaged, it is hard to locate and fix the problem.

Heat Pump

A **heat pump** is a device that acts as an air conditioner in the summer and as an electric furnace in the winter. A heat pump uses electricity to operate a system that extracts heat from one environment and moves it to another. There are two types of heat pumps: (1) air source and (2) geothermal. The air source heat pump has its outdoor heat exchanger exposed to the outside atmosphere, while the geothermal heat pump has its heat exchanger buried in the ground below the frost line. Used as a heater, a heat pump gathers heat from the outside atmosphere (air source type) or the ground (geothermal type) and moves it to the interior of a house. By using a reversing valve, a heat pump can also move heat from the inside of a house to the outside atmosphere (or the ground). This process cools the house.

Heat pumps work by circulating refrigerant through a system of pipes. In the cooling part of the cycle, the refrigerant is a cold vapor under low pressure that can absorb heat. In this state it is in a portion of the piping called the evaporator. This cooling of the surrounding air can take place either inside or outside the house depending on the position of the reversing valve. In summer, the reversing valve causes the evaporator side of the piping to be in the house so that the interior of the house can be cooled. In winter, the evaporator side would be outside the house so that the heat outside the house can be absorbed and brought into the house.

After the refrigerant has absorbed heat, an electrically operated compressor compresses the refrigerant to a high temperature liquid and sends it to the high-pressure section of the piping, called the condenser. When the refrigerant is in its hot liquid state, it heats the condenser. A fan blows air over the condenser causing the air that moves over it to warm. This heat releasing (or heating of the air) can take place either inside or outside the house depending on the position of the reversing valve. In the winter, the reversing valve would cause the condenser side of the heat pump to be in the house so that the interior of the house could be heated. In the summer, the reversing valve would cause the condenser to be on the outside of the house so that the heat taken from the interior of the house could be released to the outside air.

In areas of the country where the temperature drops below 40° F, a heat pump's efficiency drops dramatically. Therefore, an auxiliary heating system (most often electrical but occasionally natural gas or fuel oil) is incorporated into the heating systems. These homes will likely have a geothermal heat pump rather than an air-source type.

When the heat pump is working to supply heat to the interior of the house, the evaporator side of the coil, which is outside, will often be well below freezing. For this reason air-source heat pumps have defrosters designed into the coil that operate automatically to rid the system of ice.

Reportable Deficiencies - Heat Pump

- Pump not working in heating or cooling mode
- Pump is undersized for either mode

- Outdoor coil is located where water from the roof can drip on it
- Outdoor coil is located where snow can accumulate on it
- Outdoor coil is located where air flow is limited or too much
- Back-up heating system is not working
- Back-up heating system is missing altogether
- Pump is extremely old

Solar Heating

Solar heating became popular due to the combination of the need for a cheaper source for heating and the existence of tax credits from the federal government. Many homes have solar panels to heat potable water and swimming pools. Similar components are used in some solar heating systems. Two types of solar heating systems are available: (1) passive and (2) active.

The passive solar heating system depends on the construction and orientation of the home itself to capture and store the sun's energy. Typical features of a house designed to have passive solar heating include: large windows on south-facing walls and materials in the house that will be struck by the sun as it shines in these windows and absorb the sun's energy. These materials will then slowly release the heat absorbed during the day, warming the house.

Figure 9.8
Solar panels with plumbing vent roof penetration

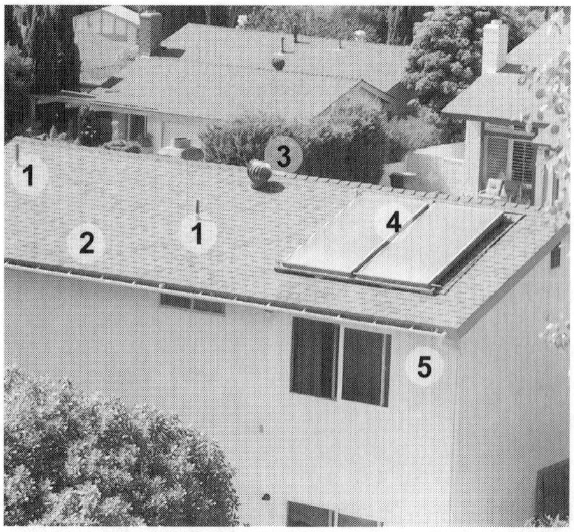

1) Plumbing vents

2) Asphalt shingle roof

3) Attic fan

4) Solar panels

5) Gutter and down spout

There are two types of **active solar heating** systems: (1) liquid and (2) air. The liquid active solar heating system can be much like the system used by solar powered water heaters. The visible part of the system is a roof-mounted arrangement of pipes, filled with a collection medium such as glycol solution or air, which collects the sun's energy by allowing it to heat the contents of the pipes. The heated liquid or air is then pumped, or carried by convection, to the various parts of the home to deliver heat to the occupants via a heat exchanger.

Not surprisingly, the parts of the country where there is lots of sunshine, such as the Southwest, are the favored locations for these systems. An active solar heating system is fairly expensive and complicated to install, but once in place will supply much of the heat needed to warm a house with no monthly fuel cost.

Parts of a Solar-Heating System

Solar-heating systems have four main components: (1) collection mechanism, (2) storage, (3) piping, and (4) controls.

Collectors

Collectors are usually roof mounted and literally soak up the suns rays. They typically consist of tubes filled with liquid. The sun's rays heat the liquid in the pipes. Once warmed, the liquid moves to the systems storage area.

Storage

Once the sun's heat energy is collected by the system's liquid or air, it is stored (depending on the system) in water tanks, masonry walls, or even a box of rocks. The storage medium is designed to release this heat slowly over time or as needed.

Piping

Piping is the component of the solar heating system that connects the other components to each other. In a liquid system, it is usually copper. In an air system, the "piping" is actually air ducts. The ducts used in an air system will be larger than the ducts in a furnace-based system because the temperature of air being moved is lower. The purpose of the pipes and ducts is the same, to distribute the heat energy collected for use in the home.

Controls

These controls are devices that monitor the temperature of the collectors and storage. They also control the pumps, which move the liquid or air through the heating system.

Other components of the solar heating system include the pump, relief valve, air vents, and tempering valve. The pump carries liquid to and from the collectors, and to the heat exchanger where the energy is stored. Relief valves eliminate the pressure that builds up in the system. The air vents release trapped air from the liquid system. This can cause the liquid to stop flowing and stop the heating system from working. The tempering valve makes sure water delivered to the water heater is the proper temperature by mixing cold water with heated water from the storage tank.

Figure 9.9
Solar home heating system

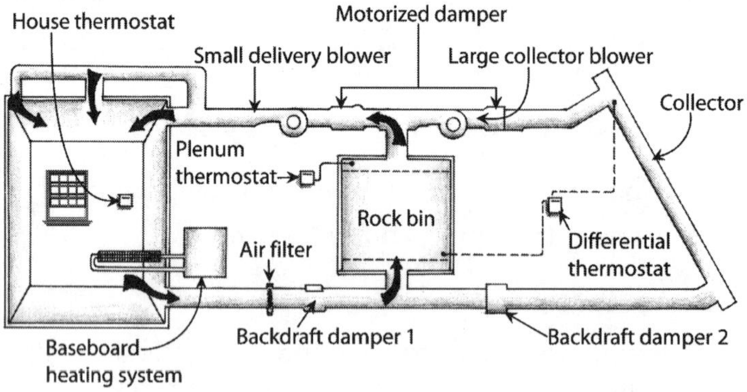

Reportable Deficiencies of Solar Heating
- Piping is not adequately insulated
- There are leaks
- Fan shrouds are not clear
- There are unusual noises coming from the pump or fan

Hydronic Heating Systems

Natural gas, fuel oil, and electric furnaces all heat air and then distribute the heated air to the different rooms of the house. However, other heating systems use different strategies.

Hydronic heating systems use hot water piped to each room to warm the air in that room. The hot water can either run through pipes in the floor or through radiators or other heat distributing devices. Water makes a good convector because it is cheap, available, easily replaced, and can hold a lot of heat.

As with all heating systems, the operation starts with a call for heat from the room thermostat. If water in the boiler is cold, this causes the boiler's burner to fire and the water in the system to begin heating. As soon as the water temperature exceeds ambient conditions, the circulation pump will begin to move the water through the system. This will cause the cool water to return to the boiler for heating.

When the heating thermostat temperature is reached, the burner shuts off; however, the circulating pump continues as long as the water in the system is above the demanded temperature. When the water temperature drops far enough, the circulation system shuts down.

Gravity Convection Water Heating

The simplest form of the hydronic water heating system uses gravity to carry the heated water. The hot water boiler is located at a low point in the home and as the water is heated in the combustion chamber, it rises through the piping and radiators where it begins to displace the cooler water. The cooler water is propelled down the pipe where it re-enters the boiler. This is a self-sustaining cycle and will continue as long as the water is heated at the boiler.

Although outdated, the gravity system is quiet and trouble free, but it is inefficient and slow to respond.

If a water pump is added to the gravity system, the response time and efficiency level improve dramatically. In an open-gravity system, the pump must be sized to lift the water column as high as the highest point in the system. If this point is thirty feet above the boiler, then the pressure will be one pound for every two to three feet of water height or 13 per square inches (PSI) at the boiler.

The Supply

Hydronic heating systems can be fueled by natural gas, bottled propane gas, coal, oil, and even electricity. The source of the fuel will vary depending on what the most available and efficient fuel was at the time the system was installed.

In these types of heating systems, water is supplied by a connection to the plumbing system and its domestic water supply.

The Boiler

In a hydronic water heating system, water is heated in a **boiler** (between 120° F and 130° F with a maximum of 200° F). This depends on the capacity of the system and outside temperatures. The system uses water to move heat through a home instead of air as with a furnace. The water actually picks up heat when it is in the boiler's heat exchanger. From there it is sent through piping under the floors and to radiators throughout the home.

State-of-the-art hydronic boilers are noiseless, and because they are designed for high temperature and rapid recovery, they can be small and compact. The data recorded on the manufacturer's nameplate is useful information that should be included in your inspection report.

A noisy hydronic system is probably caused by thermal expansion and contraction of the system's piping. Sometimes this can be cured by lubricating the pipe hangers or lining the bearing surface with a material that will allow the pipes to move laterally as they expand and contract. Other causes of noisy systems are trapped air (which needs to be bled off), partially closed valves, or defective fittings.

An automatic fill valve is usually located in the supply line to the boiler. This valve is usually placed right after the manual shut off valve. The system normally operates with water temperatures set around 130^{0} F. If the inspector observes water temperature in excess of 190^{0} F, it is possible that the system is undersized and being forced to compensate.

All boilers require the water in the system to be treated. This is done to prevent the accumulation of deposits that will eventually clog the entire system. If the water in the sight glass is dirty or rusty, the cause will be obvious. Sometimes the water in the sight glass is too clean. This can be an indication that a leak in the system is requiring a constant supply of fresh water to replenish it. If the rust line in the sight glass is well below the current water line, it may indicate a leak in the system.

Boilers need to be opened and manually cleaned every few years. If the boiler does not look like it has ever been disturbed, report this to your client.

When the boiler gets far enough ahead of the demand to allow the water temperature to rise to the level of the low limit switch plus the differential value, then the circulating pump will start again. When the circulating pump starts, heat energy is once again available to warm the living quarters.

It is important to follow the manufacturer's recommendations regarding differential spread. If the differential is too small, the boiler will cycle on and off continuously, annoying the occupants and causing wear and tear on the boiler.

Boiler Safety Controls

In order to make sure that a boiler and heating system under constant pressure are not so dangerous, safety controls are used. Several are cited and discussed below.

Relays

The relays that control the starting and stopping of the system should be enclosed in an electrical box. A home inspector should make note of any uncovered electrical connections.

Remember: fuel, plus spark, plus air = BOOM!

Pressure Relief Valve

In a hydronic system, the water is under constant pressure throughout the loop. All pressurized systems must be equipped with a functioning **pressure relief valve** to allow pressure to be released so that it does not cause an explosion. The pressure relief valve should be located on the high side of the boiler, and plumbed to a discharge point about eight inches from the floor. The terminal end of the discharge pipe should not be threaded.

The normal operating pressure for a sealed system is set at 12 to 25 PSI. The boiler should have a pressure gauge mounted in clear view. This gauge will have two needles: (1) one fixed and (2) one free to respond to fluctuating pressure. The fixed needle is pre-set 30 PSI, which is the upper safe operating limit.

If the inspector observes the free needle to be at 30 PSI or above, the system should be shut down and the appropriate service agency called to determine the cause of the high-pressure condition. High pressure in a hydronic boiler can be caused by an expansion tank or piping that is too small, a stuck fill valve, or an incorrect pressure.

High Temperature Limit Switch

This safety device is also referred to as the **aquastat**. It regulates the temperature of water and is based on the outside temperature. If the temperature of the water gets too hot, it will shut off the boiler.

It is critical for a hydronic heating system to have a functioning high temperature limit switch, because if the switch fails or is set too high, the water in the system can heat up to the point that it turns to steam. Steam occupies a volume 1,600 times as great as water and the resulting pressure will blow the system.

Low Water Shutoff

An important safety item in any boiler installation is the **low water shutoff**. This device will shut down the burner if the boiler is in danger of running out of water. If the boiler continues to fire after it runs out of water, it can damage the heat exchanger and destroy itself. This safety device can be checked by opening the dump valve for just a moment. As soon as the switch senses the falling water level, it should shut down the burner.

Backflow Preventer

The **backflow preventer** is a safety device that keeps boiler water from getting back into the home's potable water. It prevents backflow when the water to the home is shut off for repairs, and the only available water then comes from the boiler system.

The inspector should check to see that there is a backflow preventer, that it is installed correctly (not loose), and it is not leaking (if possible).

Expansion Tank

All hot water heating systems must have **expansion tanks** to deal with the fact that hot water expands. Expansion tanks are filled with both air and water to absorb the shock of pressure change.

Reportable Deficiencies - Expansion Tanks

- Filled only with water, losing the ability to absorb pressure
- Leaks
- Rust
- Too small for the system
- Poor location for the system

The Heat Exchanger

The heat exchanger of the hydronic system heats the water, which will deliver heat to the home. Some common materials used for the heat exchanger of a hydronic system include cast iron, steel, copper, and alloy.

Reportable Deficiencies - Heat Exchangers

- Leaks
- Rust
- Clogs

Distribution System

While air-based heating systems use ducts and vents to distribute air, hydronic heating systems use pumps, piping, and radiators to distribute and deliver the heat.

Pumps

The pump in a hydronic heating system has the same function as a blower or fan in the forced-air heating system. It pushes the medium that delivers the heat, in this case hot water, from the boiler source out to the rooms needing heat. The pressure put out by the pump also pushes the cool water back to the boiler where it will be reheated.

There are numerous types of pumps and ways to lubricate them. Each is relatively small and does not build up pressure on the system.

Reportable Deficiencies - Pumps

- Leaks
- Non-functional pump
- Too hot
- Too noisy

Piping

Piping in a hydronic heating system serves a similar function to ducts in a forced-air heating system—it carries the water to the rooms needing heat.

In older systems, typically the piping is black steel with steel or cast iron fittings or copper. Newer hydronic heat systems use plastic piping. The piping in heating systems lasts longer than in plumbing systems because it utilizes recycled water. Plumbing systems receive a fresh supply of water, which brings with it more oxygen and contaminants that can cause corrosion and rust. Heating pipes do not get as much exposure to these corrosion sources. Insulated piping keeps the water hot until it reaches the radiators.

Reportable Deficiencies - Hydronic System Piping

- Rusted, damaged, or crimped
- Improperly sized
- Poorly supported
- Leaking
- Improper insulation

Radiators, Convectors, and Baseboard Radiators

Radiators, convectors, and baseboard radiators are different devices that can be used by a hydronic heating system to release heat into a room. They differ in their appearance and capacity to heat.

Radiators are typically cast iron and, when on the floor, are supported by feet. They can also hang either on walls or from ceilings. They are most often uncovered because covering them reduces their ability to give off heat. Radiators are bulky, but have a greater capacity to heat a room than either convectors or baseboard radiators. They should have air bleed valves to release the trapped air in the radiator. If a "pounding" sound is heard, lift one edge of the radiator slightly to reduce the condensate blocking the pipes.

Convectors are like radiators in that they are usually made of cast iron. They differ because they are most often covered by a sheet metal cabinet with openings at the top to distribute warm air and openings at the bottom to draw in cool air. Additionally, convectors differ from radiators because they are smaller and have less capacity to heat a room.

Baseboard radiators are smaller heating components enclosed in a cabinet and located at the base of walls. They also have an opening at the top to release hot air and another at the bottom to draw in cool air. It takes a much longer baseboard radiator than a radiator or convector to heat a room due to its much smaller capacity.

Reportable Deficiencies - Radiators, Convectors, and Baseboard Radiators

- Rusted or leaking
- Covered or obstructed
- Improper location to effectively heat a room
- Not giving off enough heat
- Too small for the room
- Missing valve to release pressure
- Damage

Radiant Panels

Some hot water heating systems employ piping that is embedded in ceilings, floors, walls, and baseboards. These systems radiate heat out from a large surface to deliver a very even heat.

The piping itself can consist of wrought iron, copper, steel, or even plastics. The steel and wrought iron piping is usually only employed in floor applications as it is too heavy when filled with water for ceilings. The piping is usually laid in a grid or coil and spaced out no more than 12 inches between one another.

Occasionally a radiant panel heating system will have a boiler that will supply hot water that is too hot to put inside some surfaces, so it is blended. A hot water blender is also known as mixing or tempering valves. It blends cool water into the water from the boiler to achieve the desired temperature for use in the radiant heating pipes.

Reportable Deficiencies - Radiant Panels

Hot-water radiant heating systems can have some problems which can be very difficult to detect and very expensive to fix. Leaks in the piping itself can be big trouble as it is hard to detect when imbedded in walls or flooring. By the time it is known, extensive damage can be caused like erosion under a concrete slab, or weakening of walls or structural members.

The home inspector should:

- Locate the piping or coils of the system and check to see if the surface is being heated properly. Radiant surfaces should be warm to the touch within a few minutes of being turned on.
- Check the system for leaks. Be aware that a leak may not show unless the system is pressure tested by a service technician.
- Check the shutoff valves for each distribution area and the main balancing valves near the boiler for leaks.

Steam Heating System

In this system, steam is used to deliver the generated heat. The advantage of this system is that water absorbs a tremendous amount of heat energy in the process of turning to steam. This energy is then released when the steam condenses to a liquid. The way that this happens in a steam heating system is that the water first gets heated to steam in a boiler similar to the boiler in a hydronic heating system. Then the steam is carried through pipes to radiators that are located in each room of the house. The steam then condenses on the inside of the radiator, releasing its heat to warm the room. The condensed steam (water) is then carried back to the boiler where it is reheated.

Steam heat systems used in domestic applications are usually low-pressure systems. These systems are safer than high-pressure industrial systems. The piping can be any number of configurations.

Steam Heating Boilers and Boiler Controls

The boiler used in a steam heating system is similar to that used in a hydronic system, except that it runs about three-fourths full of water. In domestic applications, steam heat systems boilers are usually low-pressure systems, running at two to five pounds of pressure. These systems are safer than high-pressure industrial systems. Steam heating boilers are equipped with a number of monitoring and safety features. The boiler should have a water level gauge, pressure gauge, high-pressure limit switch, low water cut off, and a pressure release safety valve.

The **water level gauge** indicates how much water is in the boiler. Normal reading is about half-full. If the gauge is full of water, it means the boiler is flooded and the system requires draining. If the gauge is empty, it means that the boiler water level is too low and that it must be filled. If the gauge shows an unsteady reading, it indicates that there is sediment in the pipes. Water in the gauge should not be so dirty as to keep the inspector from reading the gauge. A **pressure gauge** indicates the amount of pressure in the boiler. A **high-pressure limit switch** turns off the burner when the boiler pressure exceeds a preset level, usually 5-7 PSI. To determine if the high-pressure cutoff switch is in good working condition, reduce the setting below the current pressure when the boiler is firing. The burner should immediately cut off. The low water cut off shuts down the burner if the boiler water gets too low. A **pressure release** (safety) **valve** allows some of the boiler contents to be discharged if the pressure exceeds 15 PSI.

Reportable Deficiencies - Steam Heating Systems

- Flooded boiler or water too low
- Sediment in the pipes
- Broken high-pressure cutoff switch
- Leaks when the system is activated
- Radiators are unevenly heating
- Pounding in the radiator

Wood Burning Heating Systems

Once used as the sole source of heat for the home, fireplaces are now used as a focal point for winter comfort. However, heating with wood was considered old-fashioned, and as soon as it became available and affordable, homeowners switched over to central heating. Recently, in response to rising energy costs and threats of energy shortages, wood heat once again is a more viable option for a heat source. Typically, wood is burned in **fireplaces** or woodstoves.

Masonry Fireplaces

Fireplaces are quite inefficient as a heat source but they are well liked for the cozy atmosphere they provide. Traditionally, masonry fireplaces have an open front fireplace and a chimney terminating above the roof.

These fireplaces may be fueled by wood alone, with natural gas assistance, or with natural gas solely. In the event the home has a natural gas fireplace with a gas log, the system should be lit and tested for functionality. Failure to light or stay lit as well as any gas leaks should be reported.

Figure 9.10
Fireplace

The main components of the masonry fireplace are the footing and foundation, firebox, hearth, damper, throat and smoke chamber, face, and chimney.

Foundation

Masonry fireplaces can be built of stone, brick, or other masonry material. They require a foundation that is tied to and consists of the same material as the foundation of the home. The exception to this would be when the fireplace is added to the home after it is built. Due to the weight of the masonry material used, it is imperative that this be a stable foundation and footing. Common problems of fireplace foundations and footings are similar to those of the home.

Reportable Deficiencies - Fireplace Foundation

- Cracks or settling
- Deterioration or damage
- Heaving or leaking

Firebox

The **firebox** is the place where the fire burns. It consists of masonry material that is rated for high temperatures of the flames and the hot embers that remain in it for hours at a time. It requires a steel supporting lintel over it.

Local codes governing the size and depth of fireboxes should be reviewed before an inspection as they vary from area to area. Combustible materials should be kept at least six inches from fireplace or firebox openings.

Reportable Deficiencies - Firebox

- Damaged or cracked
- Missing masonry
- Rusting of metal firebox parts
- Wrong materials that are not fire resistant

Hearth

The **hearth** is the floor of the firebox and the extension out in front of it. It is constructed of a non-combustible material, such as fire-rated bricks. Different parts of the hearth are sometimes referred to by different names. Some people refer to the part inside the firebox as the **inner hearth** or back hearth. Sometimes the area in front of the fireplace opening is called the **hearth extension,** outer hearth, or even the front hearth.

For safety, the hearth should extend at least eight inches on either side of the standard 36 inch wide fireplace opening and 16 inches in front.

Reportable Deficiencies - Hearth

- Too small
- Cracking or settling
- Wrong material used that is not fire resistant

Damper

The **damper** is at the top of the firebox. It is a gate allowing heated exhaust products to leave the house when a fire is burning and keeping cold air from entering or warm air from leaving the house when there is no fire.

Reportable Deficiencies - Damper

- Missing, blocked, or non functional
- Rusting
- Undersized
- Too low in the firebox

Throat and Smoke Chamber

The **throat** is the area at the top and the front of the firebox. The **smoke shelf** is an area behind the damper that is usually level and helps draw smoke upward.

The **smoke chamber** is a sloping part of the fireplace that is above the damper and throat but below the flue. These direct the exhaust gases of the large firebox into the smaller chimney flue opening. The idea is to compress the gases and create a good draft up the chimney. Problems of these parts can lead to poor draft of the exhaust gases up the chimney. Chimneys are the other major component of the fire-place and were previously reported on in the chapter on roofing.

Figure 9.11
Diagram showing details of home fireplace construction.

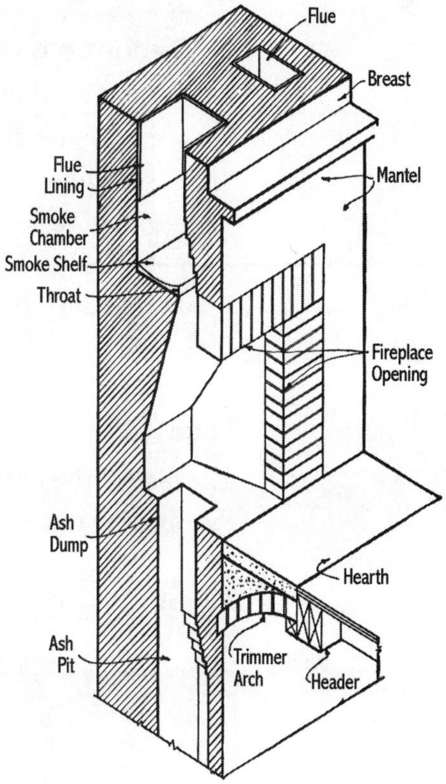

Reportable Deficiencies - Throat and Smoke Chamber

- Missing parts
- Excessive soot and debris
- Excessive or uneven slope

Flue

The **flue** is an internal passageway of the chimney which guides exhaust gases from a fireplace or other exhaust-producing appliances via vent connectors out of the home. It is usually lined with metal and is used for one fireplace. Flues may have other appliances connected to them depending on local codes. The inspector should check the flue liner for creosote deposits over 1/8" thick and report them if found. **Creosote build-up** is the burned remnants of the chemical preservative of wood known as creosote. These deposits can lead to the chimney catching on fire and potentially enveloping the entire home in flames.

Vent connectors from other appliances may connect to the flue. They must be securely connected and flush with the chimney wall. If the vent connectors in the flue are blocked, loose, or not flush, potentially fatal exhaust gases can travel back into the home.

Reportable Deficiencies - Flue

- More than one fireplace or appliance using only one flue
- Missing flue liner
- Creosote deposits build-up on flue liner
- Loose vent connectors in flue
- Incorrectly placed vent connector in flue
- Blocked vent connector in flue

Face

The **face** of the fireplace is the front wall of the chimney as well as the top of the opening to the fireplace. It is often decorated with a mantel.

Reportable Deficiencies - Face

- Cracking or loose material
- Being too thick or too thin
- Appearing to overheat

Prefabricated Fireplaces

Prefabricated fireplaces, built of steel and insulated with modern materials, can either be freestanding or open-front design. Those that are open front are sold in stock sizes to fit preframed openings. Open two-sided fireplace units are available and can be cantilevered or post-supported.

Prefabricated fireplaces, usually made of stamped steel, are sold in standard dimensions designed to fit in a pre-framed opening. These units come complete with firebox and flue. The steel flue extends through the ceiling or wall to the outside air. Safety requirements dictate that hearth extensions be constructed of brick, stone, hollow metal or other non-combustible material with a low index of thermal conductivity. These fireplaces must be located on a suitable non-combustible surface.

A home inspector should know the basic local code requirements of fireplaces as they vary from place to place.

Combustible materials such as wood framing must be kept at least two inches from the front and back of the fireplace and six inches from the flue liner. Firestops must be used wherever the flue passes framing, joists, headers, and trim.

Fireplace walls should be at least eight inches thick, and all surfaces that contact the flame should be surfaced with firebrick. The rear of the firebox is generally narrower than the front and tapers upward toward the front. This design creates a throat, which helps direct the smoke up the flue. A smoke shelf should be located above the damper to prevent back drafts.

Wood Stoves

Wood stoves are often called space heaters for their ability to heat an area, but not really an entire home. They do not have ducting or piping connected to them which makes it hard to heat other rooms.

Wood stoves are sometimes used for cooking as well. Most wood stoves now are for pleasure, like fireplaces with glass doors.

Figure 9.12
Wood stoves are used for space heating and for cooking. In earthquake areas, wood stoves should be anchored to the floor and the stovepipe secured to reduce potential fire.

Wood stoves consist of the shell and legs, the combustion chamber where the fire burns, the vent connector to the chimney for exhaust gas release and the chimney itself. They can be made of steel or iron with firebrick liners inside. They often have glass doors and employ black steel for the vent connections.

The wood stove should be centrally located by the primary living area. The home inspector should note if the wood stove is in a small confined space, as they do not get the air they need and can overheat.

Reportable Deficiencies - Wood Stoves

- Wobbly or missing legs, poor support
- Cracked or warped parts
- Smoke leaking
- Loose or poorly fitting doors
- Combustible material clearance not enough
- Malfunctioning dampers
- Lack of air for combustion
- Poor vent connection
- Too long of vent connectors
- Wrong materials used for vent connectors
- Rusting of vent connectors
- Deposits in vent connector or combustion chamber
- Multiple appliances connected to one chimney

10

Chapter

Central Cooling Systems

Introduction

Air conditioning is a central cooling system that is now a standard feature of most new homes. It can make the interior of the home very comfortable during the hot and humid summer months by lowering both the temperature and humidity to that of a cool fall day. It also allows the home to stay quieter as windows do not need to be open for air movement, thereby stopping outside noise.

An efficient air conditioning system should be able to reduce ambient temperature by 15^{0} F to 20^{0} F. The home inspector can check the cooling system by measuring the temperature at the discharge duct before and after starting the system

Basic Operation

Air conditioning is based on the principle of physics that when a solid is liquefied, or when compressed air expands, it absorbs heat. An air conditioning system contains a refrigerant that is designed to easily absorb and give off heat. The air conditioning system moves the refrigerant so that it can absorb heat when it is in a house and release the heat when it is moved to the outside of the house.

Most air conditioners are constructed as a "split system." This means that the portion of the air conditioning system that absorbs heat is located inside the house and the portion that gives up heat is located outside of the house. The air conditioning system can be thought of as one long tube with two devices on it that control the flow of the refrigerant. There are eight basic steps in the cooling cycle.

Step 1 The air conditioning cycle starts when a thermostat in the house senses that the temperature inside the house is too warm. This triggers the thermostat to turn on the air conditioning system. The first part of the system to start is the compressor. Before the compressor starts, the refrigerant in the system's pipes is close to the temperature of the air that surrounds them. That is, the refrigerant that is in the system's pipes that are inside the house is about the same temperature as the inside of the house and the refrigerant that is in system's pipes that are outside the house is about the same temperature as the outside air.

Step 2 The compressor first pulls the refrigerant that is in the house side of the system towards it. This refrigerant is in the form of gas that is under low pressure.

Step 3 The compressor then compresses the refrigerant so that it becomes a high-pressure, high-temperature gas.

Step 4 The compressor then sends this high-temperature gas to the portion of the refrigerant line that is outside the house. A part of this portion is called the outside **coil** or **condenser**. A coil is a line that winds back and forth on itself so that many feet of the line are in a small space. This allows this area of the line to function as a heat exchanger with its environment.

Step 5 A fan blows relatively cool outside air across the outside coil (condenser). The heat that the refrigerant picked up by being compressed is transferred to the air that passes over the coil. As the refrigerant gives up its heat, it condenses to a high temperature high-pressure liquid. It then passes out of the coil towards the expansion valve. It comes back inside the house at this point.

Step 6 The expansion valve controls how much refrigerant is released to an inside coil, often called an **evaporator**. The expansion valve is connected to a sensor that monitors the temperature of the inside coil. The temperature of the inside coil determines how much refrigerant the expansion valve releases. When the expansion valve releases the high-temperature high-pressure liquid refrigerant, it does so through a very small hole. Releasing this small amount of refrigerant into this relatively large space causes it to quickly expand and turn into a low-temperature low-pressure gas. It is in this state that the refrigerant enters the evaporator.

Step 7 A fan blows relatively warm inside air across the inside coil (evaporator).

Step 8 The refrigerant absorbs the heat from the air that passes over the coil and becomes a moderate-temperature low-pressure gas. As the refrigerant absorbs the air's heat, it is pulled towards the compressor where the cycle begins again. The air that passes across the evaporator is cooled. This air is circulated to the rooms of the house by ducts.

Cool air cannot hold as much humidity as warm air, so during the process of cooling, the humidity in the house air is condensed to water. This water is removed via a system of condensate drain lines plumbed to the outside.

Air Conditioning System Components

The basic components of an air conditioning system are compressor, condenser, evaporator, refrigerant lines, expansion valves, distribution ducts, and thermostat.

Compressor

The heart of a refrigeration system is the **compressor**. The purpose of the compressor is to reduce the refrigerant gas into a liquid and circulate it through the system.

The compressor is powered by an electric motor and is usually supplied with 220 volts. It is usually located in a cabinet outside the house and looks like a large, black cylinder.

There are five types of compressors: reciprocating or piston, scroll, centrifugal, screw, and rotary. Most homes have reciprocating, scroll, or rotary types.

The piston compressor uses a piston in a cylinder to compress the refrigerant and a series of valves to move the pressurized refrigerant through the piping.

The scroll type of compressor utilizes a fixed scroll and a moveable scroll to generate an infinite number of piston strokes to compress the refrigerant. A start kit prevents damage to the motor during the heavy load experienced at start-up.

A crankcase heater keeps refrigerant in the crankcase of a compressor in a vapor state, so it does not boil at start-ups and remove lubricating oil. A low ambient temperature switch keeps the fan from energizing during low outside temperature operation. This prevents low head pressure that could damage a compressor. A high-pressure switch prevents a compressor from operating if head pressure becomes too high.

A low-pressure switch prevents a compressor from operating if suction pressure drops to an unsafe level. A compressor depends on sufficient suction pressure for cooling. A principal cause of low suction pressure is a loss of refrigerant.

A time-out interlock prevents the compressor from fast cycling. This automatic delay enables the pressure in an air conditioning system to equalize before the next start cycle is initiated.

Two-Speed Compressors

Many installations employ a **two-speed compressor.** In a two-speed installation, if the cooling demand is not too great the compressor operates at low speed and conserves power. When maximum demand is reached, the compressor switches to high speed to provide additional cooling capacity.

The two-speed compressor operates automatically on either of two speeds to match cooling capacity to ambient conditions. Even during the summer months, cooling demand rarely exceeds minimum requirements. This enables the compressor to run at a low speed, resulting in substantial energy savings.

Modern reciprocating compressors are protected from the destructive consequences of "**slugging**" (entrance of freon liquid) by the use of spring loaded discharge valves and high-intake ports. The motor is engineered to run at lower temperatures by locating it within the cooler refrigerant zones.

These two-speed compressors incorporate a latent load discriminating device to increase their efficiency. This device controls the speed of the indoor evaporator blower to match it to the load requirements.

In addition to a variable speed blower, the load discriminator also uses a humidistat to sense ambient humidity. This allows the load discriminator to tailor the running requirements to the load.

Reportable Deficiencies - Compressors

- Running continuously (on mild days)
- Not running long enough (known as short cycling)
- Excessive noise like knocking
- No noise at all
- Vibration
- Incorrect fuse or breaker size (which can cause possible fire and other damage)
- Incorrect electrical wiring (which can cause poor performance or fire)
- Missing electrical shutoff (which can make maintenance difficult)
- Unit out of level (which can cause a loss of lubrication and damage)
- Unit not cooling enough (which can create high-energy costs and discomfort in the home).

Run Capacitor

The **run capacitor** reduces power surges by absorbing electrical spikes and providing power when needed to keep the flow even to the compressor. If this item is damaged it will develop a bulge and should be reported.

Condenser

The **condenser** or **condenser coil** is composed of aluminum fins installed over copper tubing that transfer the heat from the refrigerant to the outside air. The coils have a large surface area. As air is blown over them, heat leaves the refrigerant and is transferred to the outside.

A condenser fan forces the air through the condenser. The condenser needs to be clean to work efficiently. A condenser can become dirty due to yard debris, such as grass clippings, leaves, or lint, if the condenser is located too close to a clothes dryer exhaust outlet. As the refrigerant passes through the condenser's tube and its heat gets removed, it condenses from gas back to a liquid.

The compressor, condenser coil and condenser fan are all housed inside a cabinet that is often referred to as the **condenser unit**. Proper location of the condenser unit is important. If the unit is located too near the exhaust of a water heater, the acidic exhaust can corrode metal parts.

Figure 10.1
Condenser coil

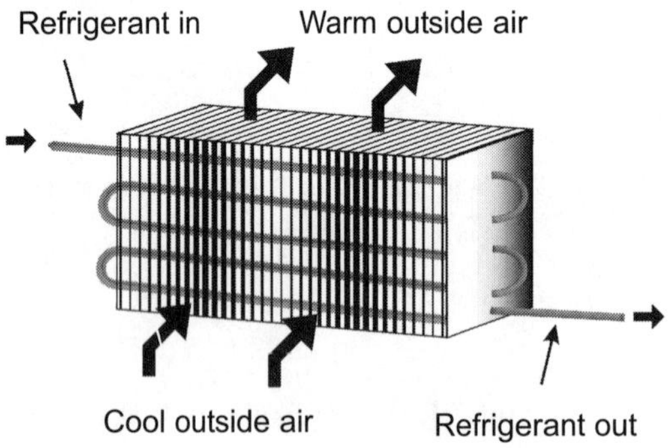

Not all condensers transfer heat to the surrounding air, some use water to cool the coil. A water-cooled condenser coil does not need to be located outside, but may be situated in the home near the evaporator coil. The advantage of this arrangement is a longer service life for the condenser due to predictable air conditions inside the home.

The downside is that some of the heat from the condenser coil is released inside the home. This causes the air conditioning system to work harder. This type of system also wastes a lot of water as the heated water from the condenser coil simply goes down the drain.

Reportable Deficiencies - Condenser Coil

- Condenser coils dirty (inhibiting their ability to transfer heat to the outside)
- Damaged parts (like corroded fins)
- Leaks (which reduce airflow and system performance)
- Exhaust of water heater too close (acidic exhaust from water heater can corrode parts)
- Exhaust of clothes dryer too close by (which clogs condenser with lint).

Evaporator

The part of the air conditioning system that actually cools the air is called the **evaporator** or **evaporator coil**. It is usually made of copper tubes with fins. It is located inside the home, and can be in an attic, basement, crawlspace, or even a closet. The purpose of the evaporator is to contain low-temperature low-pressure refrigerant, which absorbs heat from air in the house. As with the condenser coil, if the evaporator coil is dirty, its efficiency will be reduced.

Evaporator coils come in three varieties. The slab type has a rectangular shape that is placed below the lower end of the coil with one condensate tray. The "A" coil is composed of two slabs or legs that fasten together in the shape of the letter "A". It also has a condensate tray below the legs. The shape allows air to flow through the coils.

The "O" style of coil is a cylindrical evaporator that is placed in the condensate pan. The unique shape allows a more efficient airflow to the coils and removal of warm air from the home.

Reportable Deficiencies - Evaporator

- No access to the evaporator
- Dirty coils
- Damaged coils
- Corroded coils

Refrigerant Lines

The components of an air conditioning system are connected by copper tubing. One of the reasons copper tubing is used is its ability to create leak-proof joints.

A larger diameter line connects the evaporator and the compressor. It is called the **suction line**. This line is larger and insulated because it is carrying the refrigerant in a gaseous state where it occupies a greater volume.

A line that goes from the discharge side of the compressor to the inlet of the condenser is called the **hot gas line**.

A smaller line that allows refrigerant to flow from the condenser to the expansion valve and evaporator that is not insulated is called the **liquid line.**

Reportable Deficiencies - Connective Refrigerant Lines

- Leaks
- Missing insulation
- Lines that are too warm
- Lines that are too cold
- Damaged lines
- Lines that touch each other

Expansion Valve

In order for the system to work properly, the refrigerant must change from a high-pressure, high-temperature liquid to a low-pressure, low-temperature gas. This is accomplished by the use of an **expansion valve**, also known as a **metering device**.

This expansion valve comes in two forms with identical functions. The most common type to be found in homes is called the **RFC** (refrigerant flow control) or **capillary tube**. This type of metering device is a small copper tube that has no moving parts. The other type is a TEV or **thermostatic expansion valve.** This type contains moving parts that open and close. It is most often found in commercial applications.

The purpose of these controls is to regulate both the flow rate and pressure of the refrigerant. This is done to match the cooling capacity with the load.

The expansion devices of the air conditioning have common defects such as loose valves or connections, leaks, sticking valves, and clogged openings. All of these can result in a reduced refrigerant flow and performance problems with the system.

Reportable Deficiencies - Expansion Valves

- Tube defects
- Loose valves
- Loose connections
- Leaks
- Sticking valves
- Clogged openings

Distribution Ducts

The **duct** system moves cool, dry air to the rooms in the home. Some homes also have ducts that go to each room to return moist warm air to the evaporator for cooling. Most simply allow the warm air to be drawn to the evaporator via an intake grill near the evaporator. This duct system is most often the same one used for heating purposes as well.

Problems with under-sized ducting are common, especially when the air conditioning system is added to an existing heating system. Home additions and renovations are sometimes left without ducting, as it is very expensive to install. If this is the case, no cool air will be delivered to these areas, although it can drift in through an open door or window. This means insufficient or unequal cooling in the home will most likely be the result.

Figure 10.2
Air conditioning distribution ducting

Air-conditioning system supply and return registers are best set near the top of rooms, so the cool air can fall down through the warmer air and create more even temperatures. A problem arises when the ducting system is shared with a forced-air heating system. Heating systems work best when the heat enters the room near the floor, as the warmed air will rise up to provide a more even temperature. More efficient cooling is provided when the supply and returns are properly placed in the home.

There should also be adequate insulation on the ducting to prevent cooling loss as the air travels through the home. The goal is to condition the lived-in areas, not the areas that ducting travels through like the attic or even crawl space.

Reportable Deficiencies - Ducting

- Leaking
- Poor supports
- Poor connections
- Broken or crushed ducting
- Dirty ducts
- Missing dampers
- Inadequate insulation
- Undersized ducting

Thermostats

Thermostats are used to turn the cooling system on and off at the correct times to keep the room temperatures comfortable. They are put in locations that have temperatures that are representative of the entire home.

Figure 10.3
A modern thermostat can be programmed.

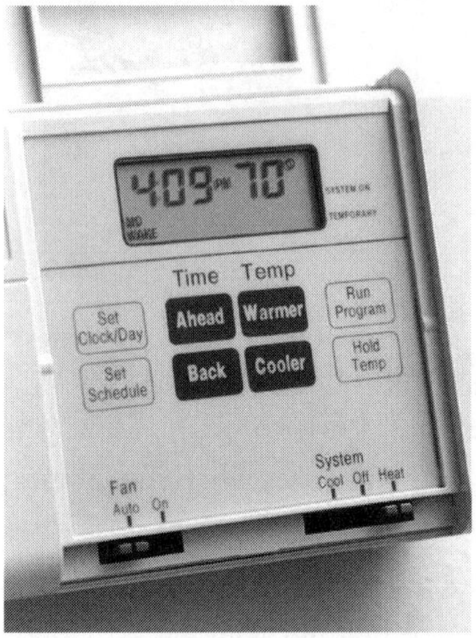

If a home has both central heating and air conditioning, a single thermostat is generally used to control both systems. This is important to avoid having both systems running simultaneously.

Many modern thermostats are programmable. The home inspector should know the different types and be able to operate them without disturbing the settings and the homeowner. It may be advisable to carry instructions for the common types in order to perform a more efficient inspection.

Reportable Deficiencies - Thermostats

- Poor location for representative home temperature
- Thermostat that doesn't function
- Thermostat that is not calibrated
- Thermostat that does not work correctly
- Loose thermostat
- Dirty thermostat

Checking the Cooling System

There is not a great deal for the home inspector to inspect in a residential air conditioning system. Check the following items:

- If the temperature in the house is above 65° F, start the system and measure the temperature of the air being delivered at a register. The system should be able to reduce the temperature by at least 15° F. If the outside temperature is below 65° F do not operate the system. You will not learn about its ability to deliver cool air, and you may damage the compressor because of low head pressure.
- Make sure that the unit starts smoothly with no unusual noise or vibration.
- Check to see that the refrigerant lines are properly insulated.
- Check to see that the hole where the refrigerant lines enter the building is sealed. Make sure that the condensate drain line is installed and unblocked.
- Check the system for leaks. The refrigerant in a home cooling system is under pressure and the inspector should be aware of any potentially dangerous leaks.

Heat Pumps

Heat pumps can be used to cool air, but they are primarily used for heating. For that reason, they are discussed in detail in the Heating chapter of this book.

Heat pumps are highly specialized and often hard to tell apart from air-conditioning units. Some ways to differentiate heat pumps from traditional air-conditioning units are:

- the data plate on it may say heat pumps or start with HP.
- an emergency heating setting is present on the thermostat.

- the thermostat has two stages. (You will have to remove the cover to determine this.)
- the unit is operating during winter.
- the two Freon™ lines are insulated.
- the unit contains a reversing valve inside of the condenser cabinet.
- the compressor is indoors.

The list of reportable deficiencies for heat pumps is located in the Heating chapter of this book.

11

Chapter

Pools, Spas, and Saunas

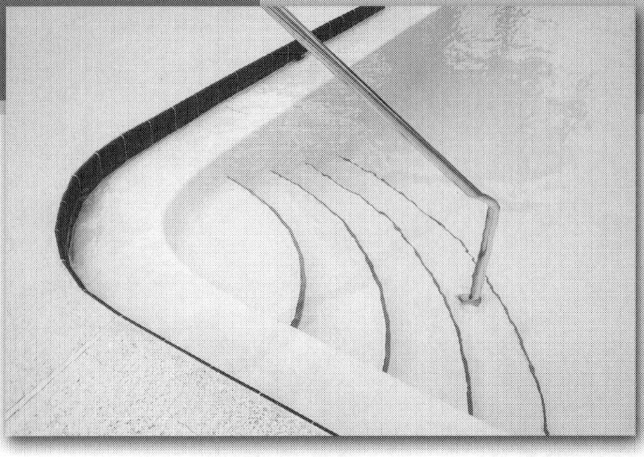

Introduction

The **swimming pool** is becoming more and more prevalent in residential areas. It may be above ground or level with the backyard. Pools are shells that can hold water without letting it leak into the ground.

A spa or hot tub is a small pool filled with circulating hot water, for therapeutic soaking. It can be freestanding, attached to a pool, above ground or even in ground.

A sauna is a Scandinavian creation that consists of a small, sealed room made of wood with the provision to heat it to a temperature of 150° F or more.

Swimming Pools

The most common materials used in pool construction are concrete, fiberglass, and vinyl. Concrete is the most popular material used for pool construction because of its strength and stability. When combined with reinforcing steel bars, concrete overcomes the forces of surrounding soil expansion and contraction.

There are two techniques used to make swimming pools when using concrete. It can be poured in place or air-sprayed into place. Of these choices, air-sprayed concrete, known as **gunite**, is the most widespread. This form of construction is relatively inexpensive and allows a great deal of design flexibility. In gunite pool construction, a mixture of sand and cement is sprayed onto a form made of steel rebar and directly onto the soil.

Figure 11.1
Concrete swimming pool

Fiberglass pools are prefabricated and shipped to the site ready to use. Advantages of fiberglass are its smooth easy-to-clean surface and its ability to absorb some movement without cracking. The disadvantage of fiberglass is that the size of the pool is limited by transportation restrictions. The fiberglass shell is set into an excavation lined with sand.

Vinyl is used as the non-leaking container for the water in the pool. The vinyl skin must be supported by a rigid wall to hold the weight of the water. After a suitable excavation is dug, a solid wall of wood, steel, or fiberglass is constructed. The vinyl liner is placed into this form and filled with water. Vinyl liners are best suited to regular shapes, such as rectangles and circles. The vinyl skin can be punctured relatively easily, but it can be repaired just as easily.

The water in a pool should be level when inspected. To check for levelness, simply observe the water line relative to the pool, using the decorative tiles as a straight edge. If the pool is more than ¼ of an inch out of level, it may indicate movement due to hydrostatic pressure.

Pool Systems

Residential swimming pool systems include the pool, filtration system, heater, timer, cleaners, fencing and gates, decking, and other various accessories.

Filtration System

The system contains the pump, filter, connecting plumbing, and skimmer. The filtration system is also used to dispense the chemicals required for proper sanitation of the water. Deficiencies in the filtration system will manifest themselves as cloudy or bad-smelling water.

Pool Pump

The **pump** or sump in a swimming pool must have adequate power to cycle the entire water volume of the pool through the filter and remove dirt and other debris in a certain number of hours. This is known commonly as the turnover rate. Requirements for this time to cycle the water will vary by pool size but most vary from 8-to-12 hours.

The **flow rate** of the pump is the number of gallons of water that are cycled through the system per minute. This is figured out by dividing the pool's water capacity by the turnover rate. This gives a gallon(s) per hour figure that then can be divided down into a gallon(s) per minute figure.

Pool Filter

At the heart of the pool's circulation system is the **filter**. The actual filter agent is available in cartridge, sand, and **diatomaceous earth (DE) types.** If properly designed for the application, all three types are equally effective. All filter systems need to be cleaned on a regular basis in order to maintain their effectiveness.

The condition of the filter is monitored by the use of a pressure gauge on the inlet side of the system. This pressure refers to the waterpressure on the filtration system. As the filter removes dirt and debris, it gets filled and the pressure increases. When the pressure increases to a predetermined level, it is time to clean the filter.

Cleaning is accomplished by rinsing the cartridge type, and back washing the sand and DE filters. The back-washing process is accomplished by temporarily reversing the water flow through the filter and disposing of the effluent or waste debris.

Pool Skimmer

An important device in the filtration system of the pool is the surface **skimmer**. This appliance is designed to filter the surface water of the pool and remove body oil, suntan lotion, leaves, and other debris. The surface skimmer traps these pollutants and keeps them from accumulating on the surface of the pool.

Pool Heater

To maximize the amount of time available for pool use, many systems employ a heater. **Pool heaters** can be fueled with gas, electricity, oil, or solar energy. When available, gas heat is the most economical. Heat can be added to the water by a solar gathering pool cover as well.

If the system has a heater, the home inspector should determine if it is operational. During cold weather, the pool temperature will indicate if the heater is working, as it should be greater than the air temperature. The inspector will not be able to check the efficiency of the pool heater however, because the effects take too long to notice during a regular home inspection.

Various health organizations recommend a water temperature of 78°F to 82°F in a heated pool.

Pool Timers

The various filtration and heating cycles are controlled by electric or solid state timers. These devices can initiate up to six different cycles per day. They can be programmed to operate the skimmer, the heater, the circulation filter, and the lights. This helps to keep the pool properly filtered and the chemicals balanced.

Pool Vacuum

Along with the skimmers and filters, some pools employ automatic **pool vacuum cleaners** to aid in filtration and maintain pool cleanliness. These vacuum cleaners travel along the bottom of the pool and collect debris. This debris is collected in a bag or piped into the main filtration system.

Fencing and Gates

The rules requiring childproof enclosures for pools are very specific, and the home inspector should be completely familiar with them.

All swimming pools should have a fence or other wall that completely surrounds the pool and obstructs access to it for safety. The top of the fence or wall should be at least 48" above the level of the pool deck with no more than two inches of clearance beneath it. The spacing of the vertical parts of the fence can be no more than four inches apart.

The gate or gates of the fence must be self-closing and open out or away from the pool. The locking mechanism of the gate should be no more than three inches from the top of the gate.

Sometimes a dwelling wall can be part of a fence or obstruction from the pool. If this dwelling wall also contains a door, it must be self-closing with an alarm.

In above-ground pools, the ladder must be removable or otherwise secured to prevent access to the pool.

Decking

The **decking** around a pool creates a frame for the pool itself and a safe walkway around it. This deck should have enough space for pool furniture and other accessories like diving boards, ladders, and slides. This decking material should not be slippery when wet, be heat reflective and have a slope away from the pool of about one inch for every six feet. This slope ensures that sprinkler or hose runoff, rainwater or even splashed water from the pool cannot drain back into the pool. Poured concrete is the most common type of decking material. Brick, stone, wood and even tile can also be used on top of a concrete slab. The material used needs to resist the acidic nature of pool chemicals, fungi, bacteria and algae growth, and even freezing.

The home inspector should check the overall condition of the decking and make sure it has the proper slope away from the pool to inhibit runoff entering.

Accessories

Pool accessories include ladders, diving boards, and slides. All of the components, if present, must be bonded or anchored to the decking.

Many pools have steps built into them. If the shallow end of a pool is deeper than two feet, steps or a ladder is required. If the pool is over 40' long, a ladder is required in the deep end. If the pool is over 30' feet wide, two ladders are required.

Diving boards are sometimes found in residential pools with a depth of more than seven and a half feet or as deep as required by local codes. There are usually minimum dimension for the size of the boards as well.

Slides need to be placed away from diving boards or ladders. There are codes for lengths and water depths but generally short slides must empty into at least four feet of water, and long slides must empty into at least six feet of water. Slides should also extend out over the water and water coming down them should fall into the pool.

Electrical Components

All electrical connections for pools must be grounded due to their proximity to water. Additional GFCI protection is required for all lighting circuits used near a pool or spa. This is done to reduce the possibility of shock or electrocution.

All GFCI units should be inspected to make sure they are in proper working order.

Plumbing Components

Plumbing included in swimming pools includes main drain piping, skimmer piping, return piping, and other piping. Most of the plumbing is buried under the pool, so it is imperative that the installation be done by a licensed, experienced plumbing contractor. The plumbing should be thoroughly tested for leaks before the concrete is poured.

The home inspector should start the circulation pump and after a few minutes check for bubbles in the plumbing system. Air bubbles in the return line piping indicate a leak in the plumbing at the suction side. A leak in the discharge side will be evidenced by wet spots in the area surrounding the pool or low water in the pool. This is a way to check for problems even though the plumbing system is buried underground and beneath the pool.

Reportable Deficiencies - Swimming Pool

- Noisy pumps
- Clogged filters
- Algae on surface of water, cloudy water
- Inoperative heater, pressure gauges, or lights
- No GFCI or other grounding for electrical components
- Bulging in wall or bottom of pool

- Cracking, chipping, or missing tiles
- Poor drainage of decking
- Unsecured or poorly secured diving board, ladder, or slide
- Missing ladder
- Missing safety fencing, gates, or inoperative gate lock

Spas and Hot Tubs

Although similar in construction to a swimming pool, a **spa** or **hot tub** is much smaller. The distinction between spa and hot tub is largely semantic, but the term "hot tub" usually refers to a round structure made from woods like cedar, redwood, cypress, oak or even teakwood.

Figure 11.2
Example of a spa attached to a pool.

Most spas are sold as portable units due to their relatively small size and only need to be filled with water and connected to power to be enjoyed. Spas must be grounded, which must be separate from the ground for pools. Spas are usually equipped with a filter, a pump, a motor and water jets that deliver a soothing stream of hot water to tired muscles. Additionally, spas have air jets that provide a massage using air bubbles.

Portable spas contain 400 to 800 gallons of water and can weigh up to four tons when full. Most spas hold around 2,000 gallons of water and will weigh over 20,000 pounds when fully filled with water and people. For this reason, they need to be placed on a concrete pad or foundation.

The volume of water is much less and the temperature is much higher than a swimming pool so attention to the chemistry is critical. The higher temperatures used in a spa promote bacteria growth and dissipate the chemicals more quickly. Hot tubs and spas are operated with temperatures between

98° F and 104° F. The maximum water depth is four feet. The maximum depth for a bench or seat is two feet below the water. Steps or a ladder should be provided if the water depth exceeds two feet. The turnover rate for water in a hot tub or spa should be no more than one hour.

Reportable Deficiencies - Spas or Hot Tubs

- Algae on surface of water, cloudy water
- Inoperative heater, pressure gauges, or lights
- No GFCI or other grounding for electrical components
- Inoperable water or air jets

Saunas

The therapeutic value of dry heat was first recognized by the Scandinavians over two-thousand years ago. Americans were introduced to the benefits of the sauna in 1638. During the last couple of decades, an increasing number of these devices have been installed in this country.

The sauna is a wooden shed-like structure equipped with a heater capable of raising the temperature inside to between 150° F and 200° F. The heat produced in a sauna is very dry. This dry heat produces increased perspiration, which aids in cleansing the skin pores. The heat also increases circulation and relaxes muscles.

The stove that supplies the heat has a shelf that holds small stones. Periodically the occupants of the sauna will throw water on the hot stones and generate a cloud of steam.

The electrical controls should be mounted outside the sauna, to protect them from the high temperatures, and to prevent perspiration-soaked individuals from electric shock.

The inside of the sauna should be equipped with a thermometer and a hygrometer. These instruments measure the temperature and humidity of the air inside the sauna.

The sauna should be allowed to dry between periods of use, and the benches should be scrubbed regularly with detergent to get rid of odors and bacteria.

Reportable Deficiencies - Saunas

- Evidence of dry rot or algae growth
- Inoperative thermostat, controls, or lights
- No GFCI or other grounding for electrical components

12 Chapter

Pests and Other Environmental Hazards

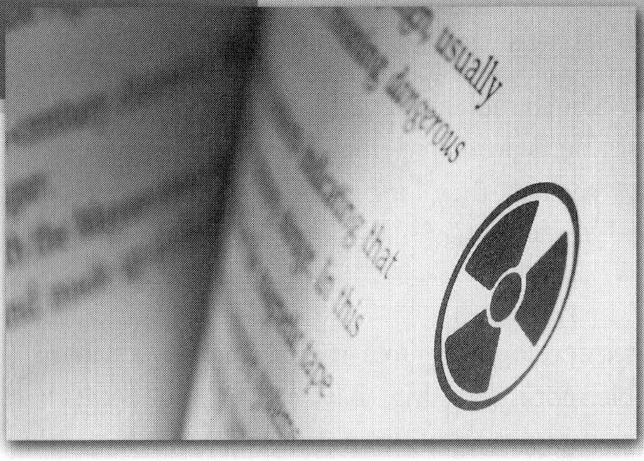

Introduction

The home inspector should be able to identify other problems in the home related to insect and animal infestations as well as plants and other environmental hazards that can cause diseases and allergies. These home invaders can weaken the structural members of the home making it uninhabitable. In many cases, a special license or advanced training is needed in order to perform these inspections.

Insects

Insects comprise the most diverse group of animals on the earth, with over 800,000 species. That is more than all other animal groups combined. Since insects are found in nearly every environment on the planet, including the oceans, it is no surprise that they invade our properties.

Termites

Most states have laws regulating the activity of termite inspectors. For this reason, home inspectors should phrase their reports in very general terms if evidence of infestation is found. Evidence of an infestation can be noted and further inspection by a professional termite inspector should be recommended. There are thousands of species of termites, but only a few pose a major problem in the United States. They are the subterranean, drywood, dampwood, and Formosan termites.

Subterranean Termites

The Subterranean termite can be found anywhere in the country because it lives in an underground nest that is protected from freezing. The inspector can recognize these termites because they look like grains of rice. These termites feed on wood and create a system of tunnels and tubes by combining saliva, sand, and excrement.

During the spring, the termites develop wings to carry them to new locations. Once they swarm to a suitable spot for nesting, they shed their wings. If the home inspector notices an accumulation of dried insect wings, it is a sure sign that there are termites nearby. Any evidence of the tubes or tunnels produced by termites should be noted on the inspection report with a callout for further investigation.

Sometimes the homeowner will attempt to treat the termite problem without professional help. This may produce a situation where the cure is worse than the disease. The inspector should notify the client if any residue of pesticide is discovered around the premises. The use of these poisons by untrained personnel can be dangerous.

Drywood Termites

These termites create their nests above ground. Because of this, they are found in the warmer parts of the country. A residential infestation of dry wood termites will usually be found in the attic or other high spot in the home. They do not require an independent source of water because they derive the needed moisture from their food source.

Evidence of infestation of these creatures is the football-shaped pellets that are pushed from the nest. These pellets can be found in the attic or outside the home. Sometimes the only sign of termite infestation is the failure of some structural member.

Figure 12.1
Drywood termite infestation

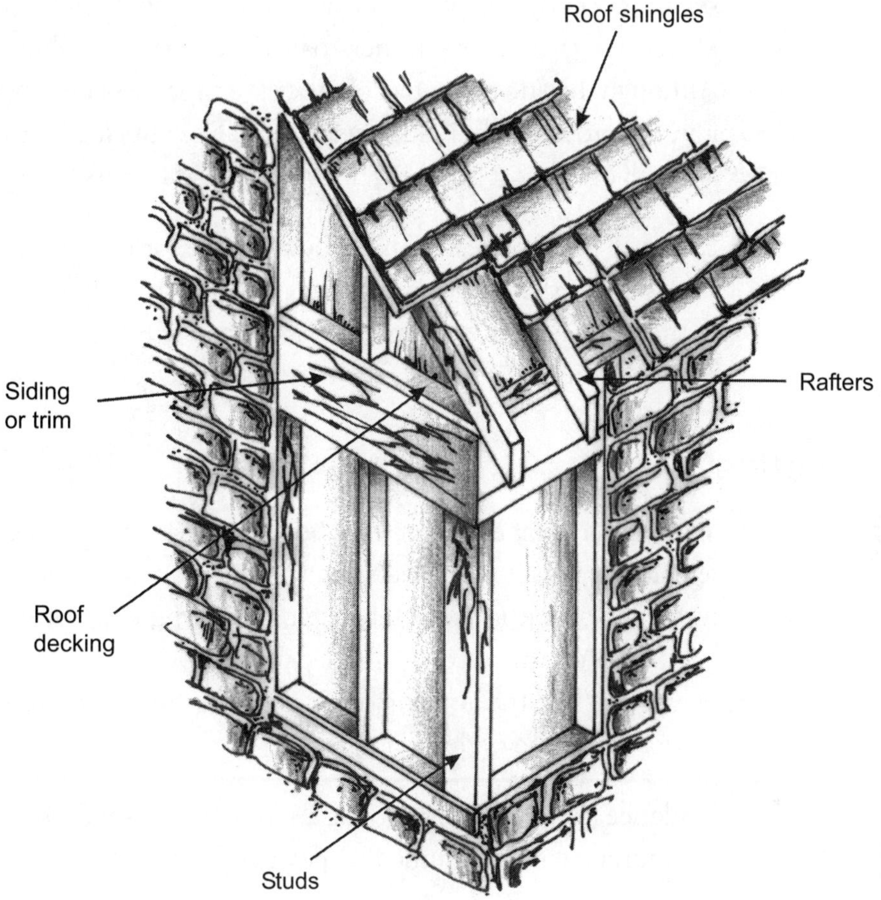

Dampwood Termites

These pests are rarely found inside the home but more likely in the areas immediately adjacent to the house where there is abundant moisture. These insects do not construct tubes.

Formosan Termites

The Formosan termite is found in Texas and Louisiana, but its range is gradually increasing. The Formosan colony is usually much larger than the subterranean termite. There are indications that this species may be able to eat through metal and plaster in order to get at the wood it uses for food.

Ants

Potentially more harmful than termites, these insects will congregate near small sources of moisture. The carpenter ant does not follow a chemical trail like the sugar ant, but rather roams the entire dwelling looking for food. Although they do not eat wood, they are capable of destroying a great deal of it in the process of building their nests. The ants feed on sugary substances, and will eat almost anything, including dead insects.

Evidence of these pests can be found in the form of sawdust-like accumulations outside the nesting area. The nests are often difficult to locate however as they may hide in obscure places and can travel great distances. Denying these pests a food source is the most effective control.

Beetles

There are a number of species of beetles whose larvae can destroy wood. The female deposits her eggs beneath the surface of the wood. The egg hatches into a larva that immediately begins digesting the surrounding wood. The larva feeds on the starch contained in the wood and excretes the rest as a fine powder. When the larva matures, it breaks out of the capsule and looks for a mate to start the cycle over again.

Evidence of beetle infestation is a series of very small holes found in a wood structural member and the fine powder deposited near them.

Roaches

These nocturnal creatures are often brought into the home in packages from the grocery store. They will eat anything they can find and contaminate any food they touch. The best defense against these hardy insects is to deny them access to any food source.

Figure 12.2
A series of very small holes in wood is evidence of beetle damage.

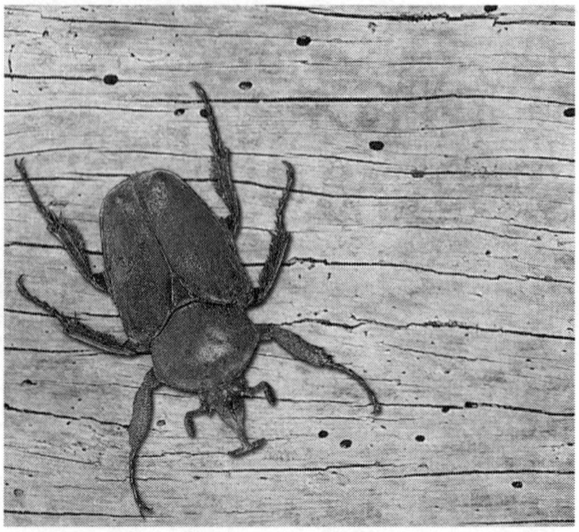

Bees and Wasps

The most obvious sign of the invasion of carpenter bees is a small hole about a $^1/_2$ inch in diameter in a piece of siding or trim. The bee digs tunnels through the wood to find sites to lay eggs.

Yellow jackets can be identified by the thin black stripes on the yellow body. These insects are aggressive about protecting their nests, and one yellow jacket can deliver several painful stings. They can be eliminated by spraying the nest with insecticide during the night when the insects are dormant.

Figure 12.3
Paper wasp nest

The paper wasp builds the typical large round beige structure that most people associate with the term wasp nest. These wasps are not particularly aggressive and do not pose any threat to the structure that they inhabit. If it becomes necessary to destroy the nest, it can be done at night when the wasps are inactive.

Animals

It is important to recognize the damage that can be caused by various types of animals on the home as well. While most are a nuisance, they can also be very destructive on the home and its components.

Mice

Mice infestation can often be determined by their characteristic droppings even before they are seen. They can sometimes be heard scurrying around the house after dark. Mice can gnaw their way through most food containers to get at grains and cereals. Mice can carry various diseases that can contaminate a home. A mousetrap baited with peanut butter will invariably produce results in one night.

Rats

Rats are much more destructive and potentially dangerous than mice. These animals are carriers of disease and are difficult to trap. If the signs of a rat problem are found, a professional exterminator should be called. A slow-acting poison is used to control rats. The rats die outside the home after ingesting the bait. A rat hole is about an inch in diameter, and the home inspector should report any evidence of these rodents.

Skunks, Opossums, and Raccoons

While these animals are not destructive, they can be dangerous because they may be disease carriers (e.g., rabies). They are easily trapped and removed from the premises. The best defense against the invasion of these night visitors is to ensure that there is no access to the home, by sealing all possible means of entrance.

Bats

Bats are harmless insect eaters contrary to popular belief. The evidence of their presence will be in the form of guano droppings beneath their roosting place. To eliminate these creatures simply seal the entrance after they leave for the night's foraging.

Squirrels

While a squirrel is not inherently aggressive, it can carry disease-causing parasites. Squirrels are often not smart enough to find their way out of a house that they have entered. In an attempt to get out, they will gnaw their way through a wall. This can have troublesome consequences for the homeowner.

Birds

Birds such as pigeons, sparrows, and starlings can be annoying houseguests. Besides the mess their droppings make, they are noisy and often infested with disease-causing organisms. To a woodpecker, a client's house is like a tree. The resulting holes will have to be repaired. Birds are territorial creatures and the house must be made unappealing to them if you want them to nest somewhere else.

Other Pests

The list of other miscellaneous pests is quite extensive and varies from region to region. Many of these creatures are more of a hazard to the inspector who is crawling around the hidden areas of the home than they are to the client. The inspector should know how to recognize the presence of common pests such as spiders, fleas, snakes, and scorpions.

Fungi

Fungi are a group of plants that lack chlorophyll and reproduce asexually through spores. They cannot make their own food so they feed off of the cells in wood by breaking it down with enzymes they secrete. This in turn reduces the strength of wood. Examples of fungi are yeast, **molds**, smuts, and mushrooms.

Figure 12.4
Mold infestation on house stucco wall

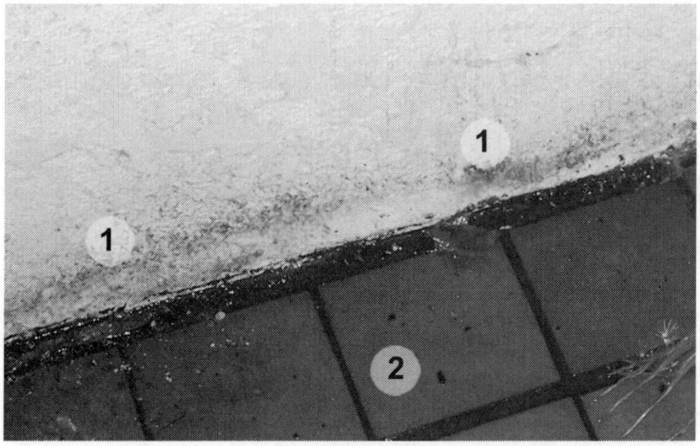

1) Mold infestation

2) Exterior tile

Fungi need three things to thrive. They need moisture, food, and a surface to grow on. Their favorite food is material with cellulose content. Unfortunately, cellulose is found in almost all building materials, including wood, insulation, and the paper that binds wallboard.

Fungi were designed by nature to promote the decay process by destroying organic material. If the conditions were right, fungi could reduce a frame house to dust.

Since wood provides two of the three requirements for fungi to flourish, the only way to stop fungus from attacking a wood structure is to limit the supply of moisture. The critical quantity of moisture in wood is 20%. If wood contains more than 20% moisture, fungal attack is inevitable.

If the content is less than 20%, fungus cannot propagate. Normally wood will not have the required moisture content to support fungal growth, but the inspector should be aware of any place where there is an accumulation of water in contact with wood.

Rotten or decayed wood is light brown in color and feels spongy when wet. When dry, it gives easily to pressure and has no strength.

Fungal growth can be recognized by a number of symptoms. There may be staining in almost any color, a scabby surface growth, a fluffy mass, or a cluster of bright colored pinhead growths.

The inspector can easily check for rotten wood by carefully probing with a sharp instrument. In addition, any damp unventilated area should be viewed suspiciously.

Once fungus has begun to attack a section of wood, the only remedy is to cure the underlying moisture problem and replace the rotten wood. The reason for the moisture is often more expensive to repair than the wood it damages.

Other Environmental Hazards

While performing a home inspection, the inspector should be aware of the presence of certain hazardous materials.

In most cases, special training is required to evaluate these environmental threats. In the last few decades, research has shown that certain materials commonly used in home construction can cause medical problems like diseases and allergies.

The major contributors to these problems are asbestos, radon gas, urea formaldehyde (UFFI), and lead poisoning.

Asbestos

Certain unique physical properties of **asbestos** made it good for use in a wide range of applications in residential construction. Asbestos is chemical resistant, non-combustible, and a good insulator. It is also light, strong, and inexpensive. The Greek derivation of the word asbestos means indestructible. Asbestos products were routinely used in flooring, cement, insulation, and various adhesives.

The health threat from asbestos comes from the inhalation of the tiny fibers. The virtual indestructibility of asbestos means that once the fibers enter the body they are there permanently. For this reason, the time period between exposure and symptoms for asbestos-related problems can be as long as forty years.

Asbestos is a known carcinogen with no safe level of exposure for man. Numerous types of cancer have been associated with it including, lung, gastrointestinal, esophageal, colon, and even stomach.

In the 1970s, the government began taking steps to eliminate the use of asbestos in construction. There may be millions of buildings that contain this potentially harmful substance. The good news, if any, is that the asbestos particles are not dangerous unless the material containing them is disturbed like in a remodeling project.

In homes built prior to the 1980s, asbestos can be found in: ventilation ductwork, boiler and pipe insulation, ironing board covers, ceiling tiles, floor tiles, sheetrock, plaster of ceilings and walls, ovens, water heater insulation and vent piping, toasters and even clothes dryers.

The home inspector should not make any specific recommendations regarding the threat of asbestos-related problems, but should report any suspect materials.

Radon Gas

Radon gas is a naturally occurring by-product of the decay of uranium. It is radioactive and therefore harmful. Since uranium is found everywhere, radon gas is present in all areas of the country.

Figure 12.5
Forced air ventilation

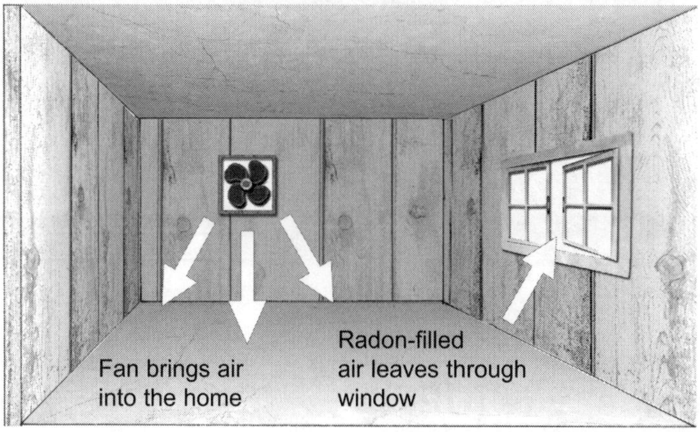
Fan brings air into the home
Radon-filled air leaves through window

The problem with radon gas is that it is radioactive and highly mobile. Radon gas enters a dwelling from the surrounding soil. The best way to prevent the entrance of radon gas is to seal all holes and penetrations near ground level, ventilate living areas to reduce concentrations, and maintain positive air pressure in the dwelling.

Radon gas is colorless and odorless, and can only be detected with special equipment. The radioactivity of radon gas is measured in units called "**picocuries**" per liter of air.

The average level of radioactivity in the U.S. is between .1 and .2 picocuries (2 pCi/L) for air outside and 1 and 2 picocuries inside the home. The Environmental Protection Agency (EPA) has recommended that levels above four picocuries (4 pCi/L) be reduced.

Newer homes, built to tighter energy conservation standards than older homes, have little natural ventilation. For this reason, a conscious ventilation plan should be employed to limit radon gas.

Care should be taken to rely more on just exhaust fans for this purpose, because the lowered air pressure in the home will only allow more radon gas to enter. Once again, if there is any question about the levels of radon gas in a home the inspector should recommend calling in an expert.

Figure 12.6
Natural Ventilation

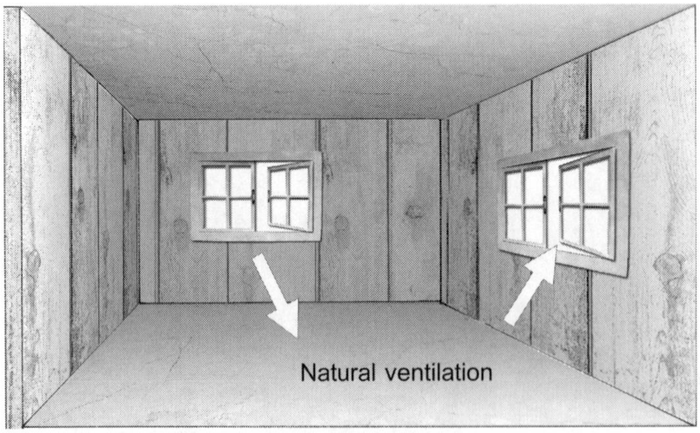

Urea Formaldehyde (UFFI)

This chemical compound was widely used as a foam insulation material prior to its ban in 1982. There is a risk of illness from the formaldehyde gas release from the foam insulation.

The insulation was manufactured at the construction site using urea formaldehyde resin and foaming agents. The mixture was pumped into the walls as foam that looked like shaving cream, where it would harden into a plastic. During the process of curing, the resin would emit formaldehyde gas that would then enter the living space.

While there is no specific threshold level that has been determined to cause illness, constant exposure should be avoided. The risks associated with urea formaldehyde insulation decrease dramatically in the first year after installation. Sensitivity to formaldehyde varies from individual to individual. Some symptoms of formaldehyde reaction are eye, nose, and throat irritation, as well as coughing, headache, and nausea.

If these symptoms persist for more than a few days but disappear when the house is vacated, a laboratory test should be conducted to determine if formaldehyde gas is present.

Lead

The human body has very little tolerance for **lead**. It is one of the few substances that normally are not found in human beings.

Before its ban in 1978, lead was used extensively in the pigments of household paint. Because of its flexibility, ductility, and resistance to corrosion, lead was also used to manufacture water piping, radioactivity shielding, roofing, electrical conduit, cable sheathing, and sewer piping.

When lead is absorbed in the human body, it concentrates in the red blood cells, kidneys, nervous system, and reproductive organs. The symptoms of lead poisoning can include fatigue, appetite disruption, disturbed sleep patterns, irritability, vomiting, and developmental problems both physical and mental.

The two most common ways that people are exposed to lead toxicity is through drinking water and inhaled lead dust. Lead is introduced into the drinking water when it is leached out of piping and into the air from surfaces painted with lead-based paints. Lead can also be found in soil surrounding the house where it has been washed off the siding paint by rain.

Because they are still developing, children are much more susceptible to lead poisoning than are adults. Common symptoms of lead poisoning are fatigue, weakness, sleep disruption, appetite disruption, irritability, developmental regression, behavioral alterations, clumsiness, vomiting, muscular difficulties, and abdominal pain.

There are lead testing kits readily available, but the home inspector should make sure that he or she is qualified to analyze the results. No liability will be incurred if the inspector simply recommends to the client that the premises be tested for the presence of lead by a professional.

13

Chapter

The Garage

Introduction

Most homes have a **garage** or **carport** to accommodate at least one car. Garages are often attached to the home and may or may not have living space above them. Sometimes they are detached structures, which are inspected in the same way as the home. The home inspector will have to check the garage during a home inspection.

Whenever a garage is attached to a home, it must have fire-rated walls separating the garage from the dwelling. The walls that separate the garage from the living space must have at least $^1/_2$" drywall or gypsum board covering them. Some localities will require even thicker $^5/_8$" gypsum board for fire prevention purposes as well. There should be no holes or penetrations in this drywall or gypsum board.

Any door that separates the attached garage from the home must be at least $1^3/_8$" thick for fire resistance. The fire door should not have any holes, loose or missing weather stripping, or sealing. These items provide a barrier from the fuels and fuel exhaust of automobiles that can lead to fires.

Detached garages have less to check regarding fire prevention, but more with regard to structural stability. Most detached garages will be slab-on-grade and have varying types of roofing. The requirements and associated defects of these structures are the same as for the house.

Garage Components

The structure of a garage is similar to that of a house, i.e., foundation, framing, roof, walls, doors, and appliances.

Garage Foundation

All garages have a foundation. More often, the foundation will consist of slab-on-grade concrete. The slab should slope slightly away from the home, or towards the large garage door or doors, to allow water to drain naturally. The garage slab should be at least four inches lower than the slab or foundation of the home to reduce the chance of exhaust or gas fumes penetrating the house.

Most cracks in the garage slab are usually related to expansion or contraction of the concrete, and are normal. If the cracks become large or have the slab rising up (heaving) or settling (sinking down), there is a potentially serious problem that should be reported. Other potential defects of the garage foundation are the same as for other concrete slabs.

Reportable Deficiencies - Garage Foundation

- Improper slope
- Slab not lower than home slab if attached
- Large cracks
- Heaving or settling of cracks

Garage Framing

The framing requirements for a garage should be the same as the home. In many cases, this is the only place for the home inspector to see the exposed wood of the wall framing. Additionally, this may be the only place to look for sill plates and the bolts used to hold the sill and wall to the foundation. Missing sill bolts or loose connection to the foundation should be reported. The bracing of the garage framing should be viewed as well. This is done to ensure it is performing its intended function and not missing when required (as in seismically active areas).

Figure 13.1
Rafters in garage

1) Underside of roof sheathing
2) Garage rafter
3) Seismic bracing/ supports

The inspector should see if the frame of the garage is racked or twisted from weather or repeatedly opening the large door. To do this, the inspector should stand about 25-50 feet away from the structure because it is difficult to see the signs of twisting or racking of the frame as the garage is approached.

The home inspector should also use an awl or screw driver to probe the wood inside of the garage to check for insect infestation and other wood-destroying conditions as well.

Reportable Deficiencies - Garage Framing

- Racking or twisting of frame
- Insufficient or loose connections to sill or foundation
- Missing or improper bracing
- Damaged or insect-infested wood

Garage Roof Structure

The requirements for the roof structure for a garage should be the same as those for the home being inspected.

Usually the structure of the garage roof is formed by prefabricated roof trusses and rafters. These parts are sometimes modified to create fold-down stairways which are added to provide access to additional storage above the garage. The added weight of stored items can sometimes overload joists and trusses, causing sagging or buckling. This sagging could also result in putting excess stress on the exterior walls of the garage.

Modifications made without the use of proper bracing, collar ties, and engineered reinforcement systems compromise the structural integrity of a garage. Over-spanning of joists and rafters puts them under too much pressure. These problems should be reported.

The inspector should make sure the garage attic or storage area is separated from the attic of the home by a firewall as well. This separation is meant to prevent or impede fire from spreading from the garage to the home.

The inspector should also probe the wood of the roof structure to check for weakness or insect infestation.

Reportable Deficiencies - Garage Roofing

- Missing or damaged rafters or joists
- Over spanning of rafters or joists
- Improper modifications of rafters or joists
- Improper or missing bracing, collar ties or engineered reinforcement
- Sagging joists
- Buckling trusses
- Insect infestation of rafters or joists

Garage Walls

Walls of a garage that are adjacent to living areas should be covered with 1/2" thick drywall to prevent toxic exhaust and gas vapors from entering the residence. This also means the walls and ceilings that separate the garage from living spaces must be free of holes or missing components to prevent these toxic gases from getting in the home and harming occupants. This also allows a measure of fire resistance so the home will not immediately catch fire if it starts in the garage. Any buckling or bowing of garage walls should also be reported, even though it may be a defect within the garage roof.

Reportable Deficiencies - Garage Walls

- Uncovered common wall or ceiling with living spaces

- Holes or other damage in common walls or ceilings
- Missing components in walls or ceilings
- Buckling or bowing walls
- Sagging ceilings

Interior Garage Doors

The door that separates the garage from the living space should be fire-resistant, installed with a curb, self-closing, and tightly sealed with weather stripping to prevent fire and toxic gas penetration into the home. It should be able to withstand fire for 20 minutes and not have holes or glass parts. Many local governments will have specific codes regarding these doors and their fire resistance.

Figure 13.2
Garage fire door

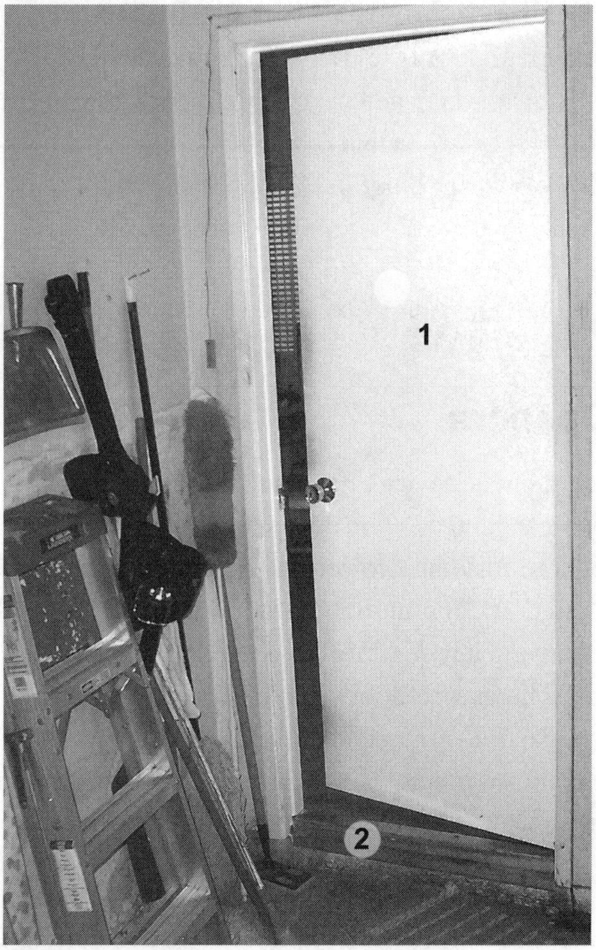

1) Fire-rated door
2) Threshold (must be min. 4" high)

Figure 13.3
An automatic garage door opener should open properly.

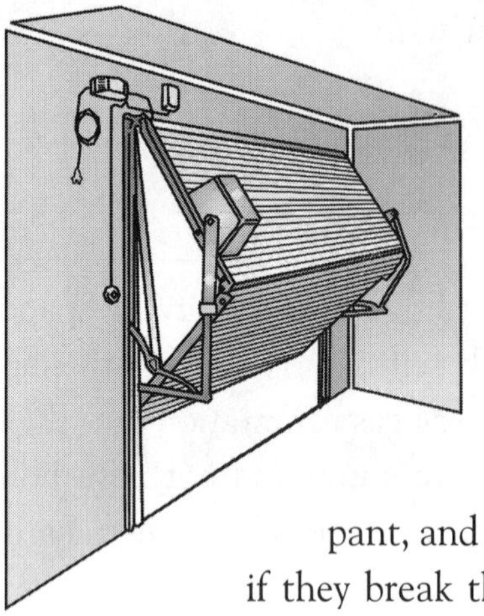

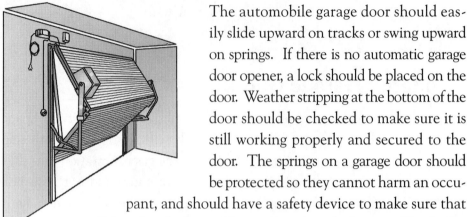

The automobile garage door should easily slide upward on tracks or swing upward on springs. If there is no automatic garage door opener, a lock should be placed on the door. Weather stripping at the bottom of the door should be checked to make sure it is still working properly and secured to the door. The springs on a garage door should be protected so they cannot harm an occupant, and should have a safety device to make sure that if they break they will not cause much damage. Tracks for garage doors should be properly greased and secured in place. The door rollers should not be bent and should move easily.

Reportable Deficiencies - Garage Doors

- Incorrect door type used for entry to home
- Missing or damaged weather stripping
- Entry door not sealed properly
- Glass or other holes in door
- Automobile garage door does not operate easily
- Tracks, rollers, or springs damaged
- Unprotected springs

Garage Door Openers

Garage door openers devices have become increasingly popular since the advent of two-car garages. The automatic garage door opener consists of an electric motor to raise and lower the door, and an electronic transmitter/receiver to direct it. The motor of the door opener should be checked for proper function and if it does not raise the door in a timely fashion, it should be reported. The garage door opener should be plugged directly into an outlet. The outlet does not need to be ground fault circuit interrupter (GFCI) protected. It must not be plugged into an extension cord, and if it is, it should be reported as deficient.

The transmitter is a small battery-powered device that is usually carried in the car. The receiver, which is programmed to a matching code, is mounted on the door assembly in the garage. It receives a signal that starts the opening of the garage door.

Figure 13.4
Garage door opener

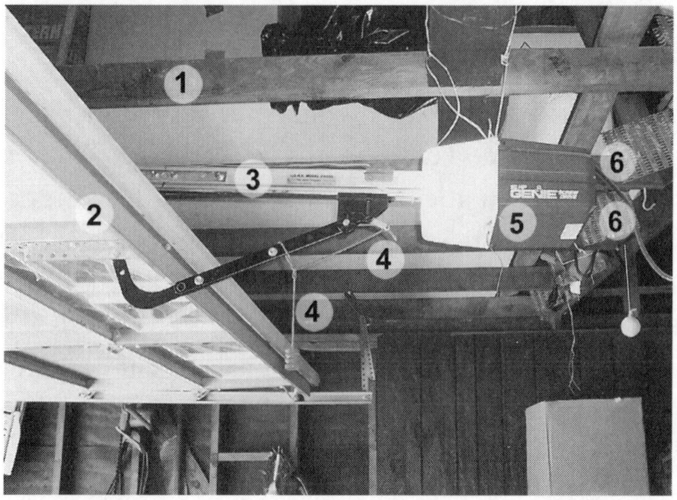

A significant safety feature of the garage door opener is the automatic reversing function. If the downward travel of the door is impeded for any reason, the reversing switch immediately stops the door and raises it. Some door systems incorporate an electric eye that will reverse the door if the beam is broken. The inspector must verify that the auto-reverse function is working properly.

Figure 13.5
Garage door safety device

Reportable Deficiencies - Garage Door Openers

- Electric eye beam is broken or malfunctioning
- Auto-reverse function not working properly
- Inoperable motor for the door opener
- Improper wiring of automatic door opener

Appliances

Appliances such as the water heater, furnace, washer, and dryer are often located in the garage. Therefore, the inspector must know the requirements for these appliances if they are included in the sale of the home. Natural gas or oil-fired furnaces must have their ignition source at least 18" above the garage floor. Water heaters are sometimes required to have energy-saving blankets wrapped around them and to be braced to walls with metal straps to keep them from toppling in an earthquake. The requirements for these appliances are dealt with in detail in the chapter on appliances.

Carports

Sometimes a home does not have a garage and the inspector will have to check the carport as the primary parking structure. The inspector looks for structural stability in its supports, complete coverage of the roof, and safety in the lighting of the carport. If the structure is leaning, has holes in its roof, is not well lit, or has a damaged foundation, it should be reported as well.

Figure 13. 6
Carport with garage

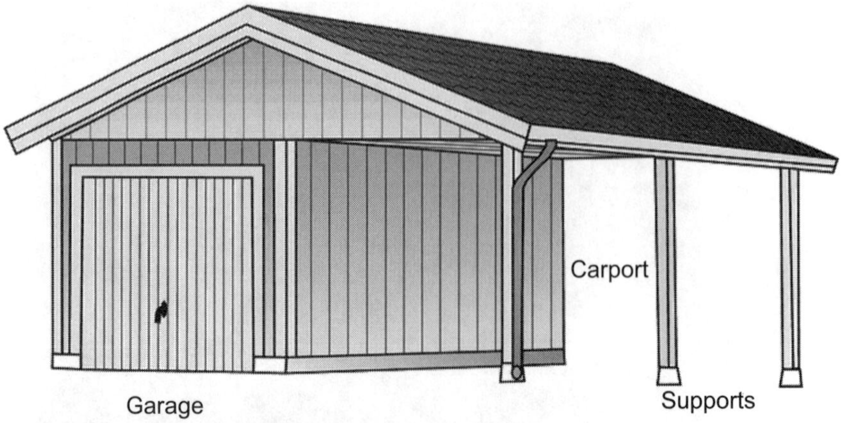

14 Chapter

The Inspection Report

Introduction

During the home inspection, some inspectors use a hand-held computer or other electronic device to assist in performing the inspection. These devices usually come with different software programs that also help in producing an inspection report.

Some home inspection programs are very advanced and allow for posting reports via the Internet or adding digital photos to them. Some examples of these software programs include: InspectVue™, Palm-Tech, HomeGauge®, and QuickStart 2000.

Other inspectors use hand-written or printed checklists (also known as field check sheets) to make notes on the differing systems and potential defects in the home. Then they complete the inspection report by handwriting, typing, or inputting the data into a software system. Many software programs for home inspection have varied checklists to print or utilize, and professional associations or societies have preferred checklists as well. We have included an example of the beginning of a printed checklist in this chapter.

Figure 14.1
An example of a personal digital assistant (PDA)

Why Create an Inspection Report?

Now that the home has been inspected and potential deficiencies identified, it is time for the home inspector to create an inspection report. Why? There are numerous reasons for creating a written inspection report.

Not all states have legislation dealing directly with home inspectors, but most inspectors will follow standards of practice from their professional association or society. Most of these professional guidelines require the inspector to complete a written report for the customer. This report reduces the liability and increases the defense for the home inspector, it helps to set expectations for the client, and it helps to build good rapport with clients, agents, and home sellers. By doing these things the written inspection report also helps to give legitimacy to the home inspection business as a whole and aids in the success of the individual home inspection business.

InspectVUE™ RESIDENTIAL

Field Check Sheet

Inspection Date: ______________________________

Start Time: ______________ End Time: ________________

Inspection Address: ______________________________

____

____

Client(s) Name: ______________________________

RE Agent's Name: ______________________________

Present During Inspection: ☐ Buyer(s) ☐ Seller(s)
☐ Buyer's Agent ☐ Seller's Agent
☐ Others: ________________

Weather Conditions: ______________________________

Temperature: ______________________________

Orientation: Property Faces: ☐ North ☐ South
☐ East ☐ West

Type of Residence: ☐ Single-family dwelling
☐ Townhouse
☐ Condominium

Year Built: ______ No. Stories: ________ Square Feet: __________

☐ Occupied ☐ Unoccupied
☐ Furnished ☐ Unfurnished ☐ Partially furnished

Table of Contents

Standards of Practice

Some states have regulations and licensing requirements that home inspectors must follow. Information about these regulations and licensing requirements can be found in Appendix A.

Home inspectors in those states not regulated by state directives may choose to follow the standards of practice of their professional organizations. It is important to note that home inspections in unregulated states are not bound legally to abide by any standards of practice, but they do so as it is in their best interest.

Many home inspection associations (listed in Appendix B) issue standards of practice and codes of ethics for their members to follow. We are highlighting the standards of practice and codes of ethics for ASHI *(American Society of Home Inspectors)* at www.ashi.com and CREIA *(California Real Estate Inspection Association)* at www.creia.org.

What to Include in the Home Inspection

Once the standards of practice are given to the client, it is appropriate for the home inspector to go over what will be inspected and what will not. This is done by verbally going over the written standards of practice with the client and explaining the items and areas included in the inspection.

Included in the Home Inspection

- Description or type of property—age, size, location, condition
- Inspection methods to be used such as probing, visual, measurement, and research
- Description of reportable deficiencies, even if the evidence is not conclusive
- Unsafe conditions that exist and need third-party evaluation
- Description of potential consequences of reportable deficiencies in the home

What to Exclude in the Home Inspection

It is very helpful to speak with clients about their expectations prior to beginning the inspection. Each area of the country has its own specific requirements. This is where the importance of explaining the governing standards of practice will be important. It is generally accepted that the inspector is not required to remove wall or floor coverings or move personal belongings that are impeding the view of a system or the inspection itself. The inspector is not required to disassemble any machinery either.

Home inspectors must also take their own safety and that of those around them into consideration when performing an inspection. This is even more important when considering entering crawl spaces, inspecting roofs, or checking the electrical and natural gas systems of the home.

Professional home inspection associations and societies have items they have determined should be inspected and/or exempted from the home inspection. Since ASHI and CREIA Standards of Practice were used as examples earlier, the limitations and exclusions of these two organizations are used in the following examples to exemplify this concept.

ASHI General Limitations and Exclusions

Inspections performed in accordance with these Standards of Practice are not technically exhaustive, will not identify concealed conditions or latent defects, and are applicable to buildings with four-or-fewer dwelling units and their garages or carports.

The inspector is not required to perform any action or make any determination unless specifically stated in these Standards of Practice, except as may be required by lawful authority.

Inspectors are not required to determine the:

- condition of systems or components that are not readily accessible.
- remaining life of any system or component.
- strength, adequacy, effectiveness, or efficiency of any system or component.
- causes of any condition or deficiency.
- methods, materials, or costs of corrections.
- future conditions including, but not limited to, failure of systems and components.
- suitability of the property for any specialized use.
- compliance with regulatory requirements (codes, regulations, etc.).
- market value of the property or its marketability.
- advisability of the purchase of the property.

- presence of potentially hazardous plants or animals including, but not limited to, wood-destroying organisms or diseases harmful to humans.
- presence of any environmental hazards including, but not limited to, toxins, carcinogens, noise, contaminants in soil, water, or air.
- effectiveness of any system installed or methods utilized to control or remove suspected hazardous substances.
- operating costs of systems or components, acoustical properties of any system or component.

Inspectors are not required to offer:

- or perform any act or service contrary to law.
- or perform engineering services, or perform work in any trade or any professional service other than home inspection.
- warranties or guarantees of any kind.

Inspectors are not required to operate:

- any system or component that is shut down or otherwise inoperable.
- any system or component that does not respond to normal operating controls.
- shut-off valves.

Inspectors are not required to enter:

- any area that will, in the opinion of the inspector, likely be dangerous to the inspector or other persons, or damage the property or its systems or components.
- the under-floor crawlspaces or attics that are not readily accessible.

Inspectors are not required to inspect:

- underground items including, but not limited to, underground storage tanks or other underground indications of their presence, whether abandoned or active.
- systems or components that are not installed.
- decorative items.
- systems or components located in areas that are not entered in accordance with these Standards of Practice.
- detached structures other than garages and carports.
- common elements or common areas in multi-unit housing, such as condominium properties or cooperative housing.

Inspectors are not required to:

- perform any procedure or operation, which will, in the opinion of the inspector, likely be dangerous to the inspector or other persons or damage the property or its systems or components.
- move suspended ceiling tiles, personal property, furniture, equipment, plants, soil, snow, ice, or debris.
- dismantle any system or component, except as explicitly required by these Standards of Practice.

CREIA Limitations, Exceptions, and Exclusions

The inspector may exclude from the inspection any system, structure, component of the building that is inaccessible, concealed from view, or cannot be inspected due to circumstances beyond the control of the inspector, or which the client has agreed is not to be inspected. If an inspector excludes any specific system, structure, or component of the building from the inspection, the inspector shall confirm in the report such specific system, structure, or component of the building not inspected and the reason(s) for such exclusion(s).

The inspector may limit the inspection to individual-specific systems, structures, or components of the building. In such event, the inspector shall confirm in the report that the inspection has been limited to such individual-specific systems, structures, and components of the building. Unless specifically agreed otherwise between the inspector and the client, there are several items excluded from the scope of a real estate inspection.

Inspectors are not required to inspect:

- systems, structures, or components not specifically identified in these Standards.
- environmental hazards or conditions, including, but not limited to, toxic, reactive, combustible, corrosive contaminants, wildfire, geologic, or flood.

Inspectors are not required to perform:

- examinations of conditions related to animals, rodents, insects, wood-destroying insects, organisms, mold, and mildew.
- services relating to geotechnical, engineering, structural, architectural, geological, hydrological, land surveying, or soil-related examinations.

Inspectors are not required to determine:

- certain factors relating to any systems, structures, or components of the building, including, but not limited to: adequacy, efficiency, durability or remaining useful life, costs to repair, replace or operate, fair market value, marketability, quality, or advisability of purchase.

The Inspection Agreement

An inspection agreement should be signed before a home inspector conducts the actual inspection and after going over the standards of practice and establishing the client's expectations. Many inspectors refer to this as their contract. The contract spells out the basic agreement between the inspector and the client. This contract includes the limitations and exemptions of the inspection. The contract reinforces that the client knows exactly what the inspection includes and what it does not include. Some basic components should be included in the inspection agreement or contract.

Items Included in the Agreement

- Person(s) performing the inspection
- Location of the inspection
- Date the inspection will be performed
- Date the report (scope of work) will be completed
- Inspection cost/fee and the means of payment
- Method for dispute resolution

Contracts should be tailored to the individual inspection business or firm to ensure a limitation of liability. Most software products for home inspection will include basic contracts that can be modified to fit the individual business or proprietor.

Reducing Liability

Home inspectors have to be wary of lawsuits that may arise after their work is completed and the report is finished. To avoid litigation and lawsuits, inspectors should give clients clear, concise, and direct information about the home they are about to purchase. The inspector should use language that is easy to understand and not coded or heavily reliant on technical jargon. Veiled problems or potential problems in a home should be spelled out very frankly for the client to evaluate. They should also follow state regulations, or, in lieu of those requirements, follow the standards of practice and ethical codes of their professional home inspection association or society.

Identifying the Three "W"s of Home Inspection

The three Ws of home inspection are "**what**", "**who**", and "**when**". The home inspector should clearly identify what defects are in a home, who should check them out for further review, and when it should be done. This three-pronged approach allows the client to understand the problem and the need for further inspection in a timely manner.

The home inspector should not recommend repairs, and is not allowed to repair defects that may be found. Any defects must be referred to another professional. For example, a damaged roof should be inspected by a licensed roofing contractor. Problems with an electrical panel should be referred to a licensed electrician for evaluation. The defects found and the need for followup by a licensed professional should always be done *before escrow closes*. Once escrow closes and the sale is final, there is no way for the client to get defects fixed or resolved unless they pay for them. Therefore, it is imperative that the home inspector make recommendations for further review by a licensed professional before the sale goes through.

Avoid Assigning Responsibility

As home inspectors should not recommend repairs, they should also avoid telling a client who is responsible for defects in a home. They should simply identify defects and not make judgments about them.

Never Re-Inspect a Home

A home inspector should never, under any circumstances, do a re-inspection on a home if a repair has been done to a defective component. This is to avoid making an inferred guarantee of the work done. There is no way to know if a certain repair has been done according to standards or has fixed the problem. Avoid this by not re-inspecting homes after they have been repaired to limit further liability.

Age and Expected Life-span of Components

The home inspector should also be very careful when describing a component of a home with respect to its expected life-span. Inspectors may be able to decipher the age of components like roofs and their typical expected life-span, but want to avoid a guarantee of remaining viability. For example, a tile roof on a home may typically be last for 40 years. The home inspector may find out the tile roof is only 8 years old but would want to avoid making a guarantee or inference that the roof should last for another 32 years.

Another example would be with a water heater. Often the manufacture date for a water heater is printed on it. Some models can last 10 years, whereas others may last much longer. Regardless, the inspector would not want to infer that it needs to be replaced based on the age or expected life-span or that it will last for a number of years to come.

Building Rapport

It is imperative for the success of the home inspector to form a rapport with not only the client, but also the agents and the sellers of the home. They are all potential future clients and should be treated as such.

It is extremely important to have proper directions to the home/location, and to show up on time. Remember, each inspection is a potential lead to others, so being on time can help establish future business.

A home inspector should also keep a clean and professional appearance while still being able to perform all the duties of the inspection. Wear clean, neat clothing that allows for climbing ladders and getting into crawl spaces. Wearing a suit and tie may be good for professional appearances, but it will not allow the home inspector to perform the duties. Looking disheveled will not help gain new business either, so there is a line between being over-dressed or under-dressed.

A home inspector should speak clearly and concisely to the parties involved in the inspection. Avoid using technical jargon or building code-related phrases like "the 8/12 pitch of the tile roof is in conflict with the area building code" or "the yard has a negative grade" to describe systems or components in the home. Remember home inspectors are not building inspectors, so citing building codes is not appropriate. Instead, the home inspector could say something like, "the tile roof is too flat to drain water properly in this climate" or "the slope of the yard is towards the house and not away from it as it should." Again, speaking plainly and directly about defects and potential problems to clients and others helps gain future business.

Keep your inspection equipment in good working order and check to be sure it is with you *before* showing up to perform the job. Dead batteries, broken electrical meters or forgotten ladders do not present a professional impression to clients and others involved.

Additionally, having a working knowledge of all equipment is essential. It does no good to have all the gadgets but little or no idea how to use them in an effective way in the home inspection. In fact, this fumbling with equipment will hurt the overall impression of the home inspection.

Finally, remember to tread lightly in the home that is inspected. Walking around in clean footwear or with covers over the footwear and being careful not to break anything will help in finding repeat business. Remember that the seller of the home will probably be buying one soon and may need home inspection services. So doing the job without being messy will help the cause in growing the home inspection business.

Appendix A
State Requirements

Alabama

License:	Home Inspection License
Req. Ed:	No required Home Inspection course
Exam(s):	Pass NHIE
Affiliation:	None
Standards:	Adhere to Alabama Standards & ASHI Code of Ethics
CE:	None
Insurance:	Liability
Regulator:	Alabama Building Commission, (334) 242-4810, email: buildcom@bc.state.al.us or www.bc.state.al.us/HI%20Menu.htm
Law:	Licensure Act of 2002-517 Licensed by the Alabama Building Commission, 334-242-4082 or www.bc.state.al.us/HI%20Menu.htm.
Insurance:	General Liability Insurance: minimum $20,000 for injury or damage to property, minimum $50,000 for injury or damage (including death) to any one person, minimum $100,000 for injury or damage (including death) to more than one person. E&O is not required at this time, but it may be in the future.

Alaska

License:	Home Inspector or Associate Home Inspector License
Req. Ed:	Educational & experience requirements of Department
Exam(s):	Pass NHIE or CRIE
Affiliation:	Not required
Standards:	Not required
CE:	At least 8 hours of CE per licensing period
Insurance:	Liability Insurance and Surety Bond
Regulator:	AK Dept. of Community and Econ. Dev., Division of Occupational Licensing; (907) 465-5470 phone, (907) 465-2974 fax, or e-mail license@dced.state.ak.us.
Law:	Chapter 134 SLA enacted 2003 - all home inspectors must be licensed by July 1, 2004. http://www.dced.state.ak.us/occ/pub/Home Inspector_Statutes.pdf

Arizona

License:	Certification required
Req. Ed:	80 hours of education; (Our course is DETC approved for 100 hours - meets criteria)

Exam(s): Pass NHIE
Affiliation: Not required
Standards: Adhere to Standards of Professional Practice
CE: None
Insurance: Errors and Omissions Insurance, Bond
Regulator: Arizona State Board of Technical Registration (BTR) Phone: (602) 364-4930 E-mail: info@btr.state.az.us www.btr.state.az.us/
Law: A.R.S. 32-101 et seq.

Arkansas

License: No license required
Req. Ed: Not required
Exam(s): Pass NHIE & ASHI Standards & Ethics
Affiliation: Not required
Standards: Conduct all inspections in adherence to the Standards of Practice and Code of Ethics of ASHI, the Arkansas Association of Real Estate Inspectors, or an equivalent professional home inspection association
CE: 14 hours of which only 4 hours per yr. as distance ed.
Insurance: Liability insurance
Regulator: Secretary of State, Division of Corporations at (501) 682-3409 registration is required. http://www.arkhomeinspectors.com_lawformatted.htm
Law: Arkansas Home Inspector Registration Act, Act 1328 of 2003 ftp://www.arkleg.state.ar.us/acts/2003/Public/Act1 328.rtf.

California

License: No license required
Req. Ed: Not required Exam(s): Not required
Affiliation: Not required
Standards: The law in California prohibits unethical home inspection practices, including repairing properties that home inspectors have inspected in the previous 12 months. The law encourages courts to consider the Standards of Practice and Code of Ethics of ASHI and the California Real Estate Inspection Association when determining whether an inspection meets the required standard of care.
CE: Not required
Insurance: Not required
Regulator: California Contractors State License Board at (916) 255-3900 or 1 (800) 321-2752 or http://www.cslb.ca.gov/
Law: Trade practice act (Chapter 338) enacted in 1996 http://www.legalinfo.ca.gov/cgibin/displaycode?section=bpc&group=070

Colorado

License:	No license required
Req. Ed.:	Not required
Insurance:	Not required
Law:	No pending legislation

Connecticut

License:	Home Inspector License or Home Inspector Intern http://dcp.state.ct.us/licensing/professions.htm
Req. Ed:	40 hours - (Allied on Board Approved List); or intern for 1 year and 200 paid inspections
Exam(s):	Pass an oral, written, or electronic competency examination
Affiliation:	Not required
Standards:	Adhere to Code of Ethics / Standards of Practice
CE:	Yes
Insurance:	Not required
Regulator:	Home Inspection Licensing Board. Phone: (860) 713-6000 e-mail: license.services@po.state.ct.us
Law:	Public Act No. 99-254 http://www.cga.state.ct.us/2001/pub/Chap400f.htm

Delaware

License:	No license required Task force is evaluating need for licensing http://legis.state.de.us/LIS/LIS142.NSF/93487d394bc01014882569a4007a4cb7/ac5d3ed7047ba52e85256cfd006 7a2e3
Insurance:	Not required

Florida

License:	No license required
Pending legislation:	http://www.flsenate.gov/cgi-bin view_page.pl?Tab=session&Submenu=1&FT=D&File=sb2016e2.html&Directory=session/2004/Senate/bills/b illtext/html/
Insurance:	Not required

Georgia

License:	No license
Req. Ed:	Not required
Exam(s):	Not required

Affiliation: Not required

Standards: Georgia law requires home inspectors to provide written documents containing certain information with regard to inspections. This written document must include the scope of the inspection, including the structural elements and systems to be inspected, that the inspection is a visual inspection, and that the home inspector will notify, in writing, the person on whose behalf such inspection is being made of any defects noted during the inspection.

CE: None

Insurance: Not required

Regulator: Secretary of State, Construction Industry License Board
phone (478) 207-1416 http://www.sos.state.ga.us/plb/construct/

Law: Trade practice act (Chapter 3, Title 8) enacted in 1994

Hawaii

License: No license required

Law: No pending legislation

Insurance: No insurance requirements

Idaho

License: No license required

Law: No pending legislation

Insurance: No insurance requirements

Illinois

License: License

Req. Ed: 60 hours of pre-license education from an education provider approved and licensed by OBRE

Exam(s): Pass the Home Inspector Examination for Illinois, which consists of the National Home Inspector Examination and a section concerning Illinois statutes and regulations NHIE

Affiliation: Not required

Standards: Licensed home Inspectors are required to perform inspections that meet the minimum standards of practice established by rule as adopted by the OBRE.

CE: Must complete the equivalent of 6 hours per year or 12 hours per renewal

Insurance: Not required

Regulator: Home Inspector Advisory Board, Office of Banks and Real Estate (OBRE) at (217) 782-3000 or http://www.obre.state.il.us/realest/home inspect.htm

Law: Illinois Home Inspector License Act (225 ILSC 441)

Indiana

License:	License
Req. Ed:	Complete a Board-approved training program or course
Exam(s):	Pass NHIE Affiliation: Not required
Standards:	Not required
CE:	Yes
Insurance:	Liability insurance
Regulator:	Home Inspectors Licensing Board, Indiana Professional Licensing Agency at (317) 234-3009
Law:	P.L. 145 enacted In 2004. This law takes effect July 1, 2004, http://www.in.gov/legislative/pdf/acts_2003.pdf

Iowa

License:	No license required
Law:	No pending legislation
Insurance:	Not required

Kansas

License:	No license required
Current legislation:	http://www.kslegislature.org/bills/2004/2100.pdf and http://www.kslegislature.org/supplemental/2004/SN2 100.pdf
Req. Ed.:	Not required
Insurance:	Not required

Kentucky

License:	License - perform 250 inspections under supervision of licensed home inspector or participate in 100 paid inspections under supervision of licensed home inspector and have letter or recommendation from that inspector.
Req. Ed.:	48 hours approved classroom training
Exam:	Pass current Kentucky Tech-Central Home Inspectors Test or equivalent test provided by Director of Division of Code Enforcement
Current Legislation:	SB 34 - effective July 1, 2006 http://www.lrc.state.ky.us/record/04rs/SB34/HCS1.d oc
Regulator:	Office of Housing, Buildings and Construction-101 Sea Hero Road, Suite100, Frankfort, Kentucky 40601 http://hbc.ppr.ky.gov/
Insurance:	No less than $250,000 operating liability insurance

Louisiana

License: License

Req. Ed: 120 hours of instruction, at least 30 hours but no more than 40 of which must be in course work containing actual practical home inspections. LA does NOT accept the correspondence course(s) as a licensing requirements and will not give applicants credit for this type of education

Exam(s): Pass NHIE

Affiliation: Not required

Standards: Adhere to the Code of Ethics

CE: 20 hours annually

Insurance: Errors and Omission Insurance

Regulator: Louisiana State Board of Home Inspectors within the Department of Economic Development at (225) 248-1334
http://www.lsbhi.info/LSBHIweb.nsf/Home? OpenForm

Law: Louisiana Home Inspectors Licensing Act, Chapter 17-A of Title37) enacted in 1999
http://la.realtorplace.com/Meetings/fall mtng98/agendas/homeinspectbill.htm

Maine

License: No license required

Req. Ed.: Not required

Insurance: Not required

Law: No pending legislation

Maryland

License: License
http://www.dllr.state.md.us/license/occprof/reappr.html

Req. Ed: Complete a minimum of 48 hours of an offsite training course at a school approved by National Home Inspection Organization. Correspondence course currently excluded

Exam(s): PSI-1-800-733-9267

Affiliation: National association

Standards: Adhere to the standards of ASHI and NAHI

CE: None

Insurance: Liability insurance

Regulator: State Commission of Real Estate
Appraisers and Home Inspectors Division of Occupational & Professional Licensing at (410) 230-6165 or hinspect@dllr.state.md.us

Law: Chapter 470) enacted in 2001
http://mlis.state.md.us/2001rs/bills/hb/ hb0379e.rtf

Massachusetts

License: Home Inspector & Associate Home Inspector
Req. Ed: Complete a Board-approved training program and assist in no less than 25 home inspections in the presence of a licensed home inspector
Exam(s): Pass NHIE
Affiliation: Not required
Standards: Adhere to the Code of Ethics
CE: 24 hours annually
Insurance: Errors and Omissions Insurance
Regulator: Board of Registration of Home Inspectors at (617) 727-4459 or http://www.state.ma.us/reg/boards/hi/
Law: Chapter 146 enacted in 1999 http://www.state.ma.us/legis/laws/seslaw 99/sl990146.htm

Michigan

License: No license required
Req. Ed.: Not required
Insurance: Not required
Law: No pending legislation

Minnesota

License: Currently no licensing requirements
Pending legislation: http://www.revisor.leg.state.mn.us/cgibin/getbill.pl?number=HF2283&session=ls83&version=latest&session_number=0&sessio n_year=2004
Req. Ed: Not required
Insurance: Not required

Mississippi

License: License
Req. Ed: Complete an approved course of study of at least 60 hours, which may include field work as required by the Commission
Exam(s): Pass NHIE
Affiliation: Not required
Standards: Follow a code of ethics and standards of practice
CE: 24 hours every two years
Insurance: Errors and Omissions Insurance & Liability Insurance

Regulator: Mississippi Real Estate Commission http://www.mrec.state.ms.us/
Real Estate Commission (Home Inspector Regulatory Board) at (601) 932-9191 or http://www.mrec.state.ms.us/
Law: (Chapter 71) enacted in 2001
http://www.mrec.state.ms.us/admindownloadsHOMEINSPECTOR REGULATORYLAWEFF.07-0101.pdf

Missouri

License: No license required
Req. Ed.: Not required
Insurance: Not required
Law: No pending legislation

Montana

License: Not required
Req. Ed: Not required
Exam(s): Pass NHIE
Affiliation: Not required
Standards: Montana law, the Home Inspection Trade Practices Act, prescribes what elements must be identified in a home inspection and defines prohibited activities by a home inspector.
CE: None
Insurance: Not required
Regulator: Office of Building Codes and Inspection at (406) 444-3933
Law: Trade Practice Act (Chapter 14, Title 30) enacted in 1999
http://data.opi.state.mt.us/bills/BillHt ml/SB0210.htm

Nebraska

License: No license required
Req. Ed: Not required
Insurance: Not required
Pending legislation: has been indefinitely postponed
http://www.unicam.state.ne.us/pdf/INTRO_ LB767.pdf

Nevada

License: Certified Residential Inspector http://www.red.state.nv.us/insp_licreq.h tm
Req. Ed: 40 hours of academic instruction in subjects related to structural inspections

Exam(s): Pass an examination approved by the Division
Affiliation: Not required
Standards: Not required
CE: 20 hours every two years
Insurance: Errors and omissions insurance and general liability insurance
Regulator: Real Estate Division of the Department of Business and Industry at (775) 687-4280
Law: (NRS 645D.120 and NAC 645D.210) enacted in 1997 http://www.leg.state.nv.us/NRS/NRS645D.html

New Hampshire

License: No license required
Req. Ed.: Not required
Insurance: Not required
Law: Legislation pending

New Jersey

License: Associated Home Inspector or Home Inspector effective January 1, 2006 http://www.state.nj.us/lps/ca/pels/hilaw s.pdf%20and%20http://www.njleg.state.nj. us/2002/Bills/S2000/1685_R3.htm
Req. Ed: There is only one curriculum approved: Carson Dunlop, which is 300 hours of instructions. Also, perform no less than 50 home inspections under the supervision of a licensed home inspector
Exam(s): Pass NHIE
Affiliation: Not required
Standards: Not required
CE: 40 hours
Insurance: General liability insurance
Regulator: Home Inspection Advisory Committee, housed under the State Board of Professional Engineers and Land Surveyors Department of Law and Public Safety, Office of Consumer Protection at (973) 504-6200
Law: Home Inspection Professional Licensing Act Chapter 8, Title 45 enacted in 1998

New Mexico

License: No license required
Req. Ed.: Not required
Insurance: Not required
Law: No pending legislation

New York

License: License as of December 31, 2005

Req. Ed.: 140 hours approved training, including 40 hours of unpaid inspection experience under direct supervision of a licensed inspector

Exam: Must pass an approved written exam

Insurance: Requirement pending

Regulator: New York State Department of State Division of Licensing Services, phone (518) 474-4429, fax (518) 473-6448, or e-mail licensing@dos.state.ny.us

Law: Legislative Bill-A00076B was signed by the Governor on September 30th, 2004. This law will go into effect on Dec. 31, 2005
http://assembly.state.ny.us/leg/?bn=A000 76&sh=t

North Carolina

License: Licensed HI or Associate Home Inspector

Req. Ed: Minimum training set by Board, must meet additional requirements other than Allied course, student must contact The Board. Licensed Home Inspector must be an Associate Home Inspector for one year. Associate Home Inspector must have a minimum of 100 home inspections. Licensed General Contractors, Architects or Professional Engineers are exempt from doing apprenticeship.

Exam(s): Pass the licensing examination prescribed by the Board

Affiliation: Not required

Standards: Not required

CE: Annual CE shall be determined by the board, no more than 12 credit hours.

Insurance: Bond

Regulator: Home Inspector Licensure Board within the Department of Insurance
(919) 661-5880 or http://www.ncdoi.com/

Law: Home Inspection Licensure Act, Chapter 143, Article 9F enacted in 1993
http://www.ncdoi.com/OSFM/Documents/Engineering/HILB/NCHILB Statutes.PDF

North Dakota

License: Home Inspector registration with state registrar; $200 original fee; $50 annual fee for renewal when it expires every June 30th

Exam: Show proof of satisfactory completion of professional association exam

Insurance: Errors and Omissions

Ohio

License: No license required

Req. Ed.: Not required

Insurance: Not required
Law: No pending legislation

Oklahoma

License: License
Req. Ed: Eighty (80) hours of home inspection training
Exam(s): Pass NHIE
Affiliation: Not required
Standards: Not required
CE: Five hours of continuing education within the preceding 12 months
Insurance: General liability insurance
Regulator: Department of Health, Occupational Licensing Committee of Home Inspector Examiners (Committee) at (405) 271-5288
http://www.health.state.ok.us/program/ol /info.html#home
Law: Oklahoma Home Inspection Licensing Act Section 858-622 of Title 59) enacted in 2001
http://www.health.state.ok.us/program/ol /HomeInspACT.pdf

Oregon

License: Certified Home Inspector
Req. Ed: Must obtain 20 points of education Exam(s): Pass the exam
Affiliation: Not required
Standards: The Oregon Standards of Practice, Standards of Behavior and Definitions are adopted from the ASHI Standards with Oregon amendments
CE: 30 continuing education credits required for renewal (only 10 from correspondence and only 3 from field training).
Insurance: Surety bond, general liability insurance
Regulator: Oregon Construction Contractors Board (CCB) at (503) 378-4621,
http://www/ccb/state/or.us
Law: Oregon Home Inspection Certification Law, ORS 701.350, 355) enacted in 1997
http://ccbed.ccb.state.or.us/WebPDF/CCB/ statutes/hi.pdf

Pennsylvania

License: No license
Req. Ed: 100 or more home inspections
Exam(s): Pass NHIE
Affiliation: Member of a nationally recognized organization that requires 100 or more inspections for membership

Standards: A home inspector shall conduct their inspection in accordance with the standards of practice set forth by a professional home inspection trade association such as ASHI or the National Association of Home Inspectors (NAHI).
CE: Not required
Insurance: General liability insurance and errors and omissions
Regulator: Pennsylvania Bureau of Consumer Protection at (717) 787-9707
Law: Trade Practice Act (Act 114 of 2000), Title 68 enacted in 2000
http://phic.info/SB1032P2140.pdf

Rhode Island

License: Home Inspector or Associate Home Inspector
Req. Ed: Licensed Home Inspector - engaged as an Associate Home Inspector for no less than one year and performed 100 paid inspections OR been registered/licensed contractor in another state in good standing for 5 years. Associate Home Inspector-must have assisted in no less than 50 home inspections in the presence of a licensed home inspector
Exam(s): Pass NHIE or other approved exam
Affiliation: Not required
Standards: Abide by standards of practice and a code of ethics
CE: Not required
Insurance: General liability insurance and errors and omissions
Regulator: RI Contractors' Registration Board at (401) 222-1268
Law: Chapter 65.1 enacted in 2000
http://www.crb.state.ri.us/docs/hilawsfi nal.pdf

South Carolina

License: License
Req. Ed: Course approved by the Commission or 1 year experience with 50 supervised inspections
Exam(s): Pass NHIE or state licensing test
Affiliation: Certified as a home inspector by an organization recognized by the Commission
Standards: Not required
CE: None
Insurance: Not required
Regulator: South Carolina Residential Builders Commission Department of Labor, Licensing and Regulation, Residential Builders Commission - (803) 896-4363 main
(803) 896-4603 for Home Inspectors, www.llr.state.sc.us/POL/ResidentialBuilders/
Law: Title 40, Chapter 59, Article 3 enacted in 1996
http://www.scstatehouse.net/coderegs/c10 6.htm

South Dakota

License:	License
Req. Ed:	At least 40 hours of approved education
Exam(s):	Pass NHIE
Affiliation:	Not required
Standards:	Not required
CE:	24 hours every two years
Insurance:	Not required
Regulator:	South Dakota Real Estate Commission (605) 773-3600 http://www.state.sd.us/sdrec
Law:	Chapter 36-21C enacted in 2000 http://www.state.sd.us/sdrec/home_inspect/homeinspectstatutes.htm

Tennessee

License:	Certification - The law only applies to inspectors in certain counties in Tennessee
Req. Ed:	Approved training by the Board
Exam(s):	Pass NHIE
Affiliation:	Certified by the Home Inspectors of Tennessee Association; or certified by ASHI
Standards:	Abide by the ethics of ASHI
CE:	Unknown
Insurance:	Not required
Regulator:	The Department of Commerce, Division of Regulatory Boards at (615) 741-3449.
Law:	Title 62, Chapter 6, Part 3) enacted in 1997 http://198.187.128.12/tennessee/lpext.dl l?f=templates&fn=fs-main.htm and scroll to Title 62, Chapter 6, Part 3

Texas

License:	Apprentice Inspectors, Licensed HI
Req. Ed:	Educational course work Texas Administrative Code, Subchapter R, Rules
Exam(s):	Pass examination of home inspectors
Affiliation:	Not required
Standards:	Abide by the Standards of Practice and Professional Conduct and Ethics
CE:	continuing education requirements
Insurance:	Unknown
Regulator:	Texas Real Estate Licensing Board at (512) 465-3900, http://www.trec.state.tx.us
Law:	Title 113A, Article 6573a, Section 23) enacted in 1991 http://www.trec.state.tx.us/pdf/rela/200 1act.PDF

Utah

License:	No license required
Req. Ed.:	Not required
Insurance:	Not required
Law:	Pending legislation: http://www.le.state.ut.us/~2004/bills/sb illint/sb0028s01.htm

Vermont

License:	No license required
Req. Ed.:	Not required
Insurance:	Not required
Law:	No pending legislation

Virginia

License:	Voluntary certification
Req. Ed:	Any educational requirements as required by the Board - 35 hours of education and perform 100 inspections or 70 hours of education and perform 50 inspections
Exam(s):	Pass NHIE
Affiliation:	Member of a national or state professional home inspector association approved by the Board, provided that the requirements for the class of membership in such association are equal to or exceed the requirements established by the Board for all applicants
Standards:	Not required
CE:	Not required
Insurance:	General liability
Regulator:	Virginia Board for Asbestos, Lead, and Home Inspectors at (804) 367-8507
Law:	Virginia Certified Home Inspectors Regulations enacted in 2001 effective date July 1, 2003, http://www.state.va.us/dpor/asb_homeinspectorreg.pdf

Washington

License:	No license required
Req. Ed.:	Not required
Insurance:	Not required
Law:	No pending legislation

West Virginia

License:	No license required
Req. Ed:	Not required
Insurance	Not required
Law:	No pending legislation

Wisconsin

License: License
Req. Ed: Not required
Exam(s): Pass NHIE and Wisconsin Statutes and Rules Exam
Affiliation: Not required
Standards: Not required
CE: 20 hours every year
Insurance: Not required
Regulator: Department of Regulation and Licensing Home Inspector at (608) 266-2112
Law: Chapter 440.97) enacted in 1998 http://www.legis.state.wi.us/statutes/99Stat0440.pdf%20and%20find% 20 section%2044 0.97

Wyoming

License: No license required
Req. Ed Not required
Insurance Not required
Law: No pending legislation

Appendix B
Home Inspection Professional Associations

American Society of Home Inspectors (ASHI)
932 Lee Street, Suite 101
Des Plaines, IL 60016
(800) 743-ASHI (2744)
www.ashi.org

National Association of Certified Housing Inspectors (NACHI)
P.O. Box 987
Valley Forge, PA 19482-0987
(610) 933-4241
www.nachi.org

National Association of Home Inspectors, Inc. (NAHI)
4248 Park Glen Road
Minneapolis, MN 55416
(800) 448-3942
www.nahi.org

Housing Inspection Foundation (HIF)
1224 North Nokomis NE
Alexandria, MN 56308
(320) 763-6350
www.iami.org/hif.html

Society of Professional Real Estate Inspectors (SPREI)
909 Summer Street
Lynnfield, MA 07940
(781) 334-4500
www.sprei.org

American Association of Home Inspectors (AAHI)
5147-D 69th Street - P.O. Box 64309
Lubbock,TX 79464
(806) 794-1190
www.aahi.com

In addition, there are other more local associations (based and practicing only in one state) of "Real Estate Inspectors" which you can find on the Internet. Two examples are:

California Real Estate Inspection Association (CREIA)
1445 N. Sunrise Way, Suite 101
Palm Springs, CA 92262
Phone (800) 848-7342
Fax (760) 318-2117
www.creia.org

Kentucky Real Estate Inspection Association (KREIA)
104 Lawson Drive Suite 103-200
Georgetown, KY 40324
www.kreia.org

Glossary

A

absorption field
(1) A group or system of absorption trenches and distribution pipes by which septic-tank waste matter seeps into the surrounding soil. (2) Also known as leaching field.

acoustical tile
Blocks of fiber, mineral, or metal with small holes or rough textured surface to absorb sound, used as covering for interior walls and ceilings.

adobe
A kind of natural clay that is sticky when wet but dries hard. Adobe soil is expansive.

aerator (fitting)
A device installed on faucets to get air into a water stream.

alarm systems
Warning devices, installed or free-standing, including but not limited to: carbon monoxide detectors, flue gas, and other spillage detectors, security equipment, ejector pumps, and smoke alarms.

algae discoloration
(1) A type of roof discoloration caused by algae. (2) Also known as fungus growth.

alligatoring
(1) A term used to describe the cracking of surfacing bitumen on a built-up roof from the limited tolerance of asphalt to thermal expansion or contraction. Produces a pattern that resembles an alligator's hide. (2) Paint can also alligator.

amperage
The measurement of the quantity of electricity in an electrical circuit available to do a given job.

ampere
(1) A measure of electrical current. (2) The steady current produced by one volt applied across a resistance of one ohm.

anchor bolt
(1) Attaches mud still to foundation. (2) Embedded in concrete foundation.

architectural style
Generally the appearance and character of a building's design and construction.

asbestos
A mineral fiber used in construction which has been implicated in causing lung and stomach cancer.

aseptic system
The "clean water" system.

ASHI
Abbreviation for the American Society of Home Inspectors.

asphalt
A tar-like substance made of a variety of bitumen, naturally occurring or obtained by evaporating petroleum.

attic
The open area above the ceiling and under the roof deck of a steep-sloped roof.

B

back surfacing
The fine mineral matter applied to the back of shingles to keep them from sticking.

backfill
Soil that is used to fill in holes or support a foundation.

base flashing
The upturned edges of a watertight membrane on a roof.

base molding
Molding used at the top of the baseboard.

baseboard
A board that goes around the room against the wall and next to the floor.

basement
The lowest story of a building partially or entirely below ground.

batten
Narrow strips of wood or metal used to cover joints on the interior or exterior of a building, also used for decorative effect.

beam
A long thick piece of wood, metal or concrete, used to support weight in a building.

beam pocket
An opening in any structural component intended to receive one or more girders or beams.

bearing wall
A wall that supports a vertical load as well as its own weight.

bird stop
In addition to preventing birds from nesting in the hollows of roof tiles, this length of formed metal or foam elevates the starter course/layer of roof tile to position it at the same angle as subsequent courses/layers.

bitumen
Mineral pitch or any material obtained as a type of asphalt residue in the distillation of coal tar, wood tar, petroleum, etc., or occurring as natural asphalt.

blacktop
Asphalt paving used in streets and driveways.

blisters
Bubbles that may appear on the surface of asphalt roofing after installation.

board foot
A unit of measurement (1'x1'x1") for lumber: one foot square by one inch thick (144 cubic inches).

bracing
Diagonal board nailed across wall framing to prevent sway.

brick ledge
The portion of a foundation upon which the first course of brick is installed.

bridging
Wood or metal pieces used to brace floor joists.

British thermal unit (BTU)
(1) A measurement that calculates heat; the amount of heat needed to raise one pound of water one degree Fahrenheit.

building paper
Waterproof paper used between sheathing and roof covering.

built-ins
Cabinets and other features built as part of the house.

built-up roof
An outer covering of a comparatively flat roof, consisting of several layers of saturated felt. As laid, each layer is mopped with hot tar or asphalt. The top layer is finished with a mineral or rock covering and a special coating.

bus bar
A heavy, rigid conductor which serves as a common connection between the electrical power source and the load circuits inside a service panel.

butt edge
The lower edge of the shingle tabs.

C

calcium carbonate
A white chalky substance often found at the evaporation line of pools and spas.

cantilever
(1) Any structural part of a building that projects beyond its support and overhang. (2) Describes the beam fixed at one end to a vertical support used to hold the structure, such as a bridge, balcony, or an arch in position.

cap flashing
(1) A sheet metal strip which covers the top edge of base flashing to prevent water from entering. (2) Also known as counter-flashing.

carbon monoxide
A colorless, odorless, poisonous gas, produced by incomplete burning of carbon-based fuels, including gasoline, oil, and wood.

casement windows
Frames of wood or metal which swing outward.

casing
The decorative wood finish trim that surrounds doors and windows.

caulk
To fill a joint with mastic or asphalt cement to prevent leaks.

cavitation
The introduction and rapid collapse of air bubbles. (Within a pump housing, this condition causes a sound like marbles churning within the housing.)

cesspool
An excavation in the earth which receives and retains drainage and sewage from a building.

chord
A component of a truss which acts as a rafter (upper chord) or joist (lower chord).

circuit breaker
An electrical device which automatically interrupts an electric circuit when an overload occurs; may be used instead of a fuse to protect each circuit and can be reset.

cladding
Any external protective skin or device for the exterior surfaces of the home.

clapboard
Narrow boards that are used for siding and that are usually thicker at one edge. The boards run horizontally with the thicker edge overlapping the thinner edge.

clay
Soil that is made of finely ground minerals and rocks other than quartz.

closed-cut valley
A method of valley (intersection of two roof slopes) treatment in which shingles from one side of the valley extend across the valley while shingles from the other side are trimmed two inches from the valley centerline. The valley flashing is not exposed.

closed sheathing
(1) Foundation for exterior siding. (2) Boards nailed to studs.

coating
A layer of viscous asphalt applied to the base material into which granules or other surfacing is embedded.

cohesive soil
Fine-grained soil which, by molecular forces of attraction, stick together when wet and hold together when dry.

collar
(1) Pre-formed flange placed over a vent pipe to seal the roof around the vent pipe opening. (2) Also known as a vent sleeve.

collar beam
A horizontal beam that connects the pairs of opposite roof rafters above the attic floor.

column
A vertical structural member that provides support for the framing. Columns that are integrated into exterior walls are known as pilasters.

combed plywood
A grooved building material used primarily for interior finish.

common area
An entire common interest subdivision except the separate interests therein.

compaction
Extra soil that is added and compressed to fill in the low areas or raise the level of the parcel.

component
(1) A part of a system. (2) Completed sections of housing parts that are delivered to a construction site and assembled into one housing unit.

concealed nail method
A roll of shingles in which all nails are driven into the underlying roofing and covered by a cemented, overlapping course.

condensate
Liquid formed by the condensation of a vapor.

conductors
Materials, such as copper, that allow the flow of electricity to move through them easily.

conduit
A flexible pipe in which electrical wiring is installed.

construction classification
(1) Type of construction. (2) A system that rates the basic frame, walls, and roof of a structure as to their relative fire resistance (e.g., Class A, B, C, or D construction. Class A being the most fireproof).

contour
The surface configuration of land. Shown on maps as a line through points of equal elevation.

convection
Gravity-caused heat transmission by the movement of air, due to the density differences between air currents of differing temperatures.

coping
(1) A protective cap or cover for masonry structures, installed to prevent water penetration. (2) The ribbon-like edge of material (usually masonry) around the perimeter of an in-ground pool (or spa) installed to prevent surface splash and rainwater from draining into the pool (or spa).

corner bead
A vertical molding used to protect the convex angle of two intersecting walls.

corner lot
A lot found at the intersection of two streets. It may be desirable because of its accessibility, but may also be noisy and expensive to maintain because of the increased frontage.

corporation
A legal entity whose rights in business are similar to that of an individual.

counterflashing
Flashing used on chimneys at roof-line to cover shingle flashing and prevent moisture entry.

course
1) The term used for each layer of materials that forms the waterproofing system or the flashing of roofs. (2) A row of shingles running the length of the roof.

coverage
Amount of weather protection provided by the roofing material. Depends on number of layers of material between the exposed surface of the roofing and the deck; i.e., single coverage, double coverage, etc.

crawlspace
An unfinished accessible space below the first floor of a building with no basement. The opening must meet building code requirements.

creosote
(1) A combustible and acidic by-product of wood fires. (2) Also obtained by distilling coal tar for use as a wood preservative.

cricket
A saddle-shaped projection on a sloping roof installed to divert water around a chimney or other obstacle.

cross connection
The condition which allows the connection between a potable water supply system and a drain.

curb appeal
A phrase, implying an informal valuation of a property based on observation and experience.

D

deadfront
A service or sub-panel cover plate which encloses the electrically energized parts.

deciduous
Plants and trees that lose their leaves seasonally in the fall.

deck
An open, unroofed structure used in conjunction with a principle building. A deck or decking is an uncovered porch (usually accessible by stairs), while a porch is a covered deck. Both structures may be attached to and accessible from the principle building.

decking
Decking is the structure around a pool that creates a frame for the pool itself and a safe walkway around it. Poured concrete is the most common type of decking material. Brick, stone, wood, or tile are often placed on top of a concrete slab.

decorative
(1) Ornamental. (2) Not required for the operation of the essential systems and components of a home.

deflection
The amount of bend in a board when under the stress of a load.

depth
Distance from the frontage of a lot to the rear lot line.

diatomaceous earth
A fine powder derived from the porous opaline shells of diatoms, sometimes used as a medium within pool and spa filters.

dielectric fitting
An adapter with a non-metallic contact surface used to connect pipes of dissimilar metals in a water supply system, in order to prevent galvanic corrosion.

differential settlement
Uneven sinking of a structure's foundation.

dip tube
A pipe within a water heater which delivers inlet water to the bottom of the tank for heating.

dismantle
To take apart or remove any component, device, or piece of equipment that would not be taken apart or removed by a homeowner in the course of normal and routine homeowner maintenance.

dormer
A framed window unit that projects through the sloping plane of a roof.

dosing pump
(1) A pump within a sewage collection tank for transfer to another location. (2) Also known as an ejector pump.

double coverage
An application of asphalt roofing where the lapped portion is at least two inches wider than the exposed portion. This creates two layers of roofing material over the deck.

downspout
A vertical pipe used to carry rainwater from a gutter to the ground. This vertical portion of the gutter system carries water away from the house, preventing basement leaks.

downwarping
The shrinking of the perimeter of a foundation relative to the center.

draft diverter
A device fitted to a flue to prevent downdrafts and admit draft air to aid in the evacuation of gasses.

drain field
The area into which the liquid from the septic tank drains.

drainage
The removal of excess surface water or groundwater from land by means of ditches or drains.

drip edge
A non-corrosive, non-staining material used along the eaves and rakes to allow water run-off to drip clear of underlying constructions.

drip flashing
An "L" shaped metal strip which extends beyond a roof edge to direct rainwater away from the structure.

drip loop
A sag in an electric cable or conduit to prevent water from entering at its ends.

dropped ceilings
A ceiling that is built below the actual ceiling, usually made of acoustic tiles and a T-bar suspension. The T-bar suspension is a framework of steel or metal channel suspended by wires that has pre-cut acoustic tiles placed into the framework.

dry rot
A wood fungus that thrives in damp conditions and turns wood fibers into powder.

drywall
Gypsum panels used in place of wet plaster to finish the inside of buildings.

dual pane (double pane)
A type of glass configuration in a window. The window has two pieces of glass with an air space between the panes. The air space provides insulation and reduces heat loss through the window.

Dutch lap method
Application of giant individual shingles with the long dimension parallel to the eaves. Shingles are applied to overlap adjacent shingles in each course as well as the course below.

E

eaves
The horizontal, lower edge of a sloped roof that hangs over the exterior walls.

eaves flashing
Layer of roofing material applied at the eaves to help prevent damage from water back-up.

edge venting
The installation of a vent material along the roof edge (starter vent) as part of a ventilation system. Edge vent material should be used in conjunction with other venting material (ridge vent), as it is not intended for use by itself.

edging strips
Boards nailed along eaves and rakes after cutting back existing wood shingles to provide secure edges for re-roofing with asphalt shingles.

efflorescence
The white powdery substance that forms on the surface of masonry by water leaching out certain chemicals.

ejector pump
See dosing pump.

erosion
The gradual wearing away of land by natural processes.

errors and omission insurance (E&O insurance)
An insurance to protect business professionals from claims due to faulty performance based on negligence, error or omission.

expansion joint
A fiber strip used to separate units of concrete to prevent cracking due to expansion as a result of temperature changes.

expansive soil
A type of soil found in many coastal areas of southern California that increases in volume when wet and decrease when dry.

exposed nail method
Application of roll roofing in which all nails are driven into the cemented, overlapping course of roofing. Nails are exposed to the weather.

exposure
Portion of the shingle exposed to the weather. Exposure is measured from the butt of one shingle to the butt of the next.

F

facade
The front face of a building, which is often more architecturally ornate than the rest of the structure.

fascia
A board nailed across rafter ends, sometimes supporting gutters.

feathering strips
(1) The tapered wood filler strips placed along the old wood shingles butts to create a level surface when re-roofing (over existing wood shingle roofs). (2) Also known as horsefeathers.

felt
(1) A flexible sheet that is saturated with asphalt and used as an underlayment or form of sheathing. (2) Also known as tar paper.

ferrous
Having iron content.

fiber cement
A roofing material that has cellulose (wood fiber) mixed into it. Cellulose absorbs water and can add greatly to the roof's weight, while reducing its longevity.

fiberglass mat
An asphalt roofing base material manufactured from glass fibers.

finish flooring
The final covering on the floor (usually decorative hardwood).

fireblocking
(1) A material which fills construction cavities to impede the spread of fire. (2) Also known as firestops.

fire rating

class "A"

The highest fire-resistance rating for roofing as per ASTM E-108. Indicates roofing is able to withstand severe exposure to fire originating from sources outside the building.

class "B"

Fire-resistance rating that indicates roofing materials are able to withstand moderate exposure to fire originating from sources outside the building.

class "C"

Fire-resistance rating that indicates roofing materials are able to withstand light exposure to fire originative from sources outside the building.

firestops
Boards nailed between studs to block the spread of fire in the walls.

flashing
Sheet metal or other material that keeps the water from seeping into a building.

flashing cement
(1) An asphalt-based cement used to bond roofing materials. (2) Also known as mastic.

flow rate
The number of gallons of water that are cycled through the plumbing system per minute.

footing
(1) The spreading part at the base of a foundation wall or pier. (2) An extended part of the foundation at the base or bottom of a foundation wall, pier, or column.

formaldehyde
A carcinogenic chemical compound found in some building materials.

foundation
The base of a house, usually concrete.

foundation plan
A drawing that shows foundation, sub-floors, footing and pier placement.

free-tab shingles
Shingles that do not have factory-applied strips of self-sealing adhesive.

French doors
Double doors hinged at either side.

French drain
(1) A drain with no pipe. (2) A small trench that will allow surface water to drain away from a building or area that is prone to surface water build-up or flooding.

frostline
The depth of frost penetration in the soil. Varies in different parts of the country. Footings should be placed below this depth to prevent movement.

fungi
A group of plants, (yeast, mold, and mushrooms) that lack chlorophyll and reproduce asexually through spores. Several types of fungi are potentially harmful to wooden structures and can cause the following: brown rot, white rot, soft rot, and dry rot.

furring
Strips of wood or metal fastened to wall to even it, form air space, or to give the wall greater thickness.

G

gable
The triangular portion at the top of a wall with a double sloping roof.

gable roof
A pitched roof with sloping planes of the same pitch on each side of the ridge. A gable roof typically contains a gable at each end.

galvanic corrosion
Corrosive breakdown which takes place when dissimilar metals are in contact in the presence of an electrolyte.

gambrel roof
Typically seen in Dutch colonial architecture, is a curbed roof, with a steep lower slope with a flatter one above. A gambrel roof usually contains a gable at each end, just like a standard gable roof.

girder
A heavy, horizontal wood or steal beam used to support other beams, joists, floors, and partitions.

glazing bead
Removable trim which holds glass panes in place at a glazed opening.

grade
Ground level at the foundation.

grade beam
The below-grade load-bearing part of a foundation system, designed as a beam, which either bears on footings or is self-supporting.

ground fault circuit interrupter (GFCI)
An electrical safety device that instantly shuts down the circuit when a short develops. Required for outlets that are used in bathrooms, kitchens, outdoors, or wherever electrical equipment might come into contact with water.

grout
Mortar which is poured or troweled into the joints between tiles or other masonry components.

gunite
Air-sprayed concrete.

gutter
Horizontal channels that are installed at the edge of a roof to carry rainwater away from the house.

guy wire
A strong steel wire or cable strung from an anchor to an antenna or tree used for support purposes.

H

hardscape
The structures and features such as retaining walls, pathways, pools, sidewalks, curbs, and gutters as part of the landscaping.

hazardous household waste
Consumer products such as paints, cleaners, stains, varnishes, car batteries, motor oil, and pesticides that contain hazardous components.

hazardous waste
Materials-chemicals, explosives, radioactive, biological-whose disposal is regulated by the Environmental Protection Agency (EPA).

header
(1) The horizontal, load-bearing board over a doorway or window opening. (2) Also known as a lintel.

hearth
The floor of a fireplace.

heat pump
A device that acts as an air conditioner in the summer and as an electric furnace in the winter.

HEX shingles
Shingles that have the appearance of a hexagon after installation.

HIF
Abbreviation for the Home Inspection Foundation.

hip
The inclined external angle formed by the intersection of two sloping roof planes. The hip runs from the ridge to the eaves.

hip roof
A pitched roof with sloping sides and ends.

hip shingles
Shingles applied to the inclined external angle formed by the crossing of two sloping roof planes.

home inspection
The process by which an inspector examines the readily accessible physical structure, systems, and condition of a home and describes those systems and components in a written report.

home inspector
A person who performs the service of making a physical inspection of homes.

hose bib
An outdoor water faucet.

household appliances
Stove, refrigerator, washer, etc., installed or freestanding, usually located in the kitchen or laundry area.

humus
Highly decomposed plant and animal residue that is a part of soil.

HVAC
The acronym for heating, ventilation and air conditioning.

hydrojet
A spa jet designed to have air injected into its water flow by a mechanical blower.

hydrostatic relief value
A valve (installed at the bottom of an in-ground pool) designed to relieve external ground-water pressure which might cause the pool structure to heave.

I

ice dam
Dam-like buildups of ice along the eaves of buildings and roofs. They can force water up and under shingles, causing leaks (even in freezing weather).

incandescent lamp
A light bulb in which a filament is energized by electric current to make light.

indirect lighting
A method of illumination in which the light is reflected from the ceiling or other object outside the fixture.

inspect
To visually examine readily accessible systems and components of a building in accordance with local standards of practice.

inspector
A person hired to examine any system or component of a building in accordance with local standards of practice.

installed
Attached in such a way that it requires removal with tools.

insulation
Any material used in building construction that slows down the transfer of heat.

insulator
A material that does not conduct electricity.

intake ventilation
The part of a ventilation system used to draw fresh air in. Usually vents installed in the soffit or along the eaves of a building.

interlocking shingles
Individual shingles that mechanically fasten to each other to provide wind resistance.

J

jalousie
Adjustable glass louvers in doors or windows used to keep out sun and rain while admitting light and air.

jamb
The side post or lining of a doorway, window, or other opening.

joint
The space between the adjacent surfaces of two components joined and held together by nails, glue, or cement.

joists
Parallel horizontal beams used to support floor and ceiling loads. The boards supporting them are girders, beams, or bearing walls.

K

knockout
A scored area in the surface of an electrical outlet box or panel, which is removed to accommodate cables, circuit breakers, or other electrical devices.

L

laminated shingles
(1) Strip shingles with more than one layer of tabs to create extra thickness. (2) Also known as three-dimensional shingles.

landscaping
The art of arranging rocks, lumber, and plants around the outside of a property for an aesthetic purpose, such as an appealing look, or for practical purposes, such as to prevent erosion or provide parking areas. Landscape may include softscape and hardscape.

lap
To cover the surface of one shingle or roll with another.

lap cement
An asphalt-based cement used to adhere overlapping piles of roll roofing.

lateral support
The support which the soil of an adjoining owner gives to a neighbor's land.

lattice
Woven strips of any material used for ornamental screening.

leaching field
See absorption field

lead flashing
When working with tile roofs, lead flashing is used. In the case of a plumbing vent flashing, the lead flashing is actually molded to the shape of the tile's surface. Then the top of the lead flashing is covered by the next tile to prevent water from seeping under the flashing.

leader
A downspout.

lean-to roof
A roof with one slope that is built against a higher wall.

limited liability company (LLC)
An alternative business that has characteristics of both corporations and limited partnerships.

limited partnership
A partnership of at least one general partner and one limited partner.

linear feet
Refers to length rather than area.

lintel
(1) A horizontal board that supports the load over an opening such as a door or window. (2) Also known as a header.

liquid line
A pipe carrying liquid refrigerant from a condenser to a metering device.

loam
Soil made from gravel, sand, clay, and a large amount of humus.

louver
An opening with a series of horizontal slats set at an angle to permit ventilation without admitting rain, sunlight, or vision.

Low-slope application
Method of installing asphalt shingles on roof slopes between two-and-four inches per foot.

M

mansard roof
A type of roof with two sloping planes of different pitch, (one each of four sides). The lower plane has a much steeper pitch than the upper, often approaching vertical. A mansard roof contains no gables.

manufactured home
A home built in a factory after June 15, 1976 and must conform to the U.S. government's Manufactured Home Construction and Safety Standards.

mastic
(1) An asphalt-based cement used to bond roofing materials. (2) Also known as flashing cement.

metal drip edge
A narrow strip of non-corrodible metal used at the rake and eave to facilitate water runoff.

metal surfaced roofing
Asphalt shingles and roll roofing that are covered with granules.

mildew
A common name for mold or fungi; often used in reference to fungal growth on bathroom tiles and fixtures.

milliampere
One thousandth of an ampere.

mobile home
A factory-built home manufactured prior to June 15, 1976, constructed on a chassis and wheels, and designed for permanent or semi-attachment to land.

modular
A system for the construction of dwellings and other improvements to real property through the on-site assembly of component parts (modules) that have been mass-produced away from the building site.

modular home
(1) Building composed of modules constructed on an assembly line in a factory. (2) See also manufactured homes.

mold
A group of organisms that belong to the kingdom Fungi. Some molds can cause disease in humans.

moldings
Usually patterned strips used to provide an ornamental variation of outline or contour, such as cornices, bases, windows, and door jambs.

mortar cap
See coping

N

NACHI
An abbreviation for the National Association of Certified Home Inspectors.

NAHI
An abbreviation for the National Association of Home Inspectors.

nesting
A method of re-roofing with new asphalt shingles over old shingles. The top edge of the new shingle is butted against the bottom edge of the existing shingle tab.

no-cut shingles
Shingles consisting of a single, solid tab.

non-veneer panels
Any board product made from chips, wafers strands, flakes, and particles of wood or wood fiber combined with adhesives. They are generally called composites, include wafer board and oriented strand board, and carry an APA span rating. Unlike plywood, they do not contain veneer.

normal operating controls
Devices such as thermostats, switches, or valves intended to be operated by the homeowner.

normal slope application
A method of installing asphalt shingles on roof slopes between 4 inches and 21 inches per foot.

nosing
(1) The horizontal projection of a stair tread beyond the riser. (2) Also known as stair tread.

O

open sheathing
Boards nailed to rafters to form foundation for roof.

open valley
A method of valley construction in which shingles on both sides of the valley are trimmed along a chalk line snapped on each side of the valley. These shingles do not extend across the valley (valley flashing is exposed).

organic felt
An asphalt roofing base material made from cellulose fibers.

organic shingle
An asphalt shingle reinforced with organic material manufactured from cellulose fibers.

oriented strand board
Oriented strand board (OSB) is manufactured sheet lumber made of strands or chip of wood glued and pressed together. It costs less than plywood, is not as strong as plywood, and does not hold nails as well as plywood. The side with the slip-resistant coating should be placed facing up.

OSHA
An abbreviation for the federal Occupational Safety and Health Administration which regulates workplace safety.

overhang
The portion of the roof structure that extends beyond the exterior walls of a building.

P

pallets
A prebuilt wooden platform used for storing and shipping bundles of shingles, tiles, and other materials.

pane
A flat sheet of glass for glazing windows and doors.

panel box
(1) A box, usually containing breakers or fuses, located at the point of entry of electric service conductors. (2) Also known as the service panel.

parapet
A low protective wall that extends above the roofline or balcony for support.

parquet floor
Hardwood flooring laid in squares or patterns.

partnership
A form of business in which two or more persons join their money and skills in conducting the business.

party wall
A wall erected on the line between two adjoining properties, which are under different ownership, for the use of both parties.

perimeter heating
Baseboard heating, or any system in which the heat register is located along the outside walls of a room, especially under the windows.

pier
A column of masonry used to support other structural members.

pier and beam foundation
A type of foundation using wood or concrete piers which rest on support beams or girders, which support the structure. It is relatively inexpensive and is rarely used for residential houses.

piles
Vertical foundation members that transfer the load to the ground and may be made of wood, steel, concrete, or a combination of these materials.

pitch
The slope, incline or rise of a roof.

planned unit development (PUD)
A planning and zoning term describing land not subject to conventional zoning to permit clustering of residences or other characteristics of the project which differ from normal zoning.

plastic cement
A compound used to seal flashings and in some cases to seal down shingles as well as for other small waterproofing jobs.

plasticity
The range of moisture content within which the soil will remain plastic.

plate
1) A horizontal board placed on a wall or supported on posts or studs to carry the trusses of a roof or rafters directly. 2) A shoe or base member, as of a partition or other frame. 3) A small flat board placed on or in a wall to support girders and rafters.

plenum
An enclosed box or changer used to aid in the distribution of conditioned air.

plumbing vent flashing
Plumbing vent flashing prevents rainwater from running into holes cut for pipes in the roof. This flashing is sold according to the size of the vent pipe of the roof angle. Roofing material is installed over the flashing.

ply
The number of layers of roofing (i.e., one-ply, two-ply).

plywood
Several thicknesses of wood glued together with grains at different angles for strength. It is usually made up in panels. It comes in many grades with ratings from A to D. Use only exterior grade plywood for decking.

pocket door
A special type of sliding door that is suspended overhead on tracks and slides into a "pocket" in the wall when open.

potable water
Fresh water that is safe and agreeable for drinking.

prefabricated house
A house manufactured and sometimes partly assembled before delivery to building site.

propane
A manufactured, liquid petroleum gas (LPG) typically used for cooking or heating.

P-trap
A "P" shaped bend in a wastewater pipe designed to seal out sewer gasses.

purlin
A structural member attached horizontally across rafters of a roof structure for strength.

purlin brace
A strut or post supporting a purlin.

Q

quarter round
A molding that presents a profile of a quarter circle.

R

racking
A roofing application where shingle courses are applied vertically up the roof (not a recommended procedure.)

rackling
The movement of structural components out of plumb, often caused by foundation settlement, wind loads, seismic stress, thermal expansion and contraction, or shrinkage.

radiant heating
A method of heating, usually consisting of coils or pipes placed in the floor, wall, or ceiling.

radon
Colorless, odorless gas that is a carcinogen detected by a spectrometer.

rafters
Slanted boards of a roof that are designed to support the roof boards and shingles. To strengthen the load bearing factor of a roof, the rafters should be placed closer together.

rail
One of the horizontal structural members of a door or window frame.

rain cap
A device installed above the opening of a chimney or flue to prevent the entry of rain.

rake board
A board or molding at the sloping edge of a gable.

rake
The inclined edge of a sloped roof over a wall from the eave in the ridge.

random tab shingles
Shingles on which tabs are different in size and exposure.

readily openable access panel
A panel provided for homeowner inspection and maintenance that is within normal reach, can be removed by one person, and is not sealed in place.

rebar
Reinforcing bar (rebar for short) is a ribbed steel bar designed to strengthen concrete. It is installed in foundation walls, footings, and columns.

receptacle
An electrical outlet for a plug.

re-cover (overlay)
The installation of a new roof system over an existing system without removing an existing system.

recovery rate
The rate at which water can be heated from 50° F to 140° F (or 90° temperature variance taking into account starting temperature and maximum allowable temperature for the water).

refractory
Any material, especially cement, brick, and concrete capable of withstanding high temperatures.

refrigerant
The medium of heat transfer in a refrigeration system.

register
A grill that is mounted at the end of the supply duct where it enters the room.

remodeling
Changes the basic design or plan of the building to correct deficiencies.

re-roofing
Installing a new roof system on a building that is not new.

retaining walls
Walls constructed to hold back soil and prevent erosion.

ridge
The highest structural part of a frame building.

ridge board
A horizontal framing member at the apex of a roof which supports the upper ends of the rafters.

ridge brace
A vertical framing member which supports the ridge board.

ridge shingles
Roof shingles used to cover the horizontal external (angle formed by the crossing of two sloping roof planes.)

rise
The vertical distance from the eaves line to the ridge.

riser
(1) The upright board at the back of each step of a stairway. (2) In heating, a duct slanted upward to carry hot air from the furnace to the room above.

roll roofing
Asphalt roofing products made in roll form.

roof drainage systems
Components used to carry water off a roof and away from a building.

roofing tape
An asphalt-saturated tape used with asphalt cements for flashing and patching an asphalt roof.

row house
See townhouse.

run
The width of a single stair tread as measured from front to back.

R-value
A rating that measures how well insulation resists heat.

S

S corporation
A corporation that operates like a corporation but is treated like a partnership for tax purposes.

saddle
(1) A cricket. (2) A threshold.

sash
Wood or metal frames containing one or more window panes.

saturation zone
The area below the water table.

scab
A gusset plate or other flat brace used for bolting, nailing, screwing, or otherwise connecting two framing components.

self-sealing shingles
Shingles containing factory-applied strips or spots a thermal sealing tab cement to firmly cement the shingles together automatically after they have been applied properly and exposed to warm sun temperatures. In warm seasons, the seal will be completed in a matter of days. In colder seasons, sealing time depends on the temperature and amount of direct sunlight hitting the shingles.

septic system
The waste removal system.

septic tank
A watertight sewage settling tank designed to accommodate liquid and solid waste, which must be at least five feet away from the improvements.

service entrance
Electric service components from the point of utility company supply to the service equipment or service panel.

shading
The small differences in shingle color that can occur as the result of normal manufacturing operations.

sheathing
Exterior grade boards used as a roof deck material.

shimming
The process raising the level of lower piers by inserting wedge shape pieces of material under them.

shingle
Building material used as siding or roofing. Usually a relatively thin and small unit composed of wood, cement, asphalt compound, slate, tile or the like and installed in an overlapping series to cover roofs and walls.

shut down
A state in which a system or component cannot be operated by normal operating controls.

sill (mud sill)
The lowest part of the frame of a house. It is a board placed level on the foundation that is used to connect the exterior wall studs and floor joists. It is fastened with bolts to the foundation and supports the upright studs of the frame.

single coverage
The asphalt roofing that provides one layer of roofing material over a deck.

site
The position, situation or location of a piece of land in a neighborhood.

skylight
A glass opening in a roof that allows natural light to enter a home.

slope
The degree of roof incline expressed as the ratio of the rise in inches and to the run in feet.

slugging
If an air conditioner's airflow is severely restricted, ice grows on the evaporator coils and can result in "slugging" the compressor with liquid refrigerant.

soffit
The exposed undersides of the eaves.

softscape
The planting and maintenance of vegetation around a house to prevent erosion and improve its aesthetic appearance.

sole plate
(1) A board, usually 2" x 4", on which wall and partition studs rest. (2) A support for studs.

sole proprietorship
A business owned and operated by one person.

solid fuel burning appliances
(1) A hearth and fire chamber or similar prepared place in which a fire may be built and which is built in conjunction with a chimney. (2) A listed assembly of a fire chamber, its chimney, and related factory-made parts designed for unit assembly without requiring field construction.

spalling
The chipping, scarring, crumbling, or splitting of concrete, and is often the result of the reinforcing steel in the concrete rusting.

span
The horizontal distance from eaves to eaves.

specialty eaves flashing membrane
A self-adhering, waterproofing shingle underlayment created to protect against water infiltration created by ice dams or wind-driven rain.

square
A unit of roof measure covering 100 square feet.

square tab shingles
Tab shingles that are all the same size and exposure.

starter strip
Asphalt roofing applied at the eaves to provide protection by filling in the spaces under the cutouts and joints during the first course of shingles.

steep slope application
The method of installing asphalt shingles on roof slopes greater than 21 inches per foot.

step flashing
Flashing application method used where a vertical surface meets a sloping roof plane. Step flashing is usually a metal piece that is bent in the middle, so that one lays on the roof and the other against the vertical wall of the dormer or chimney.

step sheathing
Sheathing used alone or in combination with solid sheathing for installation of tiles or shakes.

stile
One of the vertical structural members of a door or window frame.

stringer
(1) A timber or other support for cross-members. (2) In stairs, the support on which the stair treads rest.

strip shingles
Asphalt shingles approximately three times as long as they are wide.

structural component
A component that supports non-variable forces or weights (dead loads) and variable forces or weights (live loads).

stucco
Popular cement-like substance frequently used for wall cladding in the southwest.

studs
Vertical supporting 2" x 4" boards in the walls spaced 16" on the center.

subfloor
A wood floor, typically unfinished plywood, which is attached to a room's floor joists and to which the finished floor is attached.

suction line
The vapor line in a refrigeration loop.

sump
A pit or tank that catches liquid runoff for drainage or disposal. The sump pump is used to pump the liquid out of the pit or tank.

swale
A low area of soil in which excess surface water can flow.

system
A combination of interacting or interdependent components, assembled to carry out one or more functions.

T

tab
The exposed portion of strip shingles defined by cutouts.

tear off
Removing an existing roof system.

telegraphing
A shingle distortion that may arise when a new roof is applied over an uneven surface.

termite shield
A shield, usually of noncorrodible metal, placed on top of the foundation wall or around pipes to prevent passage of termites.

termites
Ant-like insects which feed on wood and are highly destructive to wood surfaces.

terra cotta
Unglazed fire clay used as roof or floor tiles.

thermocouple
A device which generates a voltage when heated. It is used to control fuel burning appliances.

thermostat
An electrical circuit that opens and closes at predetermined temperature.

tongue and groove 2-by-6
If a roof will be seen from the inside (no ceiling installed), tongue and groove is used. It is a wood decking that provides great insulation without additional rigid roof

insulation in moderate climates. Also, the boards can be painted or stained on the inside to match the interior.

top lap
That portion of the roof covered by the succeeding course after installation.

top plate
The horizontal framing member at the top of a stud wall.

topography
(1) Nature of the surface of land; topography may be level, rolling, mountainous. (2) Variation in earth's surface.

townhouse
One of a row of houses usually of the same or similar design with common side walls or with a very narrow space between adjacent side walls.

trade association
A voluntary nonprofit organization of independent and competing business units engaged in the same industry or trade, formed to help solve industry problems, promote progress, and enhance service.

transpiration
The removal and evaporation of soil moisture by trees and other plants.

tread
The flat part of the stair that is stepped on.

threshold
A strip of beveled wood or metal used above the finished floor under outside doors.

trim
The finish materials in a building, such as moldings applied around openings (window and door trim) or at the floor and ceiling of rooms (baseboard, cornice, and other moldings).

truss
A pre-assembled arrangement of framing members for roof or floor construction.

type of construction
Building classification, based on a structure's basic frame, wall, and floor construction.

U

under-floor crawlspace
The area within the confines of the foundation and between the ground and the underside of the floor.

underlayment
A layer of asphalt-saturated (also known as tar paper) material which is laid down on a bare deck before shingles are installed to provide additional protection for the deck.

V

valley
The internal angle formed by the junction of two sloping sides of a roof.

valley flashing
This flashing is used in the open valleys of a roof. Most often leaks are found in the valley flashings because flashing is nailed too tightly to the decking, or shingles are not trimmed far enough off the flashing.

veneer
Thin sheets of wood.

vent
(1) An outlet for air. A pipe that allows air to flow into a drainage system. (2) Any device installed on the roof, gable, or soffit for the purpose of ventilating the underside of the roof deck.

vent skirt
A roof jack, flashing, or boot used to weatherproof a vent pipe at its roof penetration.

vent sleeve
Also known as collar.

vent stack
A drain venting pipe open to the air, installed to prevent vacuum-induced siphonage from breaking the water trap seals or interfering with the free flow of wastewater.

vent system
A system of pipes and vents used to relieve pressure in a system or route gas or liquid from a building.

ventilation
The replacement of stale air with fresh air by circulation through a series of vents or an air conditioning system.

volt
The unit of electromotive force which results in a current flow of one ampere when applied across a resistance of one ohm.

voltage
The amount of pressure at which electricity is delivered

W

wainscoting
The bottom portion of a wall that is covered with wood siding; the top part is treated with another material.

water
Water flowing on the surface in a stream or underground (percolating) is real property. If it is taken and bottled, then it becomes personal property.

water pressure test
Water pressure can be tested by turning on all faucets and flushing all toilets at the same time.

water table
The natural level at which water will be found, either above or below the surface of the ground.

waterhammer
A banging noise caused by resonating water within supply pipes.

watt
The measurement of the actual amount of electrical force available to do work.

weather stripping
Material used around windows and doors to prevent drafts.

web members
A structural member which joins top and bottom chords in a truss.

weep holes
The openings in brick that allow trapped water to escape. Also used for ventilation.

weir gate
A floating gate or door at a pool skimmer inlet, designed to permit water into the skimmer while preventing debris from backwashing out into the pool.

wicking
A capillary action phenomenon caused by surface tension. It is not affected by gravity or pressure.

woven valley
A method of valley construction where shingles from both sides of the valley extend across the valley. The shingles are woven together by overlapping alternate courses when applied and do not leave the valley flashing exposed.

X

xeriscape™
A patented name that stands for landscaping that conserves water by using a wide variety of plants appropriate for the natural environment.

Y

Z

zeroscaping
The use of rock and hardscape with only a few sparse plants to create low-water landscaping.

End Notes

Photography and Illustrations

Rey Dulay, Allied Business Schools, Inc., Laguna Hills, California
Pages 17, 21, 30-31, 44, 52, 55, 60, 73, 85, 99, 100, 102, 106, 134, 216, 235

Larry Hislop, www.trustedhomeinspector.com, Mission Viejo, California
Pages 58, 67, 69, 74, 76, 77, 80, 86, 111, 113, 127, 134, 139, 149, 151, 167, 176, 178, 182, 194, 239, 247, 249, 251

Alan R. Horeis Structural Engineers, Inc., Walnut Creek, California
Pages 24, 34, 68, 78, 86, 87, 219,

Dria Kasunich, Allied Business Schools, Inc., Laguna Hills, California
Pages 241, 242

Michele Linder, Allied Business Schools, Inc., Laguna Hills, California
Pages 137, 158

Susan Mackessy, Allied Business Schools, Inc., Laguna Hills, California
Pages 163, 166

Eric Sharkey, Allied Business Schools, Inc., Laguna Hills, California
Pages 19, 75, 117, 141, 143, 153, 175, 196, 207

Index

D

E

F

I

J

K

L

M

N

O

P

Q

R

S

X

Z